THE END OF INNOCENCE

Bernadette Lally.

THE END OF INNOCENCE

Child Sexual Abuse in Ireland

Edited by Kevin Lalor

OAK·TREE·PRESS

Oak Tree Press
19 Rutland Street
Cork, Ireland
http://www.oaktreepress.com

A catalogue record of this book is
available from the British Library.

ISBN 1 86076 220 4

Printed in Ireland by Techman Ltd.

Contents

Foreword

"Some day, maybe, there will exist a well-informed, well-considered, and yet fervent public conviction that the most deadly of all possible sins is the mutilation of a child's spirit." — Erik Erikson

It has become commonplace for commentators in recent years to observe that child sexual abuse is a highly topical issue in public, professional and political life in Ireland. In so doing, authors refer to the central importance of high profile child abuse scandals which became public throughout the mid-1990s such as the X case (Holden, 1994), the Kilkenny Incest Case (McGuinness, 1993), the Brendan Smyth Affair (Moore, 1995), the Madonna House Affair (Department of Health, 1996) and the Sophia McColgan case (McKay, 1998). These developments, and their policy and practice implications, are the subjects of this book. It is our intention to provide an overview of the events of the last decade, which have brought about a radical change in our understanding of the nature and incidence of child sexual abuse in Ireland.

Chapter One, by Kevin Lalor, puts events of the last ten years in context by briefly highlighting the fact that child sexual abuse in Ireland is not a recent phenomenon. Recorded evidence can be traced to the Sixth Century AD. This chapter also examines the clinical and survey research into child sexual abuse of the last twenty years.

Chapter Two, by Niall McElwee, addresses the recent policy, service and legislative responses to our heightened awareness of child sexual abuse. Particular attention is paid to the implications for the education of social care workers.

In Chapter Three, Deirdre O'Shea and Rosaleen McElvaney of St. Clare's Child Sexual Abuse Assessment and Therapy Unit examine the range of theoretical models used in the treatment of children who have been sexually abused. The effects of sexual abuse on children are detailed, as well as issues for therapists in communicating with children and creating the therapeutic environment.

Chapter Four, also by Rosaleen McElvaney and Deirdre O'Shea, addresses current issues in therapy for adults who were sexually abused in childhood. In particular, the long-term impact of abuse is examined.

Olive Travers addresses the issue of treatment of sexual offenders in Chapter Five, with a particular emphasis on community-based treatments. The successful treatment outcomes for child sexual abuse offenders are examined in the context of this jurisdiction's meagre treatment resources.

A significant proportion of those who sexually abuse children are adolescents. Models which help us to understand this form of offending are described by Gary O'Reilly in Chapter Six, and the assessment and treatment needs of this population are detailed.

In Chapter Seven, the position of child sexual abuse victims in the legal process is described by Geoffrey Shannon. The evidence of children and their representation in court is discussed. Recent legislation dealing with the registration of sexual offenders and the reporting of child sexual abuse is analysed.

Finally, in Chapter Eight, Owen Keenan examines recent failings of the child protection system and considers children's rights as a catalyst for change. Looking to the future, he suggests that we are on the brink of a new dawn in policy and provision for children and their families but that the recent impetus to improve the lot of children in our society must be maintained and kept high on the political agenda. In his words, "it is not optimism that will make the difference. Rather, it is passion, commitment and dedication."

Irish society's "discovery" of child sexual abuse in the 1990s has implications for how we view ourselves as a people. Events in the area of child protection in recent years can leave us in no doubt that Irish children have suffered appalling abuse, sometimes by the very people charged with protecting them. In a sense, our innocence as a society is gone. This may not be a bad thing, if it allows us to recognise the realities and the dimensions of child sexual abuse. A thorough understanding, not just by child welfare professionals but by society at large, is the first step in dealing effectively with this problem. In 1998, Sophia McColgan said that "there is still far too much of the 'leave it behind' attitude. This country has to wake up." We have to strive to ensure that in ten years time other victims of child abuse shall not be in a position to so chastise society in general, and child protection professionals in particular, for having so failed them.

Kevin J. Lalor
July 2001

About the Contributors

Owen Keenan has been Chief Executive of Barnardos since 1990. He worked as a social worker in England and has held a number of practice and management positions with voluntary organisations in Ireland. He served as President of the Irish Association of Social Workers, 1983-1985. He was acting Director of the National Social Service Board, 1985-1986. He chaired the inquiry into the death of Kelly (1995). Owen was elected President of the European Forum for Child Welfare 1996 to 1998 and is currently President of the International Forum for Child Welfare (2000-2002). Owen has served on the boards of several voluntary organisations and on many official committees, and he has spoken and written extensively on aspects of child welfare and voluntary organisation management.

Dr. Kevin Lalor is Head of Department of Social Sciences at the Dublin Institute of Technology. He has published internationally in the areas of street children and juvenile prostitution and has published papers on child sexual abuse and paedagogic issues in social care in Ireland. He co-authored *Prostitution in Waterford City: A Contemporary Analysis* (1997). Current research interests include determinants of sexual behaviours amongst adolescents and young people, institutional child abuse and familial child sexual abuse in East Africa.

Rosaleen McElvaney is a Clinical Psychologist and Psychotherapist who has worked for several years with individuals who have been sexually abused. She was involved in the establishment of Laragh Counselling Service, the first Irish statutory counselling service for adults who experienced sexual abuse in childhood and worked as Director of Laragh until 1997. She then moved to St. Clare's Unit, The Children's' Hospital, Temple Street where she was involved in the expansion of the existing assessment service to incorporate a therapy service for children who have been sexually abused. She teaches on the Doctoral programme in Clinical Psychology, Trinity College, Dublin and operates a private practice in Dubh Linn Institute, Glasnevin.

C. Niall McElwee has been lecturing and researching in the field of social care for a decade. He is Head of Department of Humanities at Athlone Institute of Technology. He is founder and editor of the *Irish Journal of Applied Social Studies* and is currently President of the Irish Association of Social Care Educators. He is the author of *Children at Risk* (1996) and co-author of a number of books including *Prostitution in Waterford City: A Contemporary Analysis* (1997), *Irish Society: A Reader in Applied Social Studies* (1997) and *Worthy not worthwhile: Choosing careers in caring occupations* (2000). His forthcoming textbook is titled *Five Scenarios and Solutions for the Social Care Practitioner* (2001).

Gary O' Reilly is a Clinical Psychologist in the North Eastern Health Board. He is Regional Co-ordinator of the Board's assessment and treatment service for juveniles who engage in sexually abusive behaviour. He is currently engaged in a collaborative study between University College Dublin and the Department of Justice, Equality and Law Reform on the effectiveness of treatment for incarcerated adult sex offenders. He is currently co-editing *The Handbook of Clinical Intervention with Juvenile Sexual Offenders* with William Marshall, Alan Carr, & Richard Beckett.

Deirdre O'Shea is a psychotherapist at St. Clare's Integrated Child Sexual Abuse Assessment and Therapy Service in the Children's Hospital, Temple Street, Dublin. She formerly worked in an NCH Action for Children child sexual abuse treatment centre in the UK.

Geoffrey Shannon is a solicitor and lecturer in the Department of Legal Studies at the Dublin Institute of Technology. He is editor of the *Irish Journal of Family Law* (Round Hall Sweet and Maxwell), editor and co-author of *The Divorce Act in Practice* (Round Hall Sweet and Maxwell), general editor and co-author of *Family Law Practitioner* (Round Hall Sweet and Maxwell), co-author and general editor of *Family Law* (Blackstone Press), co-author of *Child Sexual Abuse Relationships, Trauma and Healing* (The CARI Foundation) and author of *Children and the Law* (Round Hall Sweet and Maxwell, Forthcoming). Geoffrey acts as a consultant and lecturer to the Law Society of Ireland's Professional and Advanced courses in family and child law and was appointed by the President of the Law Society of Ireland to the Society's Family Law and Civil Legal Aid Committee. He has written extensively on family and child law issues in various legal journals. Geoffrey has also had a series of articles published in several refereed international journals including the *International Journal of Law, Policy and the Family, International Family Law* and *Pennsylvania Family Lawyer*.

Olive Travers is a Senior Clinical Psychologist with 15 years experience of working with both the perpetrators and victims of sexual abuse. Along with colleagues in the North Western Health Board, she pioneered the first treatment programme for adult sex offenders in Ireland in 1985. She has done extensive media work in relation to child protection issues and has lectured widely on related topics. She is the author of *Behind the Silhouettes: Exploring the Myths of Sexual Abuse* (1999). Currently, she is the Director of COSC, a Sex Abuse Treatment and Prevention Service of the North Western Health Board and the Probation Service.

To Órla, Ciarán & Eoghan

Chapter 1

Child Sexual Abuse in Ireland: A Brief History

Kevin Lalor

INTRODUCTION

The first official reference to child sexual abuse in Ireland occurred only in 1983 (Department of Health, 1983). Since then, we have seen a dramatic increase in the awareness of child sexual abuse in Ireland. But what of child sexual abuse prior to the modern period? Can we assume that, prior to the 1980s, little or no child sexual abuse occurred in Ireland? In this chapter, an attempt is made to place recent concerns regarding child sexual abuse in an historical context. Firstly, we shall examine the historical literature and consider whether or not it is reasonable to assume that child sexual abuse has occurred throughout Irish history.[1] Secondly, the portrayal of child sexual abuse in the media in recent years is considered. Finally, the epidemiological research into child sexual abuse is reviewed.

CHILD SEXUAL ABUSE: A RECENT PHENOMENON?

Given the enormous increases in the reported incidences of child sexual abuse throughout the Western world in the last thirty years, it might be tempting to explain child sexual abuse

---

[1] Parts of this material have been previously published in the *Irish Journal of Applied Social Studies*, 1998, Vol. 1 No.1. The author gratefully acknowledges the permission of the Editor.

as a phenomenon peculiar to late 20th century Western civilisation. However, evidence does exist that the sexual abuse of children is not a modern phenomenon. Breckenridge (1992) detailed historical incidents of child sexual abuse, referring to the impregnation of girls as young as six and nine as chronicled by Savonarola (1497) and Mandelso (1658) (cited in Helfer and Kempe, 1987). She further cites statistical information from Germany where, between 1897 and 1904, recorded convictions for sexual offences against children increased from 3,085 to 4,378. Masson (1992) reviewed the French medico-legal literature initiated by Tardieu (1860) where details of horrific cases of sexual cruelty committed against children, frequently by their own parents, were reported over 140 years ago. Tardieu's *A Medico-Legal Study of Assaults on Decency* ran to seven editions between 1857 and 1878. In this book he records that, between 1858 and 1869 in France, 9,125 people were accused of rape or attempted rape of children. Bernard's *Sexual Assaults on Young Girls* (1886) reported 36,176 reported cases of "rape and assaults on the morality" of children fifteen years and younger in France between 1827 and 1870. Breckenridge (1992) argued that, historically, sexual offences against children were common and, intuitively, this seems to be a reasonable proposition. There is nothing to indicate that child sexual abuse is a novel phenomenon of the late 20th century.

EARLY CHRISTIAN IRELAND

Prior to the early Christian period, Ireland was a pre-literate society. We shall never know much of how children were treated in that time, other than what archaeologists can tell us about eating habits, clothing, housing and so on. However, to disabuse us of any romantic ideas we might have of a peaceful, child-centred Celtic civilisation, it is instructive to examine the archaeological evidence. For instance, McAllister (1928) notes the regularity with which the remains of cremated adults were accompanied by the remains of children in the cists of the Epimegalithic period (1,200–200 BC). This leads him to speculate that the children were being sacrificed to "requicken" the dead adult. In one instance, a cist found at Ballybrew in Co.

Wicklow contained the unburned remains of a middle-aged man. Prior to death, he appears to have suffered a leg injury that had failed to heal. Given the scattered remains of a young child which surrounded the dead man, McAllister speculated "the child had been 'commandeered' to provide a sound pair of legs for him in the next world" (McAllister, 1928, p. 90). Furthermore, it appears that the child was boiled, then eaten and that a share of his flesh was placed in the food-jar that was to accompany the dead man to the other world.

The Penitentials

The first written evidence of the sexual abuse of children in Ireland is to be found in the Penitentials. These texts were confessional manuals used by the clergy. They contained exhaustive lists of proscribed behaviours and recommended the appropriate penance for offenders. The Penitentials originated in Ireland in the 6th century and spread from there to England and throughout Western Europe, where they remained in use until the 12th century. It is not known how the Penitentials were used in practice but, as Payer says, their "contents permit some educated speculation" (1984, p. 8). Certainly, the Penitentials suggest that behaviours were occurring frequently enough to warrant explicit proscriptions. They contain a remarkable range of prohibited sexual behaviours, including adultery, incest, homosexuality, lesbianism, bestiality, masturbation, sodomy, fellatio, touching, kissing with and without "pollution" (ejaculation), adultery at the urging of a husband, the use of aphrodisiacs (frequently semen-based) and the use of *quasdam machinas* (certain instruments) by women. Proscriptions on incest included sexual relations with daughters, sisters, brothers, stepdaughters, god-daughters, aunts, god-mothers, mothers, infant sons, the sister of a wife and the fiancée of a son.

In Bieler's *The Irish Penitentials* there are two canons that indicate the existence of the sexual "misuse" of children in early Christian Ireland. The first is taken from the Penitential of St. Columbanus:

> If any layman or laywoman has misused their child, let them
> do penance for a whole year on bread and water, and for

two others let them refrain from wine and meats, and so first
let them be restored to the alter at the discretion of the
priest, and then let such a husband use his bed lawfully
(Bieler, 1963, p. 103).

The term "misuse" is indicative of sexual abuse in this instance
given the preceding prohibitions listed by Columbanus on fornication with beasts and fornication with widows and virgins.
Sexual abuse is further implied by the term "misuse" as it is
used in the Penitential of Cummean:

A small boy misused by an older one, if he is ten years of
age, shall fast for a week; if he consents, for twenty days
(Bieler, 1963, p. 129).

Again, sexual abuse is implied by the context of preceding
proscriptions against bestiality, mutual masturbation and femo-
ral intercourse. Payer (1984, p. 42) also highlights this canon
from the Penitential of Cummean which seems to deal with the
homosexual abuse of a young boy by an older boy. He specu-
lates that the reason the *victim* was required to do penance may
have been "educational". If this is the case, the tendency to
blame the victim of sexual assaults is not a modern phenomenon!

Further evidence of prohibitions against child sexual abuse
is found in British texts — the Canons of Theodore and the Bede
Penitentials (Payer, 1984, p. 31). Each of these texts specifies a
penance for a mother who simulates sexual intercourse with her
small son; she is to abstain from meat for three years and to fast
one day a week until vespers.

Brehon Laws

Beginning in the 7th and 8th centuries, the legal tracts that represented the ancient Celtic Brehon Laws came to be written
down. These documents provide us with some, limited, information regarding the care of children in early Christian Ireland.
The first observation that we might make is that children appear
to have been highly valued. This is reflected in the measure of
protection afforded them by law. The *lóg n-enech*, or honour-
price, of a child up to age seven was equivalent to that of a

cleric. That is, injuries to children were penalised in the same way as those against clerics (Kelly, 1988, p. 83). A second observation is that, unfortunately, our knowledge of children in early Christian Ireland is incomplete. Only fragments of the legal texts that deal mainly with children (*Cáin Íarraith*, on fosterage and *Maccslechta*, on inheritance) have survived. Furthermore, the law had little concern for the internal affairs of a family. "How a man treated a child is mainly a matter for himself, his kin and his wife's kin" (Kelly, 1988, p. 81).

In describing legitimate grounds for divorce, as detailed under Brehon Law, Cherici (1995) notes that "if a husband . . . displayed such sexual desire for other men or boys that his wife was deprived of his conjugal services, she could divorce him" (p. 134). At least in those instances in which the adult man was married, sexual relationships between men and boys were clearly not sanctioned, in that they provided legitimate grounds for divorce for the wife of the adult male.

Our final reference to adult-child sexual relations in Early Christian Ireland is found in *The Birth and Life of St. Moling*. Condren (1989), in an observation on the extreme penance performed by holy people, noted that St. Moling was angry because, having sucked the mucus from the nose of a leper, God had not appeared to him after such a feat. An angel appeared and asked in what form he would like the Lord to appear. He replied:

> In the shape of a boy of seven years, so that I may make fits of fondness around Him. He noticed nothing at the end of a time afterwards, till Christ sat on his lap in the shape of a boy of seven years, and he was fondling Him till the hour of rising on the morrow (Stokes, 1906, in Condren, 1989, p. 89).

Condren (1989) quotes this extract as evidence that homosexuality existed in Celtic Ireland. However, given the desired age of the boy, this story would appear to more accurately describe paedophilic rather than homosexual longings.

The twelfth century saw a heightened degree of concern for incestuous practices in Ireland. In 1101 a synod was held in Cashel to reform the Irish Church. The clerics "condemned the right to marry step-mother, step-grandmother, sister, daughter, brother's wife or anyone of similar degree of kindred" (Power, 1976, p. 75). Henry II's invasion of Ireland in 1169 was accompanied by a Papal Bull permitting him to reform the Irish Church and to outlaw the Brehon Law marriages which were seen as fornication. However, there is no reference to incest as we would understand it today — sexual relations between related adults and children. Rather, it refers to sexual liaisons between related adults.

CHILD SEXUAL ABUSE IN 20TH CENTURY IRELAND

The 1908 Punishment of Incest Act criminalised incest in Ireland. It is unlikely that we shall ever know the extent of child sexual abuse as it occurred in Ireland for much of the twentieth century and before but, clearly, it existed extensively enough as a phenomenon to warrant legislative action.

Ferguson (1996) has described the evolution of the Irish child protection system over the last 100 years, particularly with regard to the formation of the National Society for the Prevention of Cruelty to Children (1889) and the Irish Society for the Prevention of Cruelty to Children (1956). By the time the ISPCC split from the NSPCC in 1956, the perceived existence of incest was still very low. Ferguson (1996) notes that of the approximately half a million children which came into contact with the National Society for the Prevention of Cruelty to Children between 1889-1955, fewer than 1 per cent of the cases involved sexual abuse. Over a period of 65 years, this represents approximately 77 cases a year. By way of contrast, 970 cases of child sexual abuse were reported in 1996 in the Eastern Health Board region alone (Eastern Health Board, 1996, p. 63).

Ferguson's (1997) explanation is that "in a traditional order characterised by cultural denial, patriarchal social relations and repression, sexual abuse was not classified and worked with in practice" (p. 31). It would certainly appear to have been the case that the concept of sexual abuse of children simply did not exist within the public domain in any meaningful sense. Consequently, society was neither sensitised to its existence nor educated as to insidiousness.

Throughout the 1970s, the growing child physical abuse literature meant Irish child protection professionals were well aware of the *physical* abuse of children and the phenomenon of the "battered child syndrome". This term was first used by paediatrician C. Henry Kempe at a 1961 symposium of the American Paediatric Society and the explosion of academic literature on child abuse came in the wake of his work with physically abused children (Kempe, Silverman, Steele, Droegmueller & Silver, 1962). The identification of this syndrome came about through observations of the large numbers of unexplained broken bones and bruises in children on paediatric wards. Such was the concern for the physical abuse of children in Ireland by 1976 that the Department of Health established a Committee of Non-Accidental Injury to Children (Ferguson, 1996). This Committee's work produced a *Memorandum on Non-Accidental Injury to Children* (Department of Health, 1977) and, later, the *Guidelines on the Identification and Management of Non-Accidental Injury to Children* (Department of Health, 1980). However, the *sexual* abuse of children remained unaddressed in departmental guidelines.

The first brief reference to sexual abuse was in the 1983 *Non-Accidental Injury to Children: Guidelines on Procedures for the Identification and Management of Non-Accidental Injury to Children* (Department of Health, 1983). These Guidelines concentrated mainly on physical abuse, but included "injury resulting from sexual abuse" in the definitions of child abuse provided (Buckley, Skehill & O'Sullivan, 1997). Only in the 1987 *Child Abuse Guidelines: Guidelines on Procedures for the Identification, Investigation and Management of Child Abuse* was the sexual abuse of children specifically identified as a separate issue to that of physical abuse, or "non-accidental injury" (Department of Health, 1987). Ferguson (1996) highlights the importance of developments outside Ireland in influencing these developments; specifically, the Cleveland affair in the UK. The evolving Irish guidelines on child abuse reflected a growing awareness of child sexual abuse amongst child protection professionals. In particular, the Women's Movement and the work of Rape Crisis Centres are frequently identified as being central in the growing awareness of child sexual abuse throughout the 1980s (for example, McGuinness, 1993, p. 36; Geiran, 1996, p. 141; Buckley, Skehill & O'Sullivan, 1997, p. 15). McGrath (1996) traces the first "official" focus on child sexual abuse in Ireland to a seminar entitled "Incest", held by the Irish Association of Social Workers in January 1983. The Incest Crisis Service developed from this meeting (Irish Council for Civil Liberties, 1988). By 1985, the Sexual Assault Treatment Unit at the Rotunda Hospital, initially designed to cater for adults, was dealing predominantly with children. In 1985, 190 children were seen in the Rotunda; the following year, 530 were seen (Woods, 1987, cited in McGrath, 1996). The Unit closed in 1987 due to lack of funding. Early in 1988 the validation work of the Rotunda was taken over by units in two Dublin children's hospitals; one in Temple Street Hospital, the other in Our Lady's Hospital, Crumlin. An assessment Unit was also opened in St. Finbarrr's Hospital in Cork in 1988.

NATIONAL STATISTICAL FREQUENCIES

Beginning in 1982 the Department of Health has compiled national statistical frequencies on child abuse referrals (Department of Health, 1995). For example, the number of notifications for alleged sexual abuse in Ireland rose from 88 in 1984 to 1,242 in 1989 (Department of Health, 1996, p. 49). As we have already noted, 970 cases of child sexual abuse were reported in 1996 in the Eastern Health Board region alone (Eastern Health Board, 1996, p. 63).

Presumably, these figures reflect an increase in reporting rather than an absolute increase in the number of cases of child sexual abuse in Ireland, thus reflecting the increased public awareness of child sexual abuse and the existence of clear Departmental guidelines as to when and how this abuse should be reported.

> The increase in the number of cases reported in the last decade coincided with increased public and professional knowledge of this issue. By the late 1980s, most child care professionals had developed an awareness of child abuse, and were at least broadly familiar with the reporting re-

quirements and procedures (Department of Health, 1996, pp. 49-50).

There is nothing to indicate that the *incidence* of child sexual abuse should increase so dramatically in so short a period. This same period (the 1980s) is not marked by any particularly massive social, cultural or political changes that could explain such an increase. Rather, increased professional awareness and, to no insignificant degree, media scrutiny and public concern, led to increased *reporting* rates of child sexual abuse. Let us now consider the role of the media in more detail.

THE ROLE OF THE MEDIA IN CREATING CHILD SEXUAL ABUSE AWARENESS

We have already noted the increasing awareness and recognition of child sexual abuse by child protection professionals in Ireland from the early 1980s. Let us now consider the extent to which the media was responsible for creating the unprecedented public awareness of child sexual abuse that occurred in the 1990s.

A content analysis of child sexual abuse representations in the media appears to be a gap in the literature. The author is not aware of any such work focusing on the significant changes in media portrayal of child sexual abuse in the 1990s (the interested student of media representation is referred to Ryan's (1997) study of the portrayal of prostitutes in the Irish and British press). Thus, what follows is a description of a number of very high profile child sexual abuse scandals in Ireland that occurred throughout the 1990s and their unprecedented media coverage which ensured that this topic remained high in public consciousness.

The Kilkenny Incest Case

The so-called "Kilkenny Incest Case" (McGuinness, 1993) was the first of a series of highly publicised child abuse inquiries. The victim in the Kilkenny Incest Case ("Mary") was assaulted and sexually abused by her father over a fifteen-year period from 1976 to 1991. During these fifteen years the victim had repeated contact with hospital and Health Board personnel due to the injuries she received at the hands of her father. The investigation focused on why these contacts did not register concern and lead to an investigation of her family.

To summarise, the victim was first sexually abused at age 11, a few weeks after her family had moved to Ireland. The beatings first happened around the same time. Shortly after Christmas 1981 (at age 16), "Mary" attended a GP with a swollen stomach. The doctor told her she was approximately four months pregnant at this time. Her son was born in May 1982. Her father resumed sexual intercourse with her seven days later. Mary continued to live at home, failing to complete her education. After a serious of physical attacks over the Christmas and New Year period of 1991-1992, Mary ran from her home and sought help with her neighbours. She was brought to a GP and admitted to hospital. Upon discharge, she moved to a refuge for battered women. Her father was subsequently jailed in March 1993 for seven years.

Almost immediately after the case became public (March 1993), the Minister of Health formed an inquiry team. The report was published only nine weeks later. The impact of this report can hardly be exaggerated. In the words of Harry Ferguson:

> . . . the Kilkenny Case represents one of the most significant events in the history of welfare in this country as it is likely to reorient public awareness of family violence and child care policy and practice (Ferguson, 1994, p. 386).

He further comments:

> Sociologically, the construction of the 'Kilkenny Case' represents the kind of powerful symbolic event which appears to be required if child abuse is to become a political issue and fully recognised as a social problem (Ferguson, 1997, p. 35).

Of particular importance in this case was the victim's high public profile, including television appearances.

> To the best of my knowledge the Kilkenny case is the first inquiry situation of it's kind anywhere in the Western world

which has involved an adult survivor of the abuse under investigation herself actually speaking out (Ferguson, 1997, p. 36).

The publication of the McGuinness (1993) report resulted in an
immediate commitment from the government to release £35
million over three years to implement in full the Child Care Act
(1991).

Madonna House

Madonna House was a residential home for children, operated
by the Sisters of Charity. In 1993, allegations of sexual abuse
and other misconduct were made against a number of members of staff there. The subsequent criminal investigation led to
the conviction of a member of staff for various indecency offences. Parallel to this criminal investigation, the Sisters of
Charity and the Department of Health appointed a team to carry
out a review of the operation of Madonna House. Given ongoing
investigations and legal proceedings, the Report was not published in full. It was not until May 1996 that an abridged version
of this report was published as "Report on the Inquiry into the
Operation of Madonna House".

In addition to fuelling the continuing high public profile of
child sexual abuse, the Madonna House Report, and the recommendations it contains, has had an important effect on the
way in which residential homes are operated. Since the publication of the Madonna House report, residential facilities have
come under intense scrutiny. Perhaps the most important outcome of the Madonna House Affair is the recognition that qualified care staff are required to work with the most vulnerable
children in our society. The value of these staff needs to be recognised by providing decent working conditions, salaries and
opportunities for further training. The report highlighted the
marginalised position of child/social care professionals. Difficulties in staff retention and maintaining motivation in a poorly
resourced service leads to low staff morale, perceived low
professional status, stress and a sense that residential care is of
less value than foster care. (Department of Health, 1996, pp. 44-
45). Five years later, this position has not improved (Williams &
Lalor, 2001).

Trudder House

Another high profile case was Trudder House in County Wicklow where a boy in care was raped repeatedly by a staff member. Trudder House, now Newtown House, continues to attract intensive media scrutiny due to the death of a 15-year-old girl who ran away from there in August 2000. At the time of writing, no children reside there and its future as a care centre is uncertain.

Kelly

A further case which attracted widespread media coverage was the case of Kelly (although her surname has been widely reported, the official inquiry (Keenan, Finucane & Keogh, 1996) omits all references to Kelly's surname and requests that all subsequent publications follow suit, in order to protect the identity of her siblings).

Briefly, social workers were engaged with Kelly's family primarily because of their concerns over her sister's well being. On a November 1992 visit, a social worker reported Kelly herself as "bright, outgoing and friendly". On 1 February 1993, Kelly left for London with her elder sister. She was admitted to St. Thomas's Hospital that evening and died on the fourth of February. She was 30 pounds lighter than she should have been and had a protein level of one-third what it should have been. In December 1993 her parents were charged with wilful neglect and occasioning actual bodily harm. In November 1994 they were found guilty of wilful neglect and were sentenced to 18 months in prison.

It appears Kelly's parents resented the cost of her up-keep, particularly the cost of feeding her (Keenan et al., 1996, p. 189). It would appear that from an early stage they began to deprive her of food. It also appears that her father beat Kelly regularly, often with a belt or other object. The authors of the report take the view that Kelly was systematically beaten and deprived of food for much of her five months in Ireland (the family having previously lived in the UK). The authors are also of the view that a particularly cruel form of abuse was employed by storing bread, jam and sugar in Kelly's bedroom, which the hungry child was forbidden to eat (Keenan et al., 1996, p. 191).

The Kelly case highlighted the issue of physical abuse and neglect of children in Ireland. Whilst our primary focus in this volume is the sexual abuse of children, the Kelly case is relevant in that it was central in raising public consciousness to the general issue of child abuse.

The West of Ireland Farmer Case

In this case a child (Sophia McColgan) was sexually and physically abused by her father between the ages of six and twenty-one (1976-1991), during which time the North Western Health Board had 392 contacts with the family. Much of the media coverage of this case centred on the 1995 trial of Joseph McColgan (the West of Ireland Farmer) and his sentencing to 238 years, the longest cumulative total in Irish legal history (the sentences were to run concurrently, giving a total of 12 years). Again, in 1997, there was extensive coverage of the McColgan family's suing of the Health Board and family GP. Particularly impressive at the time was the courageous, high profile media presence adopted by Sophia McColgan.

McKay (1998) has meticulously documented the failings of the North Western Health Board, and others, in their dealings with the McColgan family. Over a fifteen-year period, the family were seen by GPs, social workers, paediatricians, Gardaí, psychologists, public health nurses, the judiciary, teachers and priests. And yet the abuse continued.

Some Concerns

The high profile coverage of child abuse scandals, and their associated official enquiries, has attracted a degree of concern. Buckley (1996) cautions that the use of child abuse enquiries as a vehicle for social change may not be appropriate. Whilst an enquiry undoubtedly informs us regarding one particular case, "it is questionable whether or not an enquiry provides a suitable theoretical foundation for the design of a set of general principles aimed at governing professional practice" (p. 41). She notes that their validity cannot compare with those of empirical research and that their recommendations would not appear to be subject to the critical evaluation of other writings. She further cautions that the increased awareness of child abuse may lead to a disproportionate or unbalanced distribution of scarce Health Board resources. For example, out of 166 non-child abuse referrals made to a community care social work team, she found that only ten received any follow up. "Most" child abuse referrals were investigated "to some degree" (Buckley, 1996, p. 49).

> This suggests the narrowing of what was originally a generic social work service to one which focuses quite narrowly on child protection, and ignores the needs of other families in the area (Buckley, 1996, p. 49).

Indeed, the investigation into the death of a child from physical abuse and neglect (Kelly), in spite of multiple contacts with the Western Health Board, highlighted the disproportionate attention given to child sexual abuse. The Inquiry team found that a "core group" of senior staff was formed in the Mayo community care area to co-ordinate the Health Board response to alleged cases of sexual abuse. The report suggests that this overemphasis on sexual abuse was a result of the sudden, dramatically increased awareness of this phenomenon at the time. Physical and emotional abuse, it would appear, came to be seen as being of a lower priority, and yet:

> [A]t any given time as many children are in the care of health boards for reasons of neglect/inadequate parenting as for all other reasons put together (Keenan, Finucane & Keogh 1996, p. 159).

The Church

Incidents of child sexual abuse by the clergy became evident in the early 1990s and attracted unprecedented levels of media attention. Of particular prominence was Brendan Smyth of the Nobertine Order, the "paedophile priest".

In 1994 the Irish Catholic Bishops' Conference convened an Advisory Committee to advise on Church response to accusations of child sexual abuse by priests and religious and to develop Church policy on this issue. This initiative was at least partly the result of a massive public outcry at the apparent lack of concern shown by the Church for the victims of child sexual abuse. The Brendan Smyth Case (Moore, 1995) seemed to indicate to the public that for many years Church authorities preferred to deny and hide his actions by moving him from parish to parish rather than recognise the criminal nature of his behaviour and, more importantly, the tremendously traumatic effects associated with child sexual abuse. Perhaps this latter reason more than any other fuelled public outrage — at a time when child sexual abuse had come to epitomise "evil" within society, it appeared that the Church was being slow in recognising the harm which sexual abuse can inflict on its victims. For example, Kirby (1995) notes that a fellow priest in Smyth's Nobertine order, Fr. Bruno Mulvihill, repeatedly reported Smyth's misconduct to the abbot's attention. Furthermore,

> The abbot disregarded a decree from the Congregation of Religions in Rome issued in the late 1960s confining Smyth to the abbey's premises and to strict supervision for the rest of his life (Kirby, 1995, p. 258).

Implicit in the Church's clumsy attempts to deal with paedophiles such as Brendan Smyth by merely moving them from place to place appeared to be a belief that the harm was not all that great; that it would be more harmful (to the Church at any rate) to publicly acknowledge the problem.

An apology from the Church followed in 1996. In the words of Cardinal Cahal Daly and John Byrne, in the Foreword of the Advisory Committee's report:

> The Church has always had its limitations and sinfulness but child sexual abuse by priests and religious is one of the saddest manifestations of this reality. Such exploitation of the vulnerability of children is a betrayal of trust of the gravest kind. We express our shame and sorrow that such incidents of abuse have occurred. On behalf of bishops, priests and religious we apologise to all who have suffered because of sexual abuse inflicted on them by priests and religious. We recognise the hurt and sense of isolation

which those who have been victims of child sexual abuse by
priests and religious have experienced (Irish Catholic Bishops' Advisory Committee, 1996, p. 9).

This public recognition of the harm caused by child sexual
abuse and the "owning" of the problem is welcome. It might
well be argued that this response should have been forthcoming many years earlier but, for now, it is an honest attempt to
re-build the trust and faith of the Irish population in an institution previously venerated.

Public abhorrence of sexual abuse committed by priests
and religious is undoubtedly aggravated by the perceived betrayal by one in a special position, that of moral guardian and
instructor. However, it is by no means clear that the religious
are any more or less likely to offend in this way than any other
group. Yet public reaction to child abuse committed by the religious has been more strident than abuse committed by any
other sector of society. This reaction is the result of four factors,
primarily. Firstly, the previously mentioned special position of
the clergy within society; the position of moral guardians. Secondly, the highly visible nature of the Church in Ireland provided a ready target for people's disgust, hurt and anger.
Thirdly, the contrast of the Church's previous venerated position in society with its more recent bruised, damaged, even
pathetic image creates a fascination not easily resisted by the
media and other public commentators. Finally, the fact that
Church was seen as tardy in dealing with this issue condemned
it in the eyes of many previous supporters.

Conclusion

Today, the sexual abuse of children is reported in the media on
a daily basis. The majority of coverage is court reporting. Occasionally, a victim will waive his or her right to privacy in order to "name and shame" the perpetrator. The offending behaviour of priests, teachers, swimming coaches, GAA activists,
civil rights leaders, child care workers etc. are reported in
great detail. Indeed, the impact on Irish society of the growth in
awareness of child sexual abuse has been extraordinary; from
disillusionment with the Church to cynicism and suspicion of

those working with children. As painful as this coverage is to us as a society and as thoroughly as it has stripped us of any delusions that we might have had regarding the rarity of child sexual abuse, it has had very important positive effects. For example, the Commission to Inquire into Child Abuse, and the Act (2000) of the same name, came into being as a direct result of the harrowing television series *States of Fear* (May, 1999). This series profiled the widespread physical and sexual abuse of children in Ireland's Industrial Schools and Schools for the disabled in the 1950s and 1960s. Many of these schools were run by religious orders but were funded by the State and subject to regular statutory inspection. Clearly, this child sexual abuse was not reported at the time and is only now, retrospectively, being recognised. Similarly, the final implementation in 1996 of the 1991 Child Care Act, the National Children's Strategy and the Social Services Inspectorate all owe, at least in part, their genesis to the ongoing public concern which is the result of prolonged media scrutiny and coverage of child abuse.

That being said, the media coverage of issues has not always been constructive. It has at times been simplistic, voyeuristic and insensitive. Let us take the example of sexual offenders. Chapters Five and Six of this text describe the reductions in recidivism rates that are the result of treatment programmes for child sex abuse offenders. Thus, the treatment of offenders should be a primary mechanism for child protection. However, this view is rarely portrayed in the media, where the demonisation of child sexual offenders is the favoured approach. Regarding the Brendan Smyth Affair, Ferguson (1995a) notes:

> Since the Smyth affair began, the media have made constant reference to the notion of 'the paedophile priest'. In tandem with the invention of a new category of sex offender, the construction of the 'paedophile priest' relied on powerful visual imagery. From the outset of the affair, the media has relentlessly used the same photograph of Brendan Smyth's face so that it has become the embodiment of the greatest demon in modern Ireland (Ferguson, 1995a, p. 249).

Within this climate, an objective analysis of the threat posed to children by the clergy becomes next to impossible. All clergy were suspect. Even now, only a few years later, we can look back and recognise that a massive over-reaction to the Smyth affair convulsed Irish perceptions of the Church and clergy, perhaps irreversibly, so powerful were the feelings of fear and betrayal which were raised. Also, there is little public awareness of the possibilities for rehabilitation of child sexual offenders by appropriate treatment. Of course, such treatment does not negate the crimes committed by sexual offenders, nor does it waive the requirement for a punishment to be served. These issues are discussed in greater detail in Chapters Five and Six.

A further feature of negative media coverage of complex child protection issues is the effect on child protection professionals. Ferguson (1995b) hypothesises that high profile scandals and inquiries push knowledge about child protection into the public domain. This, coupled with intense media coverage, creates a climate where child protection workers are under intense public scrutiny. The fear of committing an error, by doing either too much or too little, can be extremely stressful for child protection professionals.

> Individual professionals and entire systems which act primarily on the fear of blame for 'failure' can be driven into a self-defeating bureaucratic culture and a defensive practice in which 'covering yourself' takes precedence over meeting the legitimate interests of children and families (Ferguson, 1995b, p. 9).

In conclusion, the 1990s have been a period of growing public awareness of child abuse issues, fuelled by a number of high profile official Inquiries and ongoing media scrutiny.

CHILD SEXUAL ABUSE RESEARCH

What we know about the nature of child sexual abuse in Ireland has undoubtedly increased as a result of the various child sex abuse inquiries which have been held throughout the 1990s (and which continue to be held in the form of the Commission to Inquire into Child Abuse established by the government in the wake of the *States of Fear* series in May 1999). These inquires shall be discussed from a number of perspectives throughout this text, particularly in Chapter Two. Some clinical studies, also, give us an insight into the nature of child sexual abuse. For example, McKeown & Gilligan's (1991) analysis of 512 cases of child sexual abuse in the Eastern Health Board region and Cheasty, Clare & Collins' (1998) study of the relation between child sexual abuse and adult depression. In Northern Ireland, MacKenzie, Blaney, Chivers & Vincent (1993) estimated the epidemiology of child sexual abuse to be between 0.9 and 1.87 per 1,000 children by examining *reported* cases in the Province in the year 1987. Unreported episodes are not included in this calculation. A more accurate estimate of this "dark figure" of the true incidence of child sexual abuse can only be determined by large random samples of the general population.

The Report of the Child Sexual Abuse Working Party (ICCL, 1988) reports an early survey of 42 adults who had experienced child sexual abuse which was carried out in 1984. These interviews yielded some early findings on the nature of child sexual abuse in Ireland. The authors highlighted the restricted nature of the survey; that there were too few males for statistical analysis, the small sample size and the lack of a control group. Nevertheless, it marked an early attempt to gather data on child sexual abuse:

> We hope that the survey will be seen as an early contribution to recording the victim's point of view and may enable interested parties to identify more clearly which kinds of research need now to be done (ICCL, 1988, p. 3).

Also in 1984, the Incest Crisis Service carried out a survey on child sexual abuse. Nine EHB social work teams described the child sexual abuse cases they had dealt with between January 1980 and December 1983; a total of 71 cases involving 94 children. Of the 71 cases, 66 were intra-familial (ICCL, 1988).

In addition, a number of surveys of GPs and guidance counsellors were conducted in the early 1980s. These included a survey of 57 Wicklow GPs (of whom 20 replied); a survey of all GPs in the Cluain Mhuire Family Centre area (of whom 93 re-

plied); and a survey of all members of the Institute of Guidance
Counsellors (of whom 204 replied, reporting 44 cases of child
sexual abuse in the first six months of 1985) (ICCL, 1988).

There have been surprisingly few attempts to collect incidence data from large non-clinical samples in Ireland. However, from those studies that have been conducted in the last 12
years we can detect a growing rate of reporting for all forms of
child sexual abuse. This increasing rate of reporting has been
traced elsewhere (Lalor, 1999) and only a brief summary of
same is outlined below.

The earliest epidemiological investigation of child sexual
abuse in Ireland was carried out in 1987 by the Market Research Bureau of Ireland (MRBI). Five hundred adults in the
Dublin area were sampled and some 5 per cent of males and 7
per cent of females "admitted to having been sexually abused
as a child within the terms set out in the definition" (MRBI, 1987,
p. 5). For the purposes of this study, child sexual abuse was defined as:

> The involvement of dependent and immature children or
> adolescents in sexual activities they do not fully understand
> and to which they are unable to give informed consent, and
> which violate social taboos (MRBI, 1987, p. 33).

Other key findings were:

- All abusers were male, although victims were equally male
  and female.

- Thirteen of the 30 cases of reported sexual abuse happened
  whilst the child was under thirteen years of age.

- Strangers committed approximately 25 per cent of the abusive incidents. Relatives of the child or others known to the
  child committed the remainder.

- In two-thirds of the incidents, the offence was committed on
  two or more occasions.

- Only in two cases (6 per cent) was the abuse reported: one
  to the police and another to a social worker.

- Ten of the 30 victims had never told anyone of the abuse.

- Ten of the 30 felt they suffered long-term damage as a result of the abuse. The remainder felt there had been no long-term adverse effects.

In 1993 the Irish Society for the Prevention of Cruelty to Children (ISPCC), in conjunction with its counterpart organisation in the UK (the NSPCC), commissioned Irish Marketing Surveys to conduct a survey of 1,001 members of the general population regarding, amongst other things, their experiences of child sexual abuse.

The results elaborate on the picture of child sexual abuse that was described in the earlier MRBI survey. A total of 160 (16 per cent) respondents reported having experienced child sexual abuse. Twelve per cent of the total sample experienced contact sexual abuse. The breakdown of incidence figures can be seen below.

Table 1.1: Incidence of Child Sexual Abuse Reported in ISPCC/IMS (1993) Survey

	Total	Gender	
		Male %	*Female %*
Any Abuse	16	14	22
Exposure only	4	2	7
Hugged/kissed	5	4	6
Fondling organs	6	4	8
Made to touch organs	4	3	4
Attempted intercourse	2	2	3
Intercourse	1	1	1
Anal intercourse	1	1	-
Oral intercourse	1	1	-
Other	1	-	1

Fifteen per cent of the females interviewed and nine per cent of the males reported experiencing contact sexual abuse. For most, this involved being hugged/kissed and/or being touched/fondled in a sexual way. Thirty-nine per cent of contact sexual abuse victims had experienced this only once. Sixty-one per cent of contact sexual abuse victims had experienced the abuse two or more times. Regarding the age of the perpetrator, the majority of contact abuse (86 per cent) was carried out by a person aged sixteen years or older. A surprising result was that 46 per cent of those sexually abused (total number of this sub-sample is 160) reported "No real effect" from the abuse. The corresponding figure for those who had experienced contact sexual abuse (n=120) is 35 per cent. A further 25 per cent of those experiencing contact abuse said they felt upset, but got over it quickly.

In 1996/1997, 247 students of the Dublin Institute of Technology were surveyed regarding their experiences of child sexual abuse (Lalor, 1999). Notwithstanding that this does not constitute a sample of the general population, this study produced the highest levels of self-reported child sexual abuse in Ireland to date. For example:

- 31.8 per cent of the female sample had an unwanted sexual experience before the age of sixteen.

- 23.9 per cent of the female sample experienced an unwanted sexual episode prior to their teenage years. When episodes of indecent exposure are excluded, we find that 15.34 per cent of the female sample have experienced contact sexual abuse prior to their thirteenth birthday.

- 10.25 per cent of the female sample have endured unwanted sexual experiences over a period of months or years prior to their sixteenth birthday.

- Whilst under 16 years of age, respondents were significantly more likely to experience unwanted kissing, attempted intercourse, intercourse, masturbation and oral sex with somebody younger than 21 years, as compared to somebody 21 years or older.

Given the relative paucity of research on child sexual abuse in Ireland and the increasing reporting rates from each consecutive study, a continuing justification exists for ongoing epidemiological work to ascertain at which level reporting rates shall peak.

CONCLUSION

The sexual abuse of children is not a recent phenomenon in Ireland. Nevertheless, an enormous increase in the awareness and reporting of child sexual abuse took place in Ireland in recent years, specifically the middle to late 1980s. This was followed by a succession of high profile child sexual abuse cases throughout the 1990s. The aim of this book is to examine in detail the policy, practice and legislative consequences of this enormous increase in the awareness of child sexual abuse.

References

Bernard, P. (1886). *Des attentant à la pudeur sur les petites filles*. Paris: Octave Doin.

Bieler, L. (1963). *The Irish Penitentials*. Dublin: Institute for Advanced Studies.

Breckenridge, J. (1992). "An exotic phenomenon? Incest and child rape". In J. Breckenridge & M. Carmody (Eds.). *Crimes of Violence: Australian Responses to Rape and Child Sexual Assault*. Sydney: Allen and Unwin.

Breckenridge, J. & Carmody, M. (Eds.) (1992). *Crimes of Violence: Australian Responses to Rape and Child Sexual Assault*. Sydney: Allen and Unwin.

Buckley, H. (1996). Child Abuse Guidelines in Ireland: For Whose Protection? In H. Ferguson and T. McNamara (Eds.). "Protecting Irish Children: Investigation, Protection and Welfare". *Administration*, 44 (2).

Buckley, H., Skehill, C. & O'Sullivan, E. (1997). *Child Protection Practices in Ireland: A Case Study*. Dublin: Oak Tree Press.

Cheasty, M., Clare, A. & Collins, C. (1998). "Relation between sexual abuse in childhood and adult depression: case-control study". *British Medical Journal*, 316, 198-201.

Cherici, P. (1995). *Celtic Sexuality: Power, Paradigms and Passion*. London: Duckworth.

Condren, M. (1989). *The Serpent and the Goddess.* San Francisco: Harper.

Department of Health (1977). *Memorandum on Non-accidental Injury to Children.* Dublin: Department of Health.

Department of Health (1980). *Guidelines on the Identification and Management of Non-accidental Injury to Children.* Dublin: Department of Health.

Department of Health (1983). *Non-accidental Injury to Children. Guidelines on Procedures for the Identification and Management of Non-accidental Injury to Children.* Dublin: Department of Health.

Department of Health (1987). *Child Abuse Guidelines: Guidelines on Procedures for the Identification, Investigation and Management of Child Abuse.* Dublin: Department of Health.

Department of Health (1995). *Notification and Reporting of Suspected Cases of Child Abuse.* Dublin: Stationary Office.

Department of Health (1996). *Report on the inquiry into the operation of Madonna House.* Dublin: Government Publications Office.

Eastern Health Board (1996). *Child care and family support services in 1996: Review of adequacy*, Dublin: Eastern Health Board.

Ferguson, H. (1994). "Child Abuse Inquiries and the Report of the Kilkenny Incest Investigation: A Critical Analysis". *Administration*, 41 (4).

Ferguson, H. (1995a). "The Paedophile Priest: A Deconstruction0". *Studies*, 84, (335), 247-256.

Ferguson, H. (1995b). "Sitting on a Time Bomb: Child Protection, Inquiries and the Risk Society". *Irish Social Worker*, Vol. 13, No. 1.

Ferguson, H. (1996). Protecting Irish children in time: Child abuse as a social problem and the development of the child protection system in the Republic of Ireland. In H. Ferguson & T. McNamara (Eds.) "Protecting Irish Children: Investigation, Protection and Welfare". *Administration,* Vol. 44, No. 2, pp. 5-36.

Ferguson, H. (1997). "Child Abuse as a Social Problem in Post-Traditional Ireland". In C.N. McElwee (Ed.). *Irish Society: A Reader in Applied Social Studies.* Waterford: StreetSmart Press.

Ferguson, H. & McNamara, T. (Eds.) (1996). "Protecting Irish Children: Investigation, Protection and Welfare". *Administration*, 44 (2).

Geiran, V. (1996). Treatment of Sex Offenders in Ireland — The Development of Policy and Practice. In H. Ferguson and T. McNamara (Eds.). "Protecting Irish Children: Investigation, Protection and Welfare". *Administration*, 44 (2).

Helfer, R. & Kempe, R. (1987, fourth edition). *The Battered Child.* Chicago: University of Chicago Press.

Holden, W. (1994). *Unlawful Carnal Knowledge: The True Story of the Irish X Case*. London: Harper Collins.

Irish Catholic Bishops Advisory Committee (1996). *Child Sexual Abuse: Framework for a Church Response*. Dublin: Veritas Publications.

Irish Market Surveys. (1993). *Childhood Experiences and Attitudes*. Dublin: Irish Marketing Surveys Ltd.

Irish Council for Civil Liberties (1988). *Report of the Child Sexual Abuse Working Party*. Dublin: ICCL.

Kelly, F. (1988). *A Guide to Early Irish Law*. Dublin: DIAS

Keenan, O., Finucane, M. & Keogh, S. (1996). *Kelly: A Child is Dead*. Interim Report of the Joint Committee on the Family, Houses of the Oireachtas: Dublin.

Kempe, C. H., Silverman, F.N., Steele, B.F., Droegmueller, W. & Silver, H.K. (1962). "The Battered Child Syndrome". *Journal of the American Medical Association,* 181,17-24.

Kirby, P. (1995). "The Death of Innocence: Whither Now?: Trauma in Church and State". *Studies*, 84 (335), 257-265.

Lalor, K. (1998). "Child sexual abuse in Ireland: A historical and anthropological note". *Irish Journal of Applied Social Studies*, 1 (1), 37-53.

Lalor, K. (1999). "The incidence of unwanted childhood sexual experiences amongst a sample of third level students". *Irish Journal of Psychology,* 20(1), 15-28.

MacKenzie, G., Blaney, R., Chivers, A. & Vincent O. (1993). "The incidence of child sexual abuse in Northern Ireland". *International Journal of Epidemiology*, 22, (2), 299-305.

Masson, J. (1992, third edition). *The Assault on Truth: Freud and Child Sexual Abuse*. London: Fontana.

McAllister, R. (1928). *The Archaeology of Ireland*. London: Methuen.

McElwee, C.N. (1997) (Ed.). *Irish Society: A Reader in Applied Social Studies.* Waterford: StreetSmart Press.

McGrath, K. (1996). Intervening in Child Sexual Abuse in Ireland: Towards Victim-Centered Policies and Practices. In H. Ferguson and T. McNamara (Eds.). "Protecting Irish Children: Investigation, Protection and Welfare". *Administration*, 44 (2).

McGuinness, C. (1993). *Report of the Kilkenny Incest Investigation.* Dublin: Stationary Office.

McKay, S. (1998). *Sophia's Story.* Dublin: Gill & Macmillan.

McKeown, K. & Gilligan, R. (1991). "Child sexual abuse in the Eastern Health Board Region of Ireland in 1988: An analysis of 512 confirmed cases". *The Economic and Social Review*, 22 (2), 101-134.

Moore, C. (1995). *Betrayal of Trust: The Father Brendan Smyth Affair and the Catholic Church.* Dublin: Marino.

MRBI. (1987). *Child sexual abuse in Dublin: Pilot survey report.* Dublin: Market Research Bureau of Ireland Ltd.

Payer, P. (1984). *Sex and the Penitentials. The Development of a Sexual Code 550-1150.* Toronto: University of Toronto Press.

Power, P.C. (1976). *Sex and Marriage in Ancient Ireland.* Dublin: Mercier Press.

Ryan, L. (1997). *Reading 'The Prostitute': Appearance, Place and Time in British and Irish Press Stories of Prostitution.* Aldershot: Ashgate.

Stokes, W., (1906), "The Birth and Life of St. Moling". *Revue Celtique*, 27, 257-305.

Tardieu, A. (1860). "Etude médico-légale sur les sévices et mauvais traitements exercés sur les enfants". *Annales d'hygiène publique et de médecine légale*, 13, 361-398.

Tardieu, A. (1878). "Etude médico-légale sur les attentats aux moeurs". Paris: Publisher unknown.

Williams, D. & Lalor, K. (2001). "Obstacles to the professionalisation of residential child care". *Irish Journal of Applied Social Studies*, 2 (3), 73-91.

Chapter Two

Legislative and Service Initiatives: A Personal Perspective

C. Niall McElwee

INTRODUCTION

The 1980s and 1990s have seen a (re)birth in child abuse as both a medical and social phenomenon with a number of ramifications for child protection and welfare professionals increasingly under the attention of a more informed public. What, perhaps, is most shocking for many people is that we now understand that "normal" families have experienced child abuse over the years. Although child protection has traditionally tended to focus on families "at risk" or "in need", a new awareness has arisen around child abuse as an all-pervasive event. The prioritisation of child sexual abuse has fundamentally shifted the focus of child protection as it is practised in this and other countries.

This chapter assesses two recent legislative and one policy initiative beginning with the introduction of the 1991 Child Care Act, which is widely acknowledged as significant in politicising and protecting "at risk" children in the Republic of Ireland. The introduction of the Child Trafficking and Pornography Act, 1998 faces up to the very real problems of child pornography and child trafficking for sexual purposes, and is a welcome legislative development. Finally, in terms of service initiatives, the training and professionalisation of social care practitioners is viewed in the context of an increasingly legalistic and complex work environment, particularly around child abuse issues.

PART 1: LEGISLATIVE INITIATIVES

THE 1908 CHILDREN ACT

> Is it too much to ask
> I want a comfortable bed that won't
> Hurt my back
> Food to fill me up and warm clothes and
> all that stuff
>
> — From *Passionate Kisses* (lyrics by Lucinda Williams. Sung by Mary Chapin Carpenter).

The 1908 Children Act provided the legislative framework for child care in Ireland for the greater part of the 20th century.[1] This Act was widely regarded as liberal at the time of its implementation as the emphasis was now to be away from punishment towards a casework ideology, with practice based on the supervision of parent-child relations in their homes (Ferguson, 1996, p. 9). The author of the 1908 Act, Herbert Samuel, stated that the Act had three basic principles. Firstly, the separation of the child from the adult criminal with treatment meeting specified needs. Secondly, parents were made explicitly responsible for the wrongdoings of their children. The last stated intention was that a child should not be imprisoned. Industrial schools would cater for first offenders between the ages of twelve and fourteen. The role of these schools was extended to care for children whose parents were unable to control them, and to persistent truants. Provision was made for the establishment of special courts for seven to seventeen-year-olds.

> Where neglect or abuse could be proven, children could be removed from their parents to a "place of safety" and

---

[1] Justice Hugh O' Flaherty, in the Irish Supreme Court, noted that the 1908 Act was "an enlightened piece of legislation when enacted, but is now showing its age".

placed in the care of a "fit person", either a foster parent or
a residential institution (Children Act, 1908 ss. 20, 24, 58).

Although there were some provisions concerning neglected
children, child protection remained the preserve of voluntary
organisations such as the National Society for the Prevention of
Cruelty to Children and various religious congregations such as
the Oblate Fathers and the Sisters of Mercy. In 1956 the Irish
Society for the Prevention of Cruelty to Children broke away
from the NSPCC in order that it could provide a "truly distinctive Irish child protection system" (Ferguson, 1996, p. 12).

THE 1991 CHILD CARE ACT

It took 83 years for the sections dealing with neglected children
in the 1908 Act to be overhauled. The 1991 Child Care Act was
the first comprehensive legislation on the requirements of Irish
children developed by Irish parliament since the foundation of
the State, and brings together elements of public and private
law.[2] The 1991 Child Care Act is in total contrast to the 1908 Act
as the latter Act recognises that the welfare of the child is the
first and paramount consideration (section 3:(2), (b)). The rights
and duties of parents are important, but due consideration must
be given to the child's wishes. The Act attempts to balance the
rights of parents with the (emerging) rights of children and this
is a major difficulty, in itself, as there are many models of parenting, many models of effective practice and always the exceptions that cause any legislator to despair.[3]

The 1991 Act regulates the health boards in three major areas of child care: alternative care (fostering, residential care
and accommodation for homeless children); child protection
(the investigation, assessment and support of children in cases
of known suspected child abuse); and family support, and is

---

[2] Despite the plaudits given to the Act, I would suggest that the 1991 Child
Care Act did not *revolutionise* thinking on the State, the family or the child.
Rather, it crystallised contemporary thinking (McElwee, 1999).

[3] The Irish Constitution of 1937 has been criticised for its few references to the
actual rights of children.

divided into 79 sections. For the purposes of this chapter, I note only the particular section dealing with suspected abuse. These, to me, are particularly important as Kenny (1995, p. 45) points out the relationship between "the use of court orders and the identification of child abuse as the reason for reception into care".

Part IV of the Act deals with Care Proceedings and details care orders and supervision orders.

Care Order

The Act facilitates the health board with care orders where:

a. the child has been or is being assaulted, ill-treated, neglected or sexually abused, or

b. the child's health, development or welfare has been or is being avoidably impaired or neglected, or

c. the child's health, development or welfare is likely to be avoidably impaired or neglected.

This took effect as of 31 October 1995 and is seen by many commentators as the most significant part of the Act in relation to making orders for the protection and welfare of a child. A positive feature of the section is that *sexual* abuse of children should not be confined to actual physical violation of a child by rape. The publication of *Putting Children First* (1996) extends the definition of sexual abuse. In other words, the definition of sexual abuse has now been cast quite wide to include exposure to pornography, sexual exhibitionism, perverse activities and the viewing of sexual acts (Ward, 1997). Hence, a connection was established with future legislation around trafficking and pornography.

Supervision Order

The Act also allows for a health board to make an application for a Supervision Order with respect to a child who resides in its area and where the court is satisfied that there are reasonable grounds for believing that:

d. the child has been or is being assaulted, ill-treated, ne-
    glected or sexually abused, or

e. the child's health, development or welfare has been or is
    being avoidably impaired or neglected, or

f. the child's health, development or welfare is likely to be
    avoidably impaired or neglected.

This also took effect as of 31 October 1995. Under the powers of
a Supervision Order, a child may be monitored in the home by
a health board. This does not necessitate the child being formally taken into care. From the health board's perspective, the
Supervision Order has an advantage over a Care Order in the
area of producing a burden of proof as the District Court judge
needs only to "be satisfied" of reasonable grounds for concern
(meeting the grounds established in section 19(1)(a), (b) or (c).
The health board can decide where, when and how often it will
visit a child under a Supervision Order. This order has a maximum duration of twelve months and ceases either on expiry or
when the child reaches the age of eighteen.

The Act has been reviewed extensively (McGuinness, 1992;
Gilligan, 1993; Ferguson and Kenny, 1995; Ward, 1997; McElwee, 1999b) and it has brought child protection and welfare
firmly into the public gaze, which is significant in itself. The
major Irish child-centred organisations such as the Irish Association of Care Workers, the Resident Managers' Association,
the Irish Association of Social Workers, Barnardos, Focus Ireland and the Irish Society for the Prevention of Cruelty to Children, to name but some, have given considerable time over to
the Act at conferences and seminars. Comparative research has
been published on the 1991 Act with the Northern Ireland Act,
1989 (O'Halloran and Gilligan, 1996).

It is difficult to assess the 1991 Act in isolation and it is certainly ambitious. Indeed, the Act attempts to address so many
diverse areas of care for children that it sets an almost impossible agenda for itself. It is important to acknowledge the social,
economic and political climate at the beginning of this decade,
and that certain topics move in and out of the public eye depending on the media agenda. We ended the 1990s a wiser na-

tion and one far less tolerant of mistakes, cover-ups and "incompetent practice". One area of increasing attention has been that of child sexual abuse (Raftery and O'Sullivan, 1999).

THE DISCOVERY OF CHILD SEXUAL ABUSE OR "BADNESS"[4]

For decades the Irish public refused to confront the reality that child sexual abuse was taking place daily in Irish families and in residential institutions, although there is evidence to suggest that many "ordinary people" had their suspicions. I remember as a school boy in the early 1980s that there were certain characters one was told to avoid by one's older classmates as they had a reputation for "touching you up". I also have very clear memories of children from a local industrial school (which was subsequently investigated for child sexual abuse) attending my school. The inability of some residents to concentrate in school is now readily explainable.

McKeown and Gilligan (1991) suggest that the increase in referrals of child sexual abuse was due, in large part, to the advocacy of women's groups during the 1980s, but the desecularisation of society added to the opening up of the economy and social system more generally contributed to the increasing knowledge base about things formally the preserve of the few in the corridors of power (Raftery and O'Sullivan, 1999). We are all now well familiar with child sexual abuse and with the increasing number of prominent cases reported in the media involving clerics such as Fr Brendan Smyth, Fr Ivan Pane, Fr Paul McGennis and Fr Sean Fortune.[5] The end of the 1990s saw a high profile case involving a nun suspected of sexual abuse and rape being eventually overturned in court, and of a male social care practitioner being sent to prison for sexual abuse of clients

---

[4] "Badness" was the term used by children in Artane Industrial School to describe sexual abuse.

[5] Raftery and O'Sullivan (1999, p. 254) detail almost 150 religious Brothers being implicated involving Artane, Salthill, Letterfrack, Tralee, Clonmel and Upton industrial schools.

in his care. This has helped to contribute to a climate of distrust in child protection and welfare.

At the start of the 1990s, issues such as solvent abuse, homelessness and truancy received a good deal of media and academic coverage, but as the decade came to a close the public became far more interested in child protection and newspapers were more willing to print stories about suspected child abuse. Homelessness, for example, has now been (re)contextualised as child abuse. The sexual abuse of children has now taken centre stage. Better services for children and adolescents are expected as there are more resources available (unemployment fell from 17.2 per cent in 1990 to 9 per cent in 1999 and there is a surplus of billions in the national exchequer), but people disagree fundamentally as to how, and where, resources should be deployed in the area of "marginalisation". Let me outline just a few areas of concern below.

AREAS OF CONCERN IN THE 1991 CHILD CARE ACT: THE TRIUMPH OF CHILD PROTECTION OVER FAMILY SUPPORT?

Although McGuinness (1992) argues that the 1991 Act transcends the sense of negativity seen in the 1908 Act, I have to agree with Duggan (1991/1992, p. 11) who asserts that it is disappointing that it tends to focus more on the pessimistic risk side of its understanding of child welfare as opposed to the resiliency side. Since the publication of the Act in 1991, social services have increasingly concentrated their efforts on child protection at the expense of family support.[6] There are problems with this. Ferguson (1996) notes that "enormous energy is put into information gathering and investigations which, in a high percentage of cases, end up offering little or nothing to the families". As recently as August 2000 the Labour party spokesperson was calling for the Minister for Health and Children to locate substantial funding for family support services to help

---

[6] Nigel Parton (1997) has recently asked (in relation to the 1989 Children Act in the UK), is it practicable that social services should attempt to have a dual focus in providing both family support and child protection, or should one role go to another body such as a voluntary association?

families to function well and meet the needs of their children (Shortall, 2000).

USAGE OF THE 1991 ACT

Kenny (1995) makes the point that the rate of usage of the Act for child protection purposes may well vary from area to area. Something that may appear a non-controversial decision, such as the movement of the age of childhood from sixteen to eighteen, has created a further strain on resources and several child care advocates have suggested at various conferences that these two years will have significant practice implications for both "clients" and professionals.[7]

There is always the fear that the more high profile cases of children "at risk" will receive the attention of a health board that feels it is under pressure, as opposed to what might be considered by many as the more deserving cases. One thinks here of the prominent Justice Peter Kelly based in Dublin who has continually pressed health boards to provide adequate care and protection for highly disturbed young people. His comments are regularly reported in the media and are understood by social care practitioners as being influential in politicising certain cases.

WHAT HAPPENED TO THE DEVELOPMENT OF RESIDENTIAL CARE?

Residential care services in the Republic of Ireland are stretched to their very limits. The Mid-Western Health Board (1996, p. 71) acknowledges that "a very responsive and professional service cannot meet the full range of needs presenting and, in particular, the compelling and urgent need for residential care provision for older children exhibiting challenging and disturbing behaviour." With the benefit of just nine years hindsight, it seems ironic that the Act fails to regulate the care and protection of children in residential centres when one consid-

---

[7] This is for a multitude of reasons. Many young people of 17 feel they are adults in their own right and resent "being treated as children" as they have to be under the Act. See McElwee (1999a).

ers the emerging stories of some "clients" resident in children's homes over the past number of decades (Raftery & O'Sullivan, 1999; RMA, 2000). The fate of children in residential care will, perhaps, be the defining feature of the second part of this decade when we could have learned so much from the Kennedy Report (1970) and the Task Force Report on Child Care Services (1980).[8] Of course, this assumes that children can obtain a place in residential care, which is often not the case.

An increasing number of children, described in the media as "out of control", have had to be placed in wholly unsuitable care as there is insufficient space available for them in appropriate secure facilities. This includes both males and females. Such children with significant emotional and behavioural problems do not belong in Garda stations, hospital wards or adult psychiatric care, but in adequately staffed therapeutic child care facilities.

There are literally dozens of examples to choose from, but I will outline just one here. A fourteen-year-old girl described by her psychiatrist as "the saddest case I have ever seen" was forced to spend Christmas in a detention centre because there was nowhere else for her to go. The young girl had a history of drug and alcohol abuse, had exhibited suicidal thoughts and alleged that her father had sexually abused her. Needless to say, her family were "well known to the social services". Perhaps the saddest comment I can make here is that this girl's case is not unusual. In this regard, the 1991 Act has failed these children as insufficient planning has gone into developing a coherent long-term policy around considering how one might attract trained residential social care practitioners into the system. Even less has gone into a strategy of retention (McElwee, 2000b).

Perhaps the most complex area of social care practice takes place in the High Support Units and yet these units appear to have the lowest qualifications levels in residential care as few social care graduates have elected to seek employment in them. This may well result in serious contention within the vari-

---

[8] The Kennedy Report (1970) met sixty-nine times, an average of once every two weeks.

ous health board personnel offices over the next few years and
I predict that the boards will be asked to account for themselves by qualified social care practitioners. Of course, this issue might be decided if the deliberations of the Department of
Health and Children's workshops on statutory registration are
successful (McElwee, 2000c).

HOMELESS CHILDREN AND YOUNG PEOPLE

One might have thought that the area of homelessness would be
vastly improved after the implementation of the 1991 Act. Although there have certainly been improvements, the situation
remains bleak for a disturbing number of children. National
figures for homelessness stand at approximately 5,000. Some
990 children were homeless in Dublin (with either one or both
of their parents) in 1999 with a further 250 teenagers living
homeless on their own. One in five people sleeping rough are
under the age of twenty. Despite the 1991 Act, a number of
prominent charities claim that there are inadequate resources
for streetwork aimed at rough sleepers, there is no emergency
accommodation for families, there are no hostels for homeless
drug users, there is no emergency accommodation for those
with alcohol or behavioural problems and there is generally
insufficient provision for homeless youth.[9]

AN EMPIRICAL CRITIQUE

It seems a fair criticism that the 1991 Act is not well grounded in
empirical critiques of child care services, although the publication of the annual reviews of each health board since 1995 is a
welcome development for scholars, administrators and managers alike. We now have some "hard" data and can make
grounded observations and predictions. Nonetheless, it could
be stated that these documents are overly descriptive at the
expense of rigorous and critical analysis. Whilst it is interesting
to note the involvement of health boards in various sectors, it

---

[9] These charities include Simon, Threshold, Focus Ireland, Failtiu Day Centre
and the Merchant's Quay Project.

might be more valid to obtain some qualitative commentary from partners in this process.

SEEKING OUT CHILDREN "AT RISK"

I have also been, and continue to be, critical of the failure of *some* health boards to actively seek out children "at risk" despite section 3.(2) of the 1991 Act which reads:

> In the performance of this function, a health board shall (a) take such steps as it considers requisite to identify children who are not receiving adequate care and protection *and coordinate information from all relevant sources relating to children in its area* (my emphasis).

I would like to see the health boards being far more proactive in this regard than has been the case heretofore. Of course, this will have significant resource implications (see McElwee, 1999b).

INCREASING WORK LOADS FOR PRACTITIONERS: THE MCCOLGAN CASE

I am consistently informed by both social care practitioners and social workers that the 1991 Child Care Act has resulted in their work loads increasing considerably, particularly in the area of child sexual abuse cases. The work has also become more complex as procedural and legal issues assume centre stage. This point was brought to the fore in the McColgan case in the North Western Health Board where four of the six McColgan children were abused by their father Joseph from the late 1970s to the early 1990s. When this case surfaced publicly, the questions that concerned child care professionals were (a) whether or not the health board staff had an advanced understanding of child sexual abuse and (b) could the staff have done more for the children. It seems to me that the staff could have accessed international data on child sexual abuse had someone been more proactive than appears to have been the case. Indeed, sexual abuse was discussed at an Annual Conference of the Irish Association of Social Workers here in Ireland in 1983.

A clear message is that the McColgan children despaired of the professionals (adults) who entered and exited their lives and still the abuse continued. One of the chapters in McKay (1998), entitled "Trapped in a System", elaborates on this point. It documents the family's total of 392 contacts with the North-Western Health Board between 1977-1993. Sophia continually searches for a reason the abuse continued despite the intervention of various professionals. The very last line in the book speaks volumes. "There was a lot of flurry and after that, nothing", said Sophia. "A big zero".

Allied to this is the fact that there are differing numbers of children in the care of health boards as a result of child abuse. Kenny (1995, p. 44) suggests that "this may reflect different ways of identifying and responding to child abuse rather than different rates of child abuse". All of this has resulted in what Ferguson (1996, p. 7) has described as an "opening out" of the routines of the expert system and science of child protection.

THE MEDIA FOCUSES ON CHILD PROTECTION AND WELFARE

Risk is now synonymous with child protection and welfare (Ferguson, 1996; Buckley, 1996; McElwee, 1998). Attention is increasingly directed at what are variously termed "high risk", "high challenge" and "at risk" children with a child protection service concentrated on an even smaller number of cases at the heavy end of the (perceived) spectrum of risk. At the same time, as noted above, professionals feel that they have been targeted by a media insistent on sensationalising stories of neglect which adds to a general feeling of crisis and despair amongst professionals and the public.[10]

Sections of the media, over the past two decades, have attempted to single out individual child protection workers rather

---

[10] This has been a source of debate at a number of annual conferences of the Irish Association of Care Workers.

than concentrating on institutions.[11] The litany of cases where blame has focused on professionals has entered the public consciousness. The Jasmine Beckford, Cleveland affair, Pindown scandal, Orkney affair and the Kincora Boys Home in the UK and the Madonna House, Trudder House, Kilkenny incest case, the "Kelly" case to name but some child care scandals, all attest to this. The Report on "Kelly" notably recognises the dangers of blaming individuals, but at the same time is critical of the Western Health Board by pointing to a systems accountability.

There will be those who will argue that individual practitioners should be identified and held accountable. Responsibility for inadequate or ineffective intervention must be seen to be corporate rather than individual (Interim Report of the Joint Committee on the Family, 1996, p. 211).

Social workers and social care practitioners do take risks in the interest of the client, but continually argue that they have to *individually* carry the responsibility for this in terms of social policy ambiguity. This does not only affect social workers. A leading medical doctor, based for a time at the Sexual Assault Unit of the Rotunda Hospital in Dublin, has been heavily criticised by a number of parents who claim they were wrongly accused of child abuse. Her pioneering work in validating cases of child abuse during the 1980s has been called into question and the Irish Medical Council established an inquiry into complaints of her professional misconduct. This case was widely reported in the media and has yet to be resolved.

MANDATORY REPORTING OF CHILD ABUSE

A particular disappointment with the 1991 Act is that it fails to deal with the issue of mandatory reporting which was to be included in the original Child Care Bill, but was defeated in the Dáil debates and subsequently removed from the later Child Care Act. This has led to significant discussion amongst child

---

[11] Although the emphasis in Ireland has been on social workers over the past decade, there is food for thought in all of this for the country's social care practitioners as they will, increasingly, come under public scrutiny.

care professionals and academics. A great deal has been made in the press about the recently published *National Guidelines for the Protection and Welfare of Children* (1999), which states that:

> All personnel involved in organisations working with chil-
> dren should be alert to the possibility of child abuse. They
> need to be aware of their obligations to convey any reason-
> able concerns or suspicions to the health board and to be
> informed of the correct procedures for doing so (DOH&C,
> 1999).

The stated aims of the new guidelines are to "assist people in identifying and reporting child abuse and to improve professional practice in both statutory and voluntary agencies". The guidelines seek to "improve", "clarify" and "enhance" the ex-
isting situation and are to be broadly welcomed, although I have outlined a number of reservations elsewhere (McElwee, 1999b). In terms of professional practice, the onus will now be a *legal* and *professional* duty to report as distinct from the *administrative* and *bureaucratic* duties of the past (Tunstill, 1997). This point is crucial.

Let me provide just a few examples here of the complexities I have referred to earlier in this chapter. In relation to juvenile prostitution, I feel that the new document gives out mixed mes-
sages to children. On the one hand it states that the "welfare of children is of paramount importance" and yet it also acknowl-
edges that "the criminal dimension of any action cannot be ig-
nored". This creates significant issues for outreach workers in this area. What does one do about juvenile involvement in prostitution where laws are being broken? It also states "chil-
dren have a right to be heard and taken seriously. . . . They should be consulted and involved in relation to all matters and decisions that affect their lives". Again, what does one do if a juvenile states expressly that they do not want their activity reported? Perhaps most ironic of all is the statement that "early intervention and support should be available to promote the welfare of children and families, particularly where they are vulnerable or at risk of not receiving adequate care or attention". The reality is that children and adolescents are being missed by the social services safety net on a daily basis despite

the (supposed) presence of a duty social worker who is designated to deal with "cases of emergency".[12]

CHILD TRAFFICKING AND PORNOGRAPHY

In many ways, the 1991 Child Care Act set the climate for the introduction of the Child Trafficking and Pornography Act, 1998 as this Act also has the safety and welfare of children at its heart. This Act is examined in detail elsewhere (see Shannon, this volume), but let us consider some related issues.

Levels of Research on the Trafficking of Children for Sexual Purposes

There has been little academic research published on trafficking of children for sexual purposes in an Irish context with the exception of my own background paper for the Department of Foreign Affairs (McElwee, 1999c). The COPINE Project based at University College Cork (with the assistance of the Gardai, Customs and Department of Justice, Equality and Law Reform) is involved in a European study on child trafficking and is about to focus on the Irish situation.[13] Currently, the project has no hard data on trafficking of Irish minors (Delaney, 2000). The Gardai suggest that trafficking for sexual purposes is not yet a problem in this country, but outreach workers have expressed concerns, particularly around "refugee" populations and international mobility. In my (1999c) research I could find no reliable evidence to support the claim that trafficking of Irish children for sexual purposes was a *significant* problem, but I do not doubt we will have to return to this issue. Indeed, at the time of completing this chapter in July, 2000 what was described as "Ireland's first sex slave case" is under investigation by the Gardai.

---

[12] The aspiration "under no circumstances should a child be left in a dangerous situation pending health board intervention" is fine in principle, but does not easily translate in practice.

[13] COPINE's study is called "Child Sex Tourism and Child Trafficking in Europe: A Case Study Analysis for Police Training".

Child Pornography and the Internet: "Netiquette" for "Nasty" People

A survey of 1,000 adults carried out by Amarach Consulting found that 21 per cent of Irish adults said that they had come across something they considered either illegal or harmful while using the Internet and that only two of these people had phoned the Gardai (Henry, 2000). One of the most difficult areas of pornography to police is the Internet, and Internet Service Providers have recently been told by the Minister for State and Children to ensure they do as much as possible to combat child pornography (Hanafin, 2000). In relation to the Internet, the Department of Justice, Equality and Law Reform estimates that there has been approximately six convictions under the 1998 Act with two of these related to possession of computer files (McElwee, 1999c).[14] In July 2000, a German national who is a computer technician, Tobias Vollmer, was jailed for eighteen months after admitting possession of child pornography.

Ireland now has an estimated 200,000 regular Internet users (RTÉ, 9 September 1999) and the government is actively pursuing a policy of attracting children in rural and urban areas into using the Internet for educational purposes. In many households, children are fully conversant with the Internet whilst their parents feel helplessly ignorant and cannot navigate cyberspace. Parents have to trust their children in their use of the Internet and this is a cause for concern. Parents, as well as children, need to be educated on the uses of the Internet.

The Expert Working Group on the Illegal and Harmful Use of the Internet

The "down side of the net" is currently being considered by a Working Group on the Illegal and Harmful Use of the Internet. One of the points noted by the expert group was the need to make a distinction between "harmful" and "illegal" material on the net. Response strategies will, therefore, differ between

---

[14] The Department of Justice feels that (at least from anecdotal evidence) there is "not much" home produced child pornography.

states and, even, within states and this point demands a chapter in itself. Research from the COPINE project in University College Cork suggests that the net is frequently accessed by paedophiles and is the main point for distribution of pornographic material. In her assessment of child pornography images Holland (1999) downloaded pictures from 42 newsgroups including images of soft child pornography and child erotica. The COPINE project now has over 5,000 pictures analysed and entered into their database.[15]

The Expert Working Group on the Illegal and Harmful Use of the Internet note that one of the central difficulties in attempting to police the net from a legal perspective is that "the Internet operates on an international basis whilst the law operates on a territorial basis . . . the extent to which national law operates can therefore be a complex issue to decide" (Working Group, 1998, p. 3). At the end of the day, the only opportunity for policing the Internet lies with international co-operation and if, and when, Internet Service Providers agree to regulate the material they receive.[16] The main recommendations of the Working Group were self-regulation, the establishment of a non-statutory complaints hotline, the creation of a non-statutory Advisory Board, a national awareness campaign by the Information Society Commission, the "proofing" of all Internet legislation and the improvement of training programmes for Gardai, law enforcement and the judiciary (Working Group, 1998, p. 7).[17]

In November 1999, the Internet Service Providers' Association of Ireland launched a hotline (www.hotline.ie) to mixed reviews and an Internet Advisory Board has been established.

---

[15] Eighty-eight per cent of the pictures are of girls with 12 per cent showing boys.

[16] See Horgan and Daly Jermyn (1999) for a legal interpretation of child pornography and the Internet in an Irish context.

[17] A number of NGO's have expressed concern at the potential misuse of the net. Barnardos in the UK has just published a report and a video titled *Whose Daughter Next?* as a resource on children involved in prostitution and Barnardos Ireland are about to produce a leaflet, directed at families, on the Internet. This is in terms of children being de-sensitised to sexual images and the potential of Irish children to be "sucked into" pornography.

The hotline is an attempt at self-regulation as links will be constructed between members of the Association and the website. On the one hand, the Internet Service Providers have voiced concerns at the lack of government funding to the hotline and on the other hand, some commentators have raised the question of the validity of an intermediary such as a hotline. Would it not be easier to simply report one's concerns to the Gardai? (Lillington, 2000).

Linking Pornography with Child Sexual Abuse

Is there any evidence to suggest a link between pornography and sexual abuse? For me, there is. A frequent visitor to Ireland, the psychologist Ray Wyre, believes that fantasy and behaviour are directly related. He outlines that pornography is present in every stage of sexual abuse and that men masturbate with pornographic material legitimating their distorted thinking. The danger here is that this acts as a re-enforcer to the ideas and behaviour of pornography (Wyre, 1992).

Pornography can be utilised to lead children into sexual play by getting them to talk about sex. One sees countless cases of paedophiles using pornography with minors as a gate into a deviant world — one where the adult has the power and the child is powerless. Finally, Van Parijs (1999) describes child pornography as a plague which plays a real part in cases of child sexual abuse; therefore, a differentiation between "real" and "fictitious" images is not relevant.

PART 2: SERVICE INITIATIVES

TRAINING AND PROFESSIONALISATION OF SOCIAL CARE WORKERS

It should be apparent at this stage that child protection and welfare is a highly specialised and complex area of work. Children who have been abused require sustained intervention, encouragement, patience, consistency and time from staff working with them and the training of child care workers has a profound effect on whether or not they help or further harm a child that has been abused (Kuykendall, 1990).

It is of interest that social care in Ireland was born out of "serious deficiencies in the running of children's centres . . . and the recognition of the need for professionally trained staff" (Kennedy and Gallagher, 1997). Put somewhat differently, social care has traditionally been associated with *problems* rather than *solutions* in Ireland (McElwee, 2000b). One of the more enlightened comments from the Kennedy Report (1970, p. 15) in relation to staffing the Industrial Schools was that "there appears to be a tendency to staff the schools, in part at least, with those who are no longer required in other work rather than those specially chosen for Child Care work". One wonders how much the situation has really changed?

As was the case in the 1970s, there is a serious difficulty in recruiting people into specific sections of the caring professions such as mental health nursing and residential social care to name but two sub-disciplines. Anecdotal evidence available to me from over 200 social care placement visits throughout Ireland indicates that the perceived threat of allegations around abuse has been a further *disincentive*, particularly over the past five years. The reluctance of males to consider the caring professions has wide-ranging implications that pressures of space do not allow me to develop here (Wells et al., 2000).

INVESTIGATION, VERIFICATION AND NOTIFICATION OF CHILD ABUSE

Many people involved in work with vulnerable children and adolescents receive inadequate training in investigation, verification and notification of child abuse and are at a distinct disadvantage when mandatory reporting is introduced, as they continue to be unfamiliar with the now expected codes of practice. Furthermore, there is inconsistency in provision, access and continuity of training around reporting, investigating and dealing with disclosures of child sexual abuse between the health boards and voluntary agencies. The areas of training around child abuse targeted in North American child care practice focus on competence in communication, helping skills, discipline, guidance and use of self (Bausch-Rossnagel and Worman, 1985).

There is some good news. In relation to health board training, more resources are being put in place and more staff are receiving ongoing training on a consistent basis. For example, in the Eastern Health Board (the country's largest) over 300 training places were purchased from external training providers which dealt with a range of issues from child abuse to culturally sensitive practice to family group conferences to name but some (EHB, 1999, p. 78).[18] Nonetheless the Eastern Health Board does admit a shortfall in the following areas:

- Development of a regional strategic plan leading to region-wide training framework

- Further development of multi-disciplinary training

- Development of a region-wide joint training programme with An Garda Siochana

- Expanded response to service developments such as Pre-School Inspectorate, Therapeutic Crisis Intervention training, best practice and developments

- The Training and Development Unit requires enhanced administrative support (EHB, 1999, p. 79).

This is worrying given the complexities of dealing with child sexual abuse.[19]

The *Children First* (1999) document has a dedicated section on training in child protection (chapter 14) and this sets out the parameters for future training stating that "all agencies involved with children have a responsibility to ensure that such training is available on an ongoing basis" (DOHC, 1999, p. 117). Nonetheless, given the shoestring budgets that many agencies operate under, this might be difficult to achieve.

The document targets two key groups for training in child care and protection including staff in the health boards and An

---

[18] Now re-named the Eastern Regional Health Authority.

[19] It would also be useful if the health boards could break down their statistics in a little more detail and let us know the particular grades and sub-disciplines sent on these training courses.

Garda Siochana by virtue of their statutory responsibility for child protection. Finally, it is welcome news that a percentage of the annual budget in each agency has been directed explicitly to cover child protection training.

REPORT WRITING AND RECORD KEEPING

Inadequate time is given to training in recording and reporting in social care practice and this needs to be addressed at training level (Gloster, in press). I continue to see what I would term "scrappy" and colloquial accounts of proceedings and deliberations in child care practice. The introduction of the Freedom of Information Act, 1998 will go some way towards remedying this, but child protection and welfare staff will require ongoing support (Crowdle, 2000). I include here moral support (supervision) and technical support (photocopy machines, computers, discs, dictaphones) in addition to legal support.

TRAINING IN SPECIFIC AREAS OF CHILD PROTECTION: THE NEED FOR REFORM

I have written extensively on the issue of the training and professionalisation of Irish social care work in the past and a recurring theme for me is that, particularly at the lower levels of training (Introductory Certificate and Certificate), the *requirements* between the various providers differ considerably. For example, one can obtain a Certificate in Social Care through distance education with limited seminar contact from one Irish university, whilst a certificate from the Institutes of Technologies requires a minimum of two years attendance at college over six academic terms with two/three structured, supervised practice placements. This creates a scenario where there is confusion amongst the public as to what courses are valid for entry into professional social care work, amongst students attending different courses and amongst service providers and employers. It is also the case that some courses cannot allocate the same amount of time to such topics as child sexual abuse when they are of much shorter duration than other courses.

The formation of the Irish Association of Social Care Educators will go some way towards ensuring the training becomes

increasingly politicised and standardised with employers and
our colleagues in education, but there is room for much improvement.[20] The health boards themselves will have to actively
rethink the qualifications issue and will be forced to co-operate
more than has been the case in the past with the various training providers.

My own view is that no one should be permitted to work in
social care with vulnerable populations without a *minimum* certificate (two years study period in a third level environment)
and that a degree should become the standard base qualification within five years (McElwee, 2000a). Although one can understand the health boards allowing unqualified staff to work
with vulnerable children as there are so many vacancies in the
system (see McElwee, 2000c), this is not a desirable situation
and it is not one social care practitioners themselves should
permit. This is particularly the case in relation to work in the
area of child sexual abuse.

Since the mid-1990s, a degree programme has been made
available within the Institutes of Technology for social care
practitioners and has taken in graduates from allied disciplines
such as psychiatric nursing, remedial teaching and social work.
Despite this, there is some ambiguity from the health boards as
to their level of acceptance of further awards in social care and
the professional status of the awards ladder from certificate to
degree. Again, this may be redressed when, and if, statutory
registration of social care staff is passed through legislation.

MONITORING STAFF WORKING WITH VULNERABLE CHILDREN

There are a number of areas of social care that will require
close monitoring in terms of recruitment and retention of qualified staff. The entire field of residential care is experiencing a
drain to community care and other disciplines such as youth
work and community work since the early 1990s. This will be-

---

[20] The IASCE comprises membership from the Athlone Institute of Technology, the Cork Institute of Technology, the Dublin Institute of Technology, the
Institute of Technology at Sligo, the Institute of Technology at Tralee, Waterford Institute of Technology and St. Patrick's College Carlow.

come even more problematic for managers of residential centres as social care falls in behind social work in terms of legalistic approaches to work (McElwee, 2000c). Indeed, a director of a large residential care facility in the Mid-Western Health Board area recently informed me that his problem was "attracting in people with a diploma never mind a degree" as the pay rates were seen as inadequate, the work was understood to be difficult and there was a trend towards community child care work.

THE NEED FOR A PROFESSIONAL REGISTER

I have also called for the establishment of a register of staff working with vulnerable populations in social care (McElwee, 2000a) and am currently in negotiations with the Child Care Policy Unit in the Department of Health and Children on this issue. In ongoing research for a national profile of social care practitioners in Ireland, 100 per cent of respondents currently working in social care indicated that they were in favour of a national register to practice (McElwee, 2000a). As I have mentioned earlier in this chapter, the Department is holding a series of workshops on this issue with various service providers, but there are many areas to be teased out and the deliberations of these workshops must be brought to the annual conferences of all the associations involved.

IS SOCIAL CARE A PROFESSION?

Can we legitimately call social care a profession? The answer to this is both yes and no. It seems to me that social care can best be understood as an *evolving* or *emergent* profession (McElwee, 2000b). For example, drawing on my preceding discussion in this chapter, the *National Guidelines for the Protection and Welfare of Children* (1999) fail to specify a "social care worker" as a designated officer, but refer instead to "child care workers". I note that "public health nurses" are accorded their own category and not given the generic title of "nurse" (which is listed separately). This insistence by the Department of Health and Children on maintaining the older terminology (child care workers) as opposed to the terminology employed by the third level training institutes and graduates (social care workers) "keeps social care workers down" to quote an ex-student of mine. This must be proactively addressed by the representative associations.

Social care has come a considerable distance since the publication of the Kennedy Report in 1970, but it still has a long way to go. A number of opportunities have been missed. These include the harmonisation of social care and social work training, the movement between social care and mental health education, the failure of successive governments to grasp the thorny issues within social care (one thinks here of State registration and mandatory reporting) and the failure to place a fence around social care as a distinct discipline. On the other hand, the Institutes of Technology have begun to co-ordinate training and education at third level, membership of the Irish Association of Care Workers and Resident Managers' Association has grown significantly, the health boards have begun to second staff to education programmes at a number of levels and structured pay scales that take into account educational qualifications have been developed.

WHAT SHOULD WE CONCENTRATE ON?

As the key discussion in this chapter is child sexual abuse, it is worth commenting on the level of training in this area. All of the Institutes of Technology have modules on child abuse and a number of them buy in external expertise to view specific treatment programmes both nationally and internationally. There is a concern that child abuse "may just be another module" and that the colleges could concentrate on developing full modules shared from a multi-disciplinary perspective drawing from social workers, paediatricians, mental health workers and therapists. Perhaps the colleges will explore in future years the viability of their students gaining specific qualifications in the area of working with survivors of child abuse and CPD (Continuing Professional Development) is well placed to look further at this area.

TRAINING PROGRAMMES

I would like to see training programmes focusing on technological, sociological, environmental and psychological aspects of child sexual abuse. Students should be given full courses on how to safely navigate the Internet as many of them will be called on to sit patiently with children as they, in turn, use the Internet. Students should be exposed to all relevant legislation around child abuse (in the widest sense of that term) and should sit rigorous examinations in this area. Furthermore, they should complete at least one practice placement with children who have been abused *prior* to gaining their professional qualification.

Child abuse should be fully explored in group dynamics sessions and the reaction of students should be formally noted by their tutors. Individual work should then take place with students as this area is so complex. They must be adequately trained and this must be a life-long process. Colleges and the practice environment must continue to work together in partnership in the provision of courses.

CONCLUSION

This chapter has discussed the 1991 Child Care Act, the trafficking of children for sexual purposes, child pornography and some training issues pertinent to social care practitioners. All of us involved in education and training must consistently emphasise a child-centred approach. Work with children who have experienced sexual abuse must be highly individualised and use of self must be clearly thought through. Above all, the child must be nurtured and a powerful image of normalcy developed.

There are connections between the four areas discussed in this chapter. Our collective programmes must be unafraid to challenge orthodoxy and must continually push forward an empirically-led research agenda. A few years ago, none of our courses included a formal study of the Internet and its potential for further abusing children and young people who have been damaged by sexual abuse. One thinks here of the reports in the media of children "befriending" other children in Internet chat rooms only to discover that they have been communicating with adult men who are sexual predators.

Many of our courses still do not have full modules on child pornography or the trafficking of children for sexual purposes and material on how social care practitioners might best work with these very complex and emotive issues. I feel that students (and, indeed, practitioners) should be encouraged to explore their own moral value systems and how these impinge on their work practice as the personal and professional views held by them determines their choice of response to any abuse scenario. This is a point reinforced in the earlier work of Gelles (1975) over 25 years ago.

We are now aware that child sexual abuse was, and is, a reality and have actively redefined abuse through legislation and practice initiatives. We know that we need to be careful in vetting the type of people who work with vulnerable children. We owe it to children and young people to put in place protective measures, but we cannot be complacent. David Murray, who was sentenced to ten years in prison for child sexual abuse, is a case in point. He was a graduate of the first child care course in Kilkenny and worked for 25 years in centres spread throughout the State before he was arrested and prosecuted. For me, this clearly illustrates the imperative for an independent registration body dedicated to social care practitioners where professionals are consistently monitored and tracked throughout their careers in the social care system (see McElwee, 2000a for a lengthy discussion on certification and registration in social care).

Despite the letter and the spirit of the 1991 Child Care Act, it is clear that the health boards, as institutions, have failed a disturbingly significant number of "at risk" children who remain in unsuitable accommodation (if they have any), who remain addicted to chemical substances, who are involved in exploitative sex and who live in such adverse circumstances that their survival is threatened. This was bravely articulated in the Kilkenny Incest case in the South Eastern Health Board, the Kelly case in the Western Health Board and, most recently, in the McColgan case in the North Western Health Board. Indeed, surveys suggest only a minority of people now trust doctors, social workers and psychologists to take swift action when they find out a child is being abused (*Irish Times*, 22 January 1998) and we should be concerned about this.[21]

There remains too much variation within and between health boards in relation to how professionals respond to children "at risk" of sexual exploitation. We need more informed commentary around what constitutes child abuse exactly and what precisely should be done about it. In this, the role of empirical research is crucial as a tool for informed policy development. It is also disturbing that only a minority of cases of sexual abuse reach prosecution, and only a percentage of these succeed.

Both Finkelhor (1992), in an American context, and Lalor (1998) in an Irish context, suggest child sexual abuse went unnoticed for centuries, and only by highlighting it can we undo the consequences of its invisibility. In this process, an informed public awareness of child protection and welfare is essential. Mandatory reporting of child abuse has to be seen as part of a wider strategy enabling and facilitating children's participation in social and political life. Children deserve to be heard as individuals in their own right, not as something they might eventually become — adults. A difficulty here has been recognised by Kenny (1995) who discusses the relationship between law and practice.

In relation to child trafficking and pornography, State Departments and the Gardai are taking this issue seriously and a sustained and co-ordinated approach has been adopted. Ireland is co-operating with our international peers and research is being conducted at a number of sites nationally (University College Cork, Waterford Institute of Technology, Department of Health and Children, Department of Foreign Affairs, Department of Justice, Equality and Law Reform). Further arrests and convictions are expected.

Although it may appear that this chapter has dealt with very diverse areas, the link is the child and young person. Perhaps the most disturbing fact is that child sexual abuse, child por-

---

[21] A recent IMS poll of 1,400 people (1998) reported 44 per cent believed professionals could be relied upon, which of course, means that 56 per cent of people in the survey did not trust professionals.

nography and child trafficking for sexual purposes create a category of children seriously "at risk" both physically and emotionally (Kelly, 1992).

We should continue to look at embracing relevant sections of existing international legislation whilst drawing up our own law unafraid to challenge "problematic" terminology. We should look at effective ways and mechanisms of reporting and referring "at risk" children and we should continue to test the boundaries of knowledge, education and training in social care in the area of child sexual abuse.

References

Buckley, H. (1996). "Child abuse guidelines in Ireland: for whose protection?" In H. Ferguson and P. Kenny (eds.) *On Behalf of the Child: Child Welfare, Child Protection and the Child Care Act, 1991*. Dublin: A&A Farmar.

Busch-Rossnagel, N., & Worman, B. (1985). "A comparison of educators' and providers' rankings of the important competencies for day care professionals". *Child Care Quarterly*, 14(1), 56-72.

Carpenter, Mary Chapin. (1992). "Come On, Come On". Sony Music.

Children's Act, (1908). Dublin: Stationary Office.

COPINE, (1998). University College Cork. Conference Papers. Cork: UCC.

Crowdle, A. (2000). "The Freedom of Information Act, 1998". *Irish Journal of Applied Social Studies*, 2(2).

Delaney, M. (2000). Personal communication.

Department of Health. (1996). *Putting Children First. Discussion Document on Mandatory Reporting*. Dublin: DOH.

Department of Health. (1996). *Putting Children First. Promoting and Protecting the Rights of Children*. Dublin: DOH.

Department of Health and Children. (1999). *Children First. National Guidelines for the Protection and Welfare of Children*. Dublin: DOHC.

Duggan, C. 1991/1992. "Getting to grips with the Child Care Act, 1991: A delicate balancing act" *Irish Social Worker*. Winter/Spring 1991/1992. Dublin: IASW.

Eastern Health Board (1999). *Review of family support and child care services 1998*. Dublin: EHB.

Ferguson, H. (1996). Protecting Irish children in time: Child abuse as a social problem and the development of the child protection system in the Republic of Ireland. In H. Ferguson and T. McNamara (Eds). "Protecting Irish Children. Investigation, Protection and Welfare". *Administration*, 44 (2).

Ferguson, H. and Kenny, P. (1995). *On Behalf of the Child. Child Welfare, Child Protection and the Child Care Act, 1991*. Dublin: A & A Farmar.

Finkelhor, D. (1992). "What do we know about child sexual abuse?" Surviving Childhood Adversity Conference, Trinity College Dublin, July 1992.

Gelles, R. J. (1975). "The social construction of child abuse", *American Journal of Orthopsychiatry*, 44 (April), 363-71.

Gilligan, R. (1993). "The Child Care Act, 1991. An examination of its scope and resource implications", *Administration*, 4, (4), 345-70.

Gloster, B. (in press). "Record keeping and report writing", In McElwee, C. N. *Scenarios and Solutions for the Social Care Worker*. Waterford: Centre for Social Care Research.

Hanafin, M. (2000). "Minister Warns Internet Firms on Child Porn". *The Irish Times*. 15 March 2000.

Henry, M. (2000). "Home Addresses Concerns on Net's Downside". *The Irish Times*. 3 June 2000.

Holland, G. (1999). "An Analysis of Child Pornography". Paper to the Second COPINE Conference. Royal Flemish Academy of Belgium for Sciences and the Arts. April 1-2, 1999.

Interim Report of the Joint Committee on the Family (1996). "Kelly: A Child is Dead". Report of a Committee Inquiry. Dublin: Tithe An Oireachtas.

Irish Times, 22 January 1998.

Irish Independent, 8 August 1992.

Kelly, L. (1992). "Pornography and child sexual abuse". In C. Itzin (Ed.). *Pornography: Women, Violence and Civil Liberties. A Radical New View*. Oxford: Oxford University Press.

Kennedy Report (1970). *Reformatory and Industrial Schools Systems Report.* Dublin: The Stationary Office.

Kennedy, K. and Gallagher, C. (1997). "Social pedagogy in Europe". *Irish Social Worker*, 15 (1).

Kenny, P. (1995). "The Child Care Act, 1991 and the social context of child protection". In H. Ferguson & P. Kenny (Eds.). *On Behalf of the Child: Child Welfare, Child Protection and the Child Care Act 1991.* Dublin: A & A Farmar.

Kuykendall, J. (1990). "Child development: Directors shouldn't leave home without it". *Young Children*, 45(5), 47-50.

Lalor, K. (1998). "Child sexual abuse in Ireland: a historical and anthropological note". *Irish Journal of Applied Social Studies*, 1(1), 37-54.

Lillington, K. (2000). "The Web and Your Business". *The Irish Times*, 10 December 2000.

McElwee, C. N. (1996a). *Children At Risk.* Waterford: StreetSmart Press.

McElwee, C.N. (1996b) "Issues of Child Care/Social Care Policy and Practice in the Republic of Ireland. The NCEA Report on Social and Caring Studies 1992 Assessed". Child Care in Practice. *The Northern Ireland Journal of Multi-Disciplinary Child Care Practice, 3. (1). September 1996.*

McElwee, C. N. (1998). "The search for the holy grail in Ireland: Social care in perspective". *The Irish Journal of Applied Social Studies.* 1(1).

McElwee, C. N. (1999a). "Mandatory reporting and the risk society" In C. Hanly (Ed.) *Child Sexual Abuse and Rape.* Waterford: Waterford Institute of Technology.

McElwee, C.N. (1999b). "From legislation to practice: Some observations on the 1991 Child Care Act in relation to the promotion and protection of children". *Journal of Irish Family Law.* September, 1999.

McElwee, C.N. (1999c). "Moving to action: background study on child prostitution, child trafficking and child pornography for the Irish Department of Foreign Affairs". Dublin: DFA.

McElwee, C.N. (2000a). "Damned if You Do and Damned if You Don't: Self-Regulation or Formal Registration of Social Care Workers in Ireland". 11 March 2000. Annual Conference of the Irish Association of Care Workers. Ennis, Ireland.

McElwee, C. N. (2000b). "A Rose by Any Other Name. What's in a Name?" 12 March 2000. Annual Conference of the Irish Association of Care Workers. Ennis, Ireland.

McElwee, C. N. (2000c). *To travel hopefully. Views from the Managers of Residential Child Care in Ireland*. Waterford, Centre for Social Care Research: RMA.

McElwee, C. N. & Lalor, K. (1997). *Prostitution in Waterford City: A Contemporary Analysis*. Waterford: StreetSmart Press.

McGuinness, C. (1992). "Social work and the law", *Irish Social Worker*, 10 (4).

McGuinness, C. (1993). *Report of the Kilkenny Incest Investigation*. Dublin: Stationary Office.

McKay, S. (1998). *Sophia's Story*. Dublin: Gill and Macmillan.

McKeown, K. & Gilligan, R. (1991). "Child sexual abuse in the Eastern Health Board region of Ireland in 1988: An analysis of 512 confirmed cases", *Economic and Social Review*, 22(2), 101-34.

Mid-Western Health Board (1996). *Review of Child Care and Family Support Services 1995*. MWHB.

North Western Health Board. (1998). *West of Ireland Farmer Case. Report of the Review Panel*. Manorhamilton: NWHB.

O'Halloran, K. & Gilligan, R. (1996). Child Care Law. A Comparative Review of New legislation in Northern Ireland and the Republic of Ireland: The Children (N.I.) Order 1995 and the Child Care Act 1991. Dublin: CAWT.

Parton, N. (1997) "Child protection and family support: Current debates and future prospects". In N. Parton (Ed.) *Child Protection and Family Support: Tensions, Contradictions and Possibilities*. London: Routledge.

Raftery, M. & O'Sullivan, E. (1999). *Suffer the Little Children. The Inside Story of Ireland's Industrial Schools*. Dublin: New Island Books.

Report of the Working Group on the Illegal and Harmful Use of the Internet. (1998). Dublin: Department of Justice, Equality and Law Reform.

RMA (2000). Strategy document on registration. Galway: RMA.

RTE, (1999). Five seven live. 2 September Current Affairs radio broadcast.

Shortall, R. (2000). "Children at Risk". *The Irish Times,* 2 August 2000.

Task Force Report on Child Care Services (1980). Dublin: Stationery Office.

Tunstill, J. (1997). "Family support clauses of the 1989 Children Act". In N. Parton (Ed.) *Child Protection and Family Support: Tensions, Contradictions and Possibilities.* London: Routledge.

Van Parijs, T. (1999). Conference Address. Second COPINE Conference. Royal Flemish Academy of Belgium for Sciences and the Arts. April 1st-2nd.

Ward, P. (1997). *The Child Care Act, 1991.* Dublin: Round Hall Press.

Wells, J.S.G., Ryan, D., McElwee, C.N., Boyce, M. & Forkan, C. (2000). *Worthy not Worthwhile? Choosing Careers in Caring Occupations.* Waterford: Centre for Social Care Research.

Wyre, R. (1992). "Pornography and sexual violence: working with sex offenders". In C. Itzin, (Ed). *Pornography: Women, Violence and Civil Liberties. A Radical New View.* UK: Oxford University Press.

Chapter Three

Therapy with Sexually Abused Children

Deirdre O'Shea & Rosaleen McElvaney

INTRODUCTION

This chapter outlines the issues relevant for working therapeutically with children who have been sexually abused. Any discussion of such work must begin with an overview of the impact of sexual abuse, and the various theoretical frameworks which are available to help us understand what happens to children, and those around them, when they are sexually abused. Particular issues for therapists are outlined and a protocol offered for proceeding with assessing a child and family's therapeutic needs. Basic requirements for creating an environment where healing can take place are suggested and the therapy process itself is described, including a discussion of both individual and group therapy, with reference to both abuse-focused therapy and non-directive approaches. The importance of working with families is highlighted and those issues pertinent to family work are noted. Finally, a short vignette is offered to illustrate the process of what happens when a child engages in therapy. Resource materials are listed at the end of the chapter which may be useful when undertaking this work.

SERVICES

In Ireland, therapeutic services for children who have been sexually abused are primarily offered by the statutory services within each of the eight health boards around the country.

These may be accessed through local health centres, by contacting the local social worker or psychologist or they may be offered by the Child Psychiatry Services and may require a referral from a general practitioner. Within the Eastern Health Board region there are two specialist therapy services for this group of children and their families, St. Clare's Unit, The Children's Hospital, Temple St. and St. Louise's Unit, The Hospital for Sick Children, Crumlin. In the voluntary sector, Children at Risk in Ireland (CARI) provide specialist services in both Dublin and Limerick. Other voluntary organisations that provide a wide range of therapeutic services to children and their families include the Irish Society for Prevention of Cruelty to Children (ISPCC) and Barnardo's. Psychologists, social workers, psychiatrists and psychotherapists also work in the private sector and may have an interest or expertise in this area. Professionals in both the public and private sector are usually registered with their professional body and their credentials can be checked out quite easily.

IMPACT OF SEXUAL ABUSE

In any discussion of the impact of sexual abuse on an individual, it is important to acknowledge that some children who have been sexually abused do not appear to suffer adverse consequences and are able to deal with the experience without the need for professional intervention. Distress in children is not always visible or easily assessed as some children may internalise the hurt causing, for example, poor self-concept. Other children may be able to cope adequately at the time but may experience difficulties in later life which can be re-triggered by other life experiences as they grow into adulthood. Finkelhor (1990) estimated that between one-quarter and one-third of sexually abused children have adequate psychological and social resources to cope with the experience of sexual abuse without adverse long-term consequences. Considerable research has been carried out to ascertain why it is that some children are traumatised as a result of sexual abuse and other children are able to cope quite well following this experience but with little consensus on findings.

In order to assess individual impact it is necessary to take a broad perspective and include the child, the family and the broader network within which the child lives. The trauma literature suggests, according to Briere (1997), that the amount of post-traumatic symptomatology an individual experiences is a function of at least four broad variables:

- **Characteristics of the stressor**: Factors such as the duration and frequency of the abuse; the relationship between the child and the abuser; the age and sex of the abuser; the type of sexual activity; the use of physical force and violence; the age of onset; whether the child disclosed the experience and the reaction to this disclosure; whether the child participated in the abuse experience (Sanderson, 1990).

- **Variables specific to the victim**: The impact of abuse can vary according to the psychological makeup of individual children, their personal experiences prior to the abuse and resultant coping strategies. However, it is also noteworthy that a number of child molesters report that their assessment of the child's degree of loneliness and distress is a factor in targeting children for sexual abuse and the finding that vulnerable children may be more often targeted by sex offenders is supported by some research on victims (Salter, 1995). "Children are in every case hungry for love, but offenders sometimes choose children who are starving for it" (Salter, 1995).

- **Subjective response to the stressor**: how the child reacted to the abuse.

- **The response of others to the victim**: the social supports available to the child, for example, having someone to tell.

To understand the effects of sexual abuse, one must accept as a starting point that a sexually abusive experience has the potential to inflict monumental suffering on children and their families. There are potentially physical, psychological and social consequences. The Department of Health *Child Abuse Guide-*

lines (1987) details the behavioural and psychological sequelae of child abuse on the individual child.

THEORETICAL MODELS

Therapeutic interventions with children who have been sexually abused need to be firmly embedded in theoretical models of human behaviour in order to be systematically effective. There are a number of different theoretical positions which inform the therapeutic work.

Feminist theory emphasises the role of power and degradation as motivational factors in sexual violation and views child sexual abuse/incest as an endemic societal manifestation of the power imbalance between the sexes (Herman, 1992; Russell, 1986). Social conditioning into roles of power and domination versus passivity and dependency contribute to the setting for abuse to take place. There is a strong emphasis on empowerment in the therapeutic process.

Feminism stresses the subjective knowledge of the individual. The client is the expert on their own experience and therapy seeks to validate the victim's experience. There is now a widely accepted view which has its origins in Feminist theory that symptoms are a creative adaptation to highly negative circumstances. Survival skills that enable the victim to cope in the immediate aftermath may become maladaptive as the child grows into adulthood, creating secondary difficulties which need to be resolved in adulthood.

Post-traumatic Stress Disorder is defined as a traumatic event in which both of the following are present: (1) the person experienced, witnessed, or was confronted with an event or events that involved actual or threatened death or serious injury, or a threat to the physical integrity of self or others and (2) the person's response involved intense fear, helplessness or horror. In children, this may be expressed instead by disorganised or agitated behaviour (American Psychiatric Association, 1994). Finkelhor (1988) has criticised the PTSD model for its emphasis on effect, how the victim feels, without addressing many of the cognitive effects observed in children who have been sexually abused, and notes that it does not apply to all victims and is limited in its ability to describe the dynamics of sexual abuse that lead to a certain set of symptoms. Other symptoms which appear outside the PTSD model include fear, depression, self-blame, guilt and sexual problems as well as self-destructive behaviours such as suicide, substance abuse and revictimisation (Briere and Runtz, 1988).

The Traumagenic Dynamics Model of child sexual abuse (Finkelhor and Browne, 1985) proposes four dynamics which explain the impact of child sexual abuse: traumatic sexualisation, betrayal, powerlessness and stigmatisation. According to Finkelhor and Browne these dynamics are:

> not necessarily unique to sexual abuse. They occur in other kinds of trauma. But the conjunction of these four dynamics in one set of circumstances is what makes the trauma of sexual abuse unique, different from such childhood traumas as the divorce of a child's parents or even being the victim of physical child abuse. These dynamics alter children's cognitive and emotional orientation to the world, and create trauma by distorting children's self-concept, world view, and affective capacities (pp. 530-531).

The model outlines the dynamics involved in the four factors, the psychological impact of these dynamics on the child and the behavioural manifestations. The model presents a descriptive framework which accounts for the variety, diversity and extent of observed effects of child sexual abuse. It helps to explain similar effects with different manifestations. It conceptualises child sexual abuse as a process, not simply as a distinct event, and therefore takes into account the child's life prior to the abuse experience which may have made the child vulnerable to sexual abuse, such as elements of betrayal or unstable family relationships (Sanderson, 1990). This model reinforces the importance of individualised therapy for each child rather than adopting a formalised, structured therapeutic framework or model.

Developmental Psychology and Object Relations Theory suggests that chronic abuse by family members inevitably alters the full development of the child (Courtois, 1988). It involves the sacrifice of the self to the satisfaction or care of the family which can lead to serious damage to the child's sense of self, often causing a fragmented identity to develop. Children often talk about having a sense of "not being myself". The sense of a "normal self" is lost as defences and symptoms become entrenched into the child's developing personality. According to Van der Kolk (1987):

> The earliest and possibly most damaging psychological trauma is the loss of a secure base. When caregivers who are supposed to be sources of protection and nurturance become simultaneously the main sources of danger, a child must manoeuvre psychologically to re-establish some sense of safety, often becoming fearfully and hungrily attached, unwillingly or anxiously obedient, and apprehensive lest the caregiver be unavailable when needed (p. 32).

To survive, the child must resort to primitive ego defences to protect him/herself. These include denial, projection, introjection, splitting, avoidance, and distancing. Children become confused and the meanings of love and sexuality become intertwined. It is necessary for the child's survival to perceive their parents as "good" yet what is happening is clearly bad, thus the child sees themselves as "bad", deserving the parent's treatment, therefore maintaining the image of the parent as good. Roland Summit (1983), in the *Child Sexual Abuse Accommodation Syndrome*, describes how the sexually abused child psychologically adapts to the sexual abuse and accommodates so that life is turned into a seemingly normal event allowing for psychological survival. Secrecy and helplessness and possible unpredictability and threat to life are constantly reinforced in renewed invasions into the child's physical and mental integrity and autonomy. Although this helps the child maintain an illusion of control, it can have very serious consequences for the child's sense of themselves and self-esteem. Child abuse in its many forms inevitably interferes to some extent with the achievement of the various developmental tasks which the healthy child needs to complete to grow into a healthy adult.

In this model, therapy is about the search for the "true self", the dismantling and dissolution of the "false self" that developed in order to protect the child from psychological disintegration. Therapeutic work referred to as "inner child work" draws to a large extent on this model and is about helping the individual to both remember the trauma and to feel the emotions which were split off at the time in order to survive the abuse ordeal. Work focuses on family patterns and how the child's development fitted into these patterns. This model emphasises the importance of the therapeutic environment being one of safety, consistency and reliability.

Grief Theory: Victimisation of any sort involves loss — of control of life assumptions, of innocence, of a sense of safety in the world, and very often of the self as it was before the victimisation, of self-esteem, sense of personal worth and body integrity; loss of trust. Many adult survivors refer to their sense of "lost childhood"; children refer to not having a sense of themselves as "a child". This can show itself in the growing child developing a compulsive pattern of seeking out lost opportunities in a futile search for what was denied them in their childhood. Kubler Ross (1982) has written extensively on both theories of loss and the process of recovery. According to this model, in order to heal, the individual must accept the losses, stop trying to heal the family and stop the self-sacrifice entailed in the effort. This involves admitting the inability to control the circumstances. It is through this process that the pain associated with grief is experienced and the grieving process takes over.

Tilman Furniss' Syndrome of Secrecy (1991) highlights the difference between child sexual abuse and other forms of child abuse. Child sexual abuse as syndrome of secrecy for the child is determined by external factors, by specific aspects of secrecy in the abusive interaction itself and by internal psychological factors. External factors relate to the lack of corroborative evidence, implicit and explicit pressure on the child not to tell and anxiety about the consequences of disclosure. Interactional aspects of secrecy describe the nature and process of the abuser's relationship with the child and how this contributes to the powerful dynamic of secrecy. Internal psychological factors refer to internal processes within the child and how this maintains the secret. There is a similarity between Bastiaans' (1957) (cited in Furniss, 1991) description of the concentration camp syndrome and the process of sexual abuse in that in both situations an extreme survival mechanism of normalising the experience can occur. A psychological state can evolve in which the experience is psychologically wiped out and "forgotten about", only to re-emerge in later life when new stressful events result in flashbacks which threaten to flood and overwhelm entirely the coping mechanisms and defences of the survivor. A further similarity between the experience of childhood sexual abuse and concentration camp experience is that the perpetrator in both scenarios is often also the caretaker and provider, sometimes of positive emotional attention. This element is crucial in understanding the seemingly bizarre attachments and loyalties between victim and perpetrator.

These models do overlap although they place different emphases on different issues and all contribute significantly to the understanding of child sexual abuse. However, they can only be valuable in the context of a thorough knowledge of child development and how the impact of child sexual abuse varies according to developmental stage. Also, there are different impact issues for boys and for girls which have not been adequately explored in these models. It is therefore important to take account of gender but also of race, culture, class, sexuality, disability and religion which will influence the child and family's perception/beliefs about and response to the abuse.

ISSUES FOR THERAPISTS

Working therapeutically with children places demands on therapists. This section therefore applies to any therapeutic work with children but certain issues are particularly relevant to the area of sexual abuse. Firstly, an understanding of the dynamics of child sexual abuse, theoretical models, abnormal psychology and a thorough knowledge of child development is essential. Regular access to supervision and support which should involve formalised regular supervision is necessary, both case management supervision in relation to decision making and clinical supervision in relation to the therapeutic process. Conscious awareness of one's own family history, potential personal issues, attitudes to sexuality and child sexual abuse as well as a willingness to seek help with unresolved conflicts are essential. The therapist's own life experiences influence their belief systems and how they work in therapy.

Transference and counter-transference issues will operate and influence the therapeutic work. In therapy, children can often experience the therapist as a symbolic representation of other psychologically important authority figures in their lives and respond to the therapist in this way (both behaviourally and emotionally). Similarly, the child or the therapy process may evoke some unresolved conflictual feelings which need to be recognised as counter-transference and brought to an appropriate forum such as supervision or personal therapy.

Gender differences need to be acknowledged and how this might impact on the therapeutic relationship. There are advantages and disadvantages to both female and male therapists depending on the gender of the child, the gender of the abuser, the emotional relationship between child and abuser, the child's relationship with both parents, the child and family's attitudes to men or women and the possible need for an alternative role model. It is important to emphasise that the gender of the therapist is an issue for both the child and the therapist as transference issues for the child can raise significant counter-transference issues for the therapist. The impact of abuse material on the therapist is also significant. Secondary post-traumatic stress or vicarious traumatisation can arise for therapists when working with children who have experienced trauma. This can take the form of a tendency to discuss sexual abuse excessively outside of work, feeling overwhelmed by the abuse material, feelings of numbness and listlessness, experiencing a lack of safety in the world or experiencing flashbacks, dreams or nightmares with abuse content. Boundary issues need particular attention when working with children who have been sexually abused, given that the trauma they have experienced has been one of boundary violation. It is the role of the therapist (similar to the parent) to create safety in the therapy through the establishment and maintenance of appropriate boundaries. Difficulties which may arise include moving appointment times, ending on time, touch, and therapist's self-disclosure (see Pearlman and Saakvitne (1997) for a full discussion of vicarious traumatisation and boundary issues).

ASSESSMENT FOR THERAPY

Assessment for therapy is primarily about identifying the impact of the abuse on the child and their family, determining whether therapy is appropriate and necessary at this time and deciding what form the therapy should take. A systemic approach involves assessing children in their context, their family or care system and planning therapeutic interventions for the whole system. For those children in residential care it may be important to offer consultation and/or support in the issues that arise in caring for children who have been sexually abused.

A thorough assessment involves a three-stage process, each of which are examined below: (1) obtaining information relevant to the therapy, (2) the initial assessment appointment(s) between the child, family and therapist and (3) planning the therapeutic intervention.

Obtaining Information Relevant to the Therapy

The information needed can be obtained from three sources: the referring agency or other agencies involved with the family, the assessment report and the family. In our legal context it is necessary for a forensic interview to have been undertaken with the child before engaging the child in therapy that is specifically abuse-focused. It is important to draw a distinction between a forensic assessment which is for legal purposes and a therapeutic assessment which is primarily to ascertain the child's needs. A thorough assessment would require the following information:

- Detailed family history including attitudes to sexuality, any other traumatic experiences that the child or family may have had, support available to the child and family

- Specific abuse details, how the abuse was discovered/disclosed, the current situation regarding the child's safety, legal proceedings, contact with the abuser and the family's reaction to the disclosure

- Child's presentation and level of functioning; communication skills, developmental level (cognitive, emotional, sexual), how the child is doing educationally, interests and hobbies, the effects of the abuse on the child — emotions, behaviour, relationships, current concerns about the child and strengths in the child's life

- The impact of the abuse on the family — the parents and siblings, parents' psychological functioning, parenting issues and level of support available to them.

- Previous experiences of therapy, if any, and the child's view of this, parents' expectations and views of therapy.

Assessment is an ongoing process throughout therapy. Some of this information becomes available in the course of therapy and may change over time, for example, family reaction to disclosure. Disclosure is generally not a one-off incident but an ongoing process that often continues during therapy as the child develops trust and a sense of physical and emotional safety.

The Initial Therapy Assessment

This is often the first meeting between the therapist and the child and family and so is the beginning of the therapeutic relationship. A significant aim is to make a connection with the child and their family. It involves a dual focus — information for the child and family about therapy and information for the therapist. This sharing of information is essential in order to empower the child and family to make an informed choice about therapy and gives them a sense of choice and control in their lives. This creates the sense of therapy as a collaborative process.

Planning the Therapeutic Intervention

The following decisions need to be considered:

- Who in this family requires help and what form should this be — individual, group or family therapy, support group for parents?

- How to match this child with a therapist in terms of models of working, skills, experience and gender.

- Should the therapy be short term, focussed and directive or more longer term, non-directive? In many cases it is appropriate to follow a combination of the two approaches. It is important for the child and family that the initial contract is clear. It may be that the therapy contract requires constant reassessment and only becomes clearer as therapy proceeds.

- Where there are criminal/legal proceedings pending, consideration needs to be given regarding preparing the child to give evidence in court. It may be that the therapist is the best placed person to undertake this work as the court case is likely to have an impact on the child. However, for some children it is better that this piece of work is undertaken by someone independent, for example, victim support workers.

- Communication media: the media through which the child is likely to engage and is best able to express themselves, for example, art, play, drama, music, movement, writing, poetry.

CREATING A THERAPEUTIC ENVIRONMENT

Our understanding of the dynamics of child sexual abuse informs our decisions as to how we create a space for the child where they can feel safe enough to engage in therapy and hopefully to benefit from it. Although many of the following points are relevant to working with children in distress, some are particularly important for the child who has been sexually abused because of the nature of sexual abuse.

Child Safety

What makes a child feel safe? Firstly, the child needs to be in a stable environment in order for them to engage in and benefit from therapy. This may involve considerable work on the part of the community services to ensure, for example, that the child has no ongoing contact with the alleged abuser. Alternatively, there may be a lot of disruption and chaos in the child's family following a disclosure of child sexual abuse and this situation may need to be addressed before the child will feel safe enough to engage in therapy. This does not exclude the possibility of supporting a child through a time of crisis but this support might best be offered by another health care professional, for example, a child care worker or social worker in the community. Thus, it is important to distinguish between therapy and support. Therapy can be distressing in itself and children need to have a network of supports available to help them cope with the possible secondary distress arising from attending therapy. It is also true that after a child is engaged in therapy other issues which are going on in their life (for example, placement issues) indicate that a more supportive therapy is more appropriate for a period of time when difficult material would not be explored and the focus may be on more practical day-to-day issues in the child's life.

The Therapeutic Frame

It is the responsibility of the therapist to ensure that all the necessary supports are established prior to engaging the child in therapy.

Children need both practical and emotional support in coming. They need to be brought, collected, and have an adult nearby to call on if they are distressed and looking for a parent/caregiver.

Consistency and predictability are important. Thus, children should be confident that the same therapist will see them in the same location, in the same room, at the same time, for the same length of time, without interruptions, on a regular basis, usually once a week. If for any reason this pattern has to change, it is important to signal this in advance so that the inconsistency is balanced with knowledge (predictability). Talking through as much as possible what might or might not happen during the course of the therapy helps the child develop a sense of security and confidence that there will be no nasty surprises in store. This is particularly relevant to establishing the therapeutic contract. This involves talking about why they are coming, what will happen (for a useful aid see Nemiroff and Annunziata

(1990) in Children's Book section at end of chapter), what information will remain confidential between the child and the therapist and what type of information will need to be given to the child's parents or caretakers and what reports may be requested. It is usually best practice not to make promises about never sharing information, but rather attempt to develop trust and ensure that the child understands that if information is going to be shared, they will be informed of this in advance.

Confidentiality — what is appropriate? This is an ongoing issue for therapists working with children. It is important that children feel they have their own space to express thoughts and feelings that they are unable to do elsewhere. They may be afraid to distress their parents or feel misunderstood at home. However, if a child is sharing information about difficulties at home which need to be addressed with the family, it is not in the child's best interests to keep this information confidential. Also, if the child shares information indicating a risk to their own welfare or the welfare of other children, it is the therapist's obligation to act on this information, with or without the consent of the child. There are limitations to confidentiality and when these are outlined in the beginning and incorporated into the therapeutic contract, later difficulties can be easily avoided.

The physical environment is also important — the waiting area and consultation rooms need to be child-friendly, with a ready availability of toys for appropriate age levels, books, crayons, paper. A comfortable warm welcoming room — homely but not at home, a room that the therapist feels comfortable in. Some children need to have very little stimulation in the room depending on distractibility levels, and one may have to remove toys; for others, they need to engage with material at their own pace and be able to explore the room.

It may be necessary to establish rules, for example, the child may only play with one toy at a time. Practical safety also needs to be attended to — plug covers, scissors, knives or sharp instruments kept in a safe place.

COMMUNICATING WITH CHILDREN

There are a variety of theoretical approaches which influence one's therapeutic orientation, namely psychoanalysis, child psychoanalytic psychotherapy, Jungian analysis, constructivist psychotherapy, systemic psychotherapy, integrated psycho- therapy, cognitive-behavioural therapy, gestalt therapy, psy- chosynthesis, transpersonal theory and the person-centred ap- proach. (Boyne, 1993). Those most featured in the literature on child abuse are behaviour therapy, cognitive therapy, systemic therapy and psychoanalytic psychotherapy. There is also a va- riety of therapeutic media that are very useful in communicat- ing with children: art therapy, play therapy, drama therapy, music therapy, body psychotherapy and verbal therapies. There is specialist training available in these areas, some in Ireland and others are available in England.

Communicating with children requires a comprehensive understanding of child development, particularly children's language skills and their comprehension. Too often adults can expect children to adapt to the adult world rather than adults trying to get in touch with the child's world. An ability to get in touch with children is related to an ability to get in touch with the child within oneself, that is, an ability to recall what it is like to be a child and an ability to be playful.

A holistic approach to working with children is very impor- tant. This entails taking account of the whole child and all that has and is happening to them as well as focusing on the abuse. There is a risk that the abuse can become the central focus of the work and other significant issues can get lost. For all victims it is im- portant that they are not just seen as the sexually abused child but that their whole self/life is taken into account. A holistic ap- proach therefore involves meeting the child where they are at. Therapy can only work if children feel heard and understood.

The therapeutic relationship with the child is the vehicle through which children are able to explore their most painful experiences and feelings. It can also provide an opportunity for re-learning about relationships and about boundaries. The re- lationship is also an opportunity for the child to address issues and experiences from other relationships through transference.

Some children are able to talk directly about their experiences and feelings and benefit from the use of workbooks and
focussed techniques. For other children, direct verbal communication may not be possible. Children tend to think symboli-
cally rather than literally. It is especially difficult to talk about
painful and traumatic experiences as children often do not have
a language to communicate about sexual abuse and the resulting emotional trauma. It is therefore important that we try to
find and understand each child's own unique way of communicating. Very often children can show us how they feel through
the use of different media. Therapy using art and play is a
helpful way for children to explore their inner worlds. The process of playing itself may be therapeutic for children (Winnicott, 1971). Some children are able to immerse themselves with
this media and to work through their painful experiences in the
context of the therapeutic relationship. In other situations, it is
necessary for the therapist to help them make sense of their
feelings through the use of interpretation, reflection and making connections.

It may be possible to have a play therapy room, a music
room and an art therapy room that are specifically equipped for
these purposes. More often therapists have to adapt other therapy rooms and so may require play bags with different play
equipment available and art therapy boxes.

Therapeutic work with children can be either through individual or group therapy and may be directive or non-directive.
Directive work involves having a pre-planned focus or agenda.
This is related to the child's ability to work in a direct focused
way and the therapist's assessment of the issues and feelings
that the child needs to explore. A number of workbooks have
been written that suggest different ways of addressing the issues (see resource list at end of this chapter). *Non-directive
therapy* involves following the issues that the child brings into
the room either directly/verbally or through the play/art or
other media. In non-directive therapy the therapist may take
the role of following the child or may follow the child's engagement in art/play and be involved in guiding this. If a child
chooses to play with puppets the therapist may follow this and
use reflection or interpretation or may introduce a relevant

theme/issue/feeling into the play and see how the child engages with this.

It is important for parents to have some sense of how their child is doing in therapy and to have feedback if there are any concerns. This is an important boundary issue to discuss with children when arranging the therapeutic contract. Discussing with children what they think their parents need to know from the session is an important way for children to feel that they have some control and ownership over what is happening.

GROUP THERAPY

Group therapy can be very beneficial. It helps to reduce isolation, can normalise feelings and can facilitate children in being able to identify and explore feelings particularly through a sense of not being the only one. It can help reduce shame and embarrassment. Often children who find individual therapy too intense can find that the group experience encourages and facilitates an exploration of issues related to the abuse. Also, discussion with others who have had similar experiences can trigger previously unexplored or unacknowledged issues for children. Undertaking group therapy requires knowledge and understanding of group processes which also involves a comprehensive understanding of the role of the group and group leaders.

When considering groupwork there are a number of key questions to consider:

- **Timing**: It may be appropriate to start with individual or group therapy. However, it may also be that a combination of therapies is appropriate, for example, individual then group, group then individual. Children who are experiencing crises may require individual therapy alongside group therapy.

- **Age range**: It is important to take account of not only the child's developmental and cognitive level but also their level of social and emotional functioning.

- **Gender mix**: Generally, for younger children it is possible to have mixed gender groups, whilst for teenagers it is better to have same gender groups.

- **Group numbers**: Minimum participants should be five, maximum eight to ten, depending on age of participants, developmental level and number of facilitators.

- **Mix of group membership**: While it is good to match group members according to similar issues, the benefits of group-work may be undermined if one group member has markedly different issues (for example, intrafamilial v. extrafamilial; gender of abuser). This is important in reducing isolation and stigmatisation.

- **Gender of therapists**: Where possible it can be very beneficial to have leaders of mixed gender as this is useful role modelling for children and also opens opportunities to explore transference.

- **Focussed or process-oriented group**: A focused group involves a prepared programme that aims to address particular themes/issues/feelings. A process-oriented group works on two levels — to address the issues that are most pertinent to the group members each week/at that time and to use the group process to explore relationships. Children may play out roles in the group that are reflective of family patterns of relationships or peer relationships.

- **Open or closed groups**: Closed groups have defined membership from beginning to end and tend to provide more safety and security which is vitally important for members to be able to engage in therapy. A continually changing membership may raise difficulties in developing trust and encouraging people to share their innermost feelings/thoughts/worries. However, an open group may be appropriate if there are predetermined entry and exit times.

- **Length of groups**: This will vary according to the needs of the children and their age. Generally, a minimum of eight weeks is required for a focussed group. Process-oriented groups usually require a longer period which can vary from 12 to 18 weeks or longer.

WORKING WITH FAMILIES

When a child has been sexually abused it has an impact on the whole family. A circular pattern of mutual influence can develop in that the emotional impact on each family member will impact on and influence how the child copes and vice versa. It is therefore important to take account of the whole family's needs, for their benefit and for the benefit of the child. Work with the family may involve parents, siblings and other extended family members.

Working with parents involves allowing them the time and space to discuss the emotional impact of their child's abuse on themselves and to explore how this has influenced their relationships. It is important to assess how the family is dealing with the child's disclosure. The range of family reactions may include: trying to pretend that it has not happened, focussing all their energy and time on the abuse so that their life becomes organised around this, over-protectiveness, disbelief of the child and failing to take action to protect the child. Many parents feel tremendously guilty about the abuse, often questioning how did they not know, did not realise, did not see the signs. They may feel responsible for the abuse if they left their child in the care of the person who abused them. Parents also question why their children may not have told them or delayed in telling them. Parents' own level of distress influences their behaviour which impacts on their relationship with their child and can lead to miscommunication and misunderstandings of each other's behaviour and actions. Children may choose not to talk about the abuse with their parents in order to protect them from further distress. Parents may interpret this as the child not trusting them and feeling very angry with them. Parents may feel very angry about the abuse of their child and children may interpret this as anger with them for "letting it happen" or "not telling". Some parents may wish to compensate for the abuse and do so by removing/reducing boundaries, which can be very frightening and confusing for children.

Parents can be overwhelmed by their own feelings of guilt or anger which may influence how emotionally available they are to their children. It is difficult for children to express their feelings if their parents have unresolved feelings of their own.

Clearly the impact of the abuse on the family is affected by whether the abuse is intrafamilial or extra-familial, which creates different dynamics for family members. There may be different alliances for family members depending on the nature and history of their relationship with the abuser. Where one child is abused by an older adolescent sibling the issues are especially complicated. Parents may have divided loyalties and feel joint obligations to both children, as well as strong feelings of guilt — how did this happen? In situations where the abuser is a partner or one of the parents there may be ambivalent feelings about them and complex feelings of loyalty to their child, their partner and to themselves. They may feel guilty for choosing an unsuitable partner and putting their child at risk.

In our experience, addressing the wider systemic issues is vital for therapy for the child to be effective and to reduce the longer-term detrimental effects of the abuse.

The other key focus of work is in relation to parenting a child who has been sexually abused. Meeting and talking with other parents is often a very important way to share ideas and experiences. However, when one's child has been sexually abused this is more complex and difficult for parents. They may feel very isolated and stigmatised and so do not know how to seek help or advice. Parents often raise questions: should we talk to our children about the abuse? How do we do this? How do we help our child to cope with learning how to trust, or to cope with the feelings of sadness and anger? How do we cope with the changes in their behaviour? A support group for parents of children who have been sexually abused can be invaluable. Groups such as this can also be educational, for example, sharing information about the impact of abuse on children, ways of managing concerning behaviour. Support groups for parents are usually set up by individual services where children are attending therapy, when there is a demand for such groups and sufficient numbers to constitute a group.

Thus, assessment for therapy involves assessment of the whole family's needs. In considering family work, it is important to think about the timing. Sometimes family therapy is indicated from the outset and needs to be part of a parallel process alongside the therapy with the child. In other cases, it may be too painful and difficult for the family to meet and talk together at the outset and it may be that the child requires time in individual therapy initially and the parents also require some time to explore their own issues first. In our experience it can be beneficial to find a way of re-joining the child and parents once the child's individual therapy is drawing to a close. The child may need the opportunity to explore particular issues in their relationship with family members.

Couples therapy may be required to explore the impact of the abuse on the parents' relationship (for example, sexual difficulties). Also, the abuse may raise issues for parents about their own experiences and they may require individual personal therapy.

It is necessary to consider the other children who are in the family, that is, the non-abused siblings. These can often be the "lost children". It can be helpful to explore what the siblings know about the abuse. Is the abuse a secret in the family? How does this affect family relationships? How do they understand and make sense of the abuse? How has the abuse affected family dynamics? Siblings can often sense that something serious is happening in their family and may fear that it is something to do with them. They may also feel left out, possibly feel jealous of the time and attention given to the victim. Some siblings may feel guilty for not having known, not protected or not believed. If siblings are not given some information then it is difficult for them to make sense of what is happening in their family. These issues need to be explored with parents. Is it appropriate to tell siblings about the abuse? How will the victim feel about this? What is appropriate to tell them given their age and understanding? Family therapy can provide a useful forum for exploring these issues, particularly to look at family communication and relationships.

Finally, family therapy does not necessarily require that the whole family attend together initially. Sessions may be offered to the parents, the parents with the victim, the parents with the siblings, the victim and siblings together, the siblings on their

own. Various meetings may be appropriate and it is important
to consider the individuality of each family.

CASE VIGNETTE: SEAN

Family History

Sean, aged 4, has three older siblings, Seamus (8 years), Siobhan (10 years) and Donal (13 years). They live with their parents Teresa and Mark. All identifying details have been
changed to protect the family's confidentiality.

Background to the Referral

Sean was referred by a social worker from the local community
care team. Some weeks earlier whilst playing outside in the
front garden Sean had gone missing. The Gardai were called
and searched for Sean, who was found approximately two hours
later further up the street. Sean said a neighbour, Michael (17
years) had taken him to his house. Sean had extensive bruising
to his body and a medical examination was arranged. Sean told
the Gardai that Michael had "hit him and hurt him on his pri-
vates".

Following an assessment it was confirmed that Sean was
sexually and physically abused by Michael. The sexual abuse
involved penetrative anal abuse. Sean was then referred for
therapy.

Therapy Intake

Sean attended this appointment with his parents. Teresa and
Mark explained that since the abuse Sean's sleep pattern had
become very disrupted, he did not like to sleep in his own bed,
had lots of nightmares, appeared more angry and aggressive,
was very fearful of Michael returning and had become sexually
curious with his peers, was using sexual language particularly
with his brothers and wanting to engage in sexual play. Sean
was colouring a picture whilst his parents talked. He then got
up, moved a chair to the corner and commented "this is the
naughty chair where Michael should sit". The therapist re-

peated what Sean had said and acknowledged that Michael had been very hurtful to him and that he might want to come and get some help with the feelings that this has left him with.

Decision

It was agreed that Sean would be offered individual play therapy and that sessions would also be offered to the parents with a different therapist. Family sessions were to be considered at a later time.

Therapy with Sean

Sean was seen by a female therapist (there were no male therapists available). He attended a total of 38 sessions over a period of one year.

In view of Sean's age and developmental level the therapist decided to undertake non-directive play therapy initially and follow the child's lead, keeping an open mind to use more directive approaches if indicated. Sean chose to explore the play materials available and showed a particular interest in the sand, the play figures and the dolls' house.

Through the play Sean started to explore and express his feelings about the sexual abuse. Sean played with the toy soldiers in the sand, splitting them into "goodies and baddies". Initially the baddies would always win the fights and would kill the goodies. Elements of his own experience were represented in the play, for example, the goodies were often trapped by the baddies and unable to get away, the goodies were hidden in the sand and could not be found by anyone. The therapist would reflect on the symbolic themes in the play and explore with Sean the feelings connected with this, for example, the fears of the trapped soldiers, feelings about being hurt. One week Sean put a "bad" soldier in the slime commenting that "he had taken a child away and assaulted him". As the sessions progressed Sean's play changed so that the goodies began to develop more strength and would win the fights, indicating Sean's attempts to have a sense of mastery over his experiences.

Sean then moved into pretend play — choosing the scary face mask and pretending to take away the soft toys. Sean talked about the big boy killing the teddy bear. This indicated Sean playing more directly about his own experience and possibly expressing fears that he was going to die. He engaged in play fights with the swords, pretending that he was the baddie who had hit Teresa's little boy. The therapist started to make connections with Sean's own experience and ask questions about this.

Following this Sean began to talk more directly about Michael — he would comment that Michael was not allowed to come to this special room. He started asking questions, for example, did his Mum and Dad like Michael? Why did Michael take him away? Why could his Mum and Dad not find him? And he described how he had tried to get away. This led to a different stage in the therapy. Sean started expressing feelings of anger towards Michael and towards his parents, which related to his sense of feeling let down.

Sean spoke about his bad dreams and his fears that Michael would try and take him away again. He used the clay to make the dragon from his dreams and then a magic wand so that he could make the dragon go away. Sean practised using the magic wand in the sessions and spoke directly to the dragon about his fears and his anger. He continued with pretend play where he was the policeman who arrested Michael and sent him away.

Sean's play then changed to curiosity about the differences between boys and girls. The therapist introduced some focused work on bodies, exploring Sean's questions, good and bad touches, good and bad secrets, safe places and safe people.

Three review appointments were held with Sean and his mother — at the 6th session and then at 12 session intervals. His parents began to report considerable improvement in Sean — reduced preoccupation with the abuse and with Michael, reduction in his level of anger and nightmares, and describing him as becoming more like "his old self". It was agreed to work towards ending therapy and appointments were changed from weekly to fortnightly for the final six sessions as a way of preparing Sean. Sean began to express some anger and frustration with the therapist. The therapist considered the possibility of this being transference of Sean's earlier feelings of being let down and abandoned or whether in fact it was an inappropriate time to end. Through regular supervision she was able to explore her own feelings about finishing with Sean and her fear that she was "abandoning" Sean. She was then able to explore these issues in the play with Sean and look at creating positive experiences of endings.

Work with Parents

Teresa and Mark were offered and attended eight sessions. They used the time to talk about their own feelings about Sean's abuse and to discuss parenting issues. They discussed feelings of shock, disbelief, anger with Michael and his parents, distress at the thought of what Sean went through and feelings of guilt for not having protected him. They spent time recalling the details of the day Sean went missing and when he was found, which seemed to help them process the experience and feelings attached to it. They also raised questions about the abuse — Why did Michael do it? What would happen to him now? And how it would affect Sean in the future?

A number of sessions focused on parenting issues — how to talk to Sean and his siblings about the abuse, ways of helping Sean with the nightmares and with his anger.

Family Sessions

Four sessions were held with Teresa, Mark, Seamus, Siobhan, Donal and Sean. These focused on the children's understanding of what had happened to Sean and answering their questions about it. Time was also spent discussing Teresa and Mark's concerns about sexual play, normalising sexual curiosity, looking at how children can find safe ways to raise their questions and creating safety rules and boundaries.

RESOURCES

Play Equipment

Play people, farm and zoo animals, dinosaurs, sea animals, monster people spiders/snakes. Cars, car mat, police cars, fire engine and ambulances. Farm yard. Toy soldiers, tanks and trucks. Hand and finger puppets — people, animals and "feelings face" puppets. Dolls, dolls house, dolls bed, bath, potty, baby's bottle. Play kitchen and play food, toy money. Telephone. Face masks. Dressing up box, including doctor's bag, police hat, gun, and handcuffs. Face paints. Soft toys. Play dough, shapes and plasticine.

Art Equipment

A variety of colours of poster paints, powder paints and finger paints. Clay, clay boards, clay tools and hardener. Paint brushes, water pots, trays, rollers, sponges, splatter tools, aprons. Pens, pencils, crayons, felt tip pens — large and small, chalk, charcoals, pastels. Crêpe paper, tissue paper, and a selection of colours and sizes of art paper. White board and pens.

Children's Books

Curtis, J.L. (1998). *I feel silly today and other moods that make my day*, New York: Joanna Cotler Books.

Crary, E. (1992,1992,1994) *Dealing with Feelings Series*, Seattle, WA: Parenting Press.

Davis, N. (1996) *Once upon a time: Therapeutic stories that teach and heal*. Oxon Hill, MD: Psychological Association of Oxon Hill.

Nemiroff, M. & Annunziata, J. (1990). *A Child's First Book about Play Therapy* Washington, DC: American Psychological Association

Patterson, S. & Feldman, J. *No No and the Secret Touch,* California: The National Self-Esteem Resources and Development Center.

Rouf, K. (1989). *Mousie,* London: The Children's Society

Books on fairy tales, books on feelings, sex education books.

Resource Packs and Books

Celano, M. Hazzard, A., Simmons, M. & Webb, C. (1991) *Recovery from Abuse Project.* Atlanta, GA: Emory University School of Medicine.

Karp, C & Butler, T. (1996) *Treatment Strategies for Abused Children,* Thousand Oaks, CA: Sage.

Karp, C & Butler, T. (1997) *Activity Book for Abused Children.* Thousand Oaks, CA: Sage.

Karp, C & Butler, T. (1997) *Treatment Strategies for Abused Adolescents.* Thousand Oaks, CA: Sage.

Karp, C & Butler. T. (1998) *Activity Book for Abused Adolescents.* Thousand Oaks, CA: Sage.

Madell, J.G. & Damon, L. (1989) *Group Treatment for Sexually Abused Children.* New York: Guildford Press.

Spinal-Robinson, P. & Easton-Wickham, R (1992) *Flip Flops, a workbook for children who have been sexually abused, ages 7–9.* Notre Dame, IN: Jalice Publishers.

Sunderland, M. & Engleheart, P. (1993). *Draw on your Emotions, Creative ways to explore, express and understand important feelings.* Minneapolis, MN: Winston Press.

References

American Psychiatric Association (1994) *Diagnostic and Statistical Manual of Mental Disorders* (4th ed.). Washington, DC: American Psychiatric Association.

Bastiaans, J. (1957). *Psychosomatische gevolgen van Onderdrukking en Verzet.* Amsterdam: NoordHollandische Uitgevers Maatschappij.

Boyne, E. (1993). *Psychotherapy in Ireland.* Dublin: Columba Press.

Briere, J. (1997). *Psychological Assessment of Adult Posttraumatic States* Washington, DC: American Psychological Association.

Briere J. & Runtz, M. (1988). "Symptomatology associated with childhood sexual victimization in a nonclinical adult sample", *Child Abuse and Neglect*, 12, 51-59.

Courtois, C. (1988) *Healing the Incest Wound: Adult Survivors in Therapy*, New York: Norton.

Department of Health (1987) *Child Abuse Guidelines,* Dublin: Department of Health.

Finkelhor, D. & Browne, A., (1985) "The traumatic impact of child sexual abuse: A conceptualisation", *American Journal of Orthopsychiatry*, 55, 530-541.

Finkelhor, D., Williams, L.M. & Bums, N. (1988) *Nursery Crimes: Sexual Abuse in Day Care.* Newbury Park, CA: Sage.

Finkelhor, D. (1990) "Early and long-term effects of child sexual abuse: An update". *Professional Psychology: Research and Practice,* 21, 325-330.

Furniss, T. (1991) *The Multiprofessional Handbook of Child Sexual Abuse*, London: Routledge.

Herman, J. (1992) *Trauma and Recovery*, London: Basic Books.

Kubler-Ross, E. (1982). *On Death and Dying,* London: Tavistock.

Pearlman, L.A. & & Saakvitne, K.W. (1997) *Trauma and the Therapist*, New York: Norton

Russell, D. (1986). *The Secret Trauma: Incest in the Lives of Girls and Women.* New York: Basic Books.

Sanderson, C. (1990) *Counselling Adult Survivors of Child Sexual Abuse,* London: Jessica Kingsley Publishers.

Salter, A. (1995) *Transforming Trauma,* Thousand Oaks, CA: Sage.

Summit, R. (1983) "The child sexual abuse accommodation syndrome", *Child Abuse and Neglect,* 7, 177-193.

van der Kolk (1987b) "The role of the group in the origin and resolution of the trauma response". In B. van der Kolk (Ed.). *Psychological trauma.* Washington, DC: American Psychiatric Press

Winnicott, D. (1971) *Playing and Reality,* London: Tavistock.

Chapter Four

Current Issues in Therapy for Adults Sexually Abused in Childhood

Rosaleen McElvaney & Deirdre O'Shea

INTRODUCTION

In recent years in Ireland there has been a growing number of
adults approaching counselling services seeking help in dealing with difficulties associated with childhood experiences of
sexual abuse. This population of clients has grown steadily. In
the early 1980s the majority were attending Rape Crisis Centres
around the country. Some of these clients had been raped in
adulthood but most were not. Similarly in the public health
services, the numbers of adults presenting for therapy with the
problem "sexually abused in childhood" were increasing. In
addition, many adults already engaged in therapy began disclosing childhood experiences of sexual abuse. These new disclosures were no doubt influenced by the growing public recognition of the existence and prevalence of child sexual abuse.
However, there was also a growing awareness among health
care professionals of the secrecy surrounding such experiences
and the reluctance on the part of both children and adults to
disclose sexual abuse. These professionals were therefore
more open to hearing about sexual abuse, and so less likely to
inhibit clients from talking about these difficult experiences.
Detailed statistics of adults seeking help were not available
across all the health board regions but concern about the demand for counselling resources resulted in the Eastern Health

Board (now the Eastern Regional Health Authority) establishing a separate service specifically to deal with this client group. The LARAGH Counselling service, established in 1993, was the first statutory counselling service established within the UK and Ireland to offer an exclusive service to adults who had been sexually abused in childhood. In 2000 the brief of the LARAGH service has broadened to incorporate those clients who have experienced physical abuse in childhood in line with the work of the Child Abuse Commission and the establishment of other counselling services throughout the public health service in Ireland.

The previous chapter considered in detail therapeutic work with children who have been sexually abused. Many of the points discussed are also relevant to working with adults. This chapter will focus on those issues which we feel are particularly pertinent as we enter a new millennium when health care professionals are seeking to place a new emphasis on the broad range of childhood abuses which are prevalent in our society.

LONG-TERM IMPACT OF SEXUAL ABUSE

Factors Influencing Impact

Those factors which have been identified as influencing the impact of child sexual abuse have been outlined in the previous chapter. The time delay between the abuse itself and seeking help can contribute to difficulties or ameliorate difficulties depending on certain exacerbating or mediating factors.

Life experiences prior to the abuse are relevant when considering the impact of childhood experiences. These include attachment history to parents or relevant carers, other significant life events including the occurrence of other traumatic experiences. Coping mechanisms used over the years influence how the individual and his or her family cope with the disclosure of sexual abuse. Many adults present in therapy, having made attempts over the years to tell others, only to feel rejected, dismissed and determined to tell no one ever again. The impact of a negative reaction to disclosure can for many individuals be as significant as the impact of the experience itself.

The extent to which they were believed if they did disclose, any action taken as a result of their disclosure (either by family or by authorities), or opportunities for therapy, are all relevant. Also significant is the level of secrecy which has been maintained and the effort required to do so. Many clients, particularly those who have been abused by family members, have continued to have close contact with the offender; indeed, the abuse may have continued into adulthood. There may have been pressure, internal or external, to maintain the outward appearance of a positive relationship with the offender.

The individual's current life situation including current relationships which may be either supportive or abusive can be a mediating or exacerbating factor. Support networks available to the client throughout childhood and into adulthood are crucial, including those available to the client at the time of seeking therapy.

The reason for seeking help is particularly important for adults who maintained silence around their experience of childhood sexual abuse. Significant life events may act as triggers for seeking therapy: consensual sexual relationships; marriage; birth of children; children reaching the age at which the adult was when they were abused; deaths of family members, close friends, or the offender; other traumatic events such as car accidents; hearing of other instances of child sexual abuse, either through the media or through acquaintances; sexual abuse of their own children.

Effects of Trauma

When considering the specific difficulties with which adults may present in therapy it is more helpful to think in terms of the effects of exposure to traumatic events rather than the effects of child sexual abuse per se. Often children not only experienced sexual abuse but also emotional abuse and perhaps physical abuse. The effects of these experiences are not neatly categorised. As Berliner & Briere (1999) note, exposure to traumatic events can be associated with a wide variety of subsequent psychological difficulties, including post-traumatic and acute stress, dissociation, anxiety, depression, low self-esteem, guilt, psychosomatic symptoms, sexual difficulties, relationship problems, substance abuse and suicidality (for example, Boney-McCoy & Finkelhor, 1995; Briere, 1992; Davidson & Foa, 1993; Herman, 1992; Kulka et al., 1990; Singer, Anglin, Song, & Lunghofer, 1995; Suedfeld, 1990; Weaver & Clum, 1995; Yule & Williams, 1990). Difficulties may persist over many years, depending on the varying influence of certain mediating or exacerbating factors mentioned above, resulting in adults seeking help as late in life as their sixties and seventies.

THEMES IN THERAPEUTIC WORK WITH ADULTS

It is helpful to have a theoretical framework for understanding the impact of child sexual abuse which informs the therapeutic work. Different theoretical models are outlined in the previous chapter. Browne & Finkelhor (1986) have provided the most comprehensive framework to date to offer an understanding of the aetiology and effects of childhood sexual abuse and how the impact of the abuse can manifest itself in adulthood. Their Traumagenic Dynamics theory outlines four dynamics which encompass the range of difficulties experienced: Traumatic Sexualisation, Betrayal, Powerlessness and Stigma. While this model is useful, it is our belief that it needs to be incorporated with a systemic approach which takes account of the impact on the family and how the family coped at the time of the abuse as well as how this then impacts on the child and later the adult. A holistic approach would take account of both intrapersonal and interpersonal perspectives on understanding the impact of the abuse. The intrapersonal perspective may well address the level of self-blame and guilt the person feels in relation to the abuse which impacts on self-esteem and sexual identity among other issues. However, it is also necessary to explore how the child/adult's relationships have both impacted on these personal issues and vice versa. The systemic family therapy approach stresses the importance of looking at individuals within the context of their family lives, past and present, and how this influenced, and continues to influence, their constructions of who they are. Individual one-to-one therapy needs to take account of this. No one exists in isolation but in the context of many relationships and the dynamics of the sexual abuse occur within this context and need to be addressed as such.

Hall and Lloyd (1993) identify the following themes in therapeutic work: issues around "the child within", being believed, the nature of the abuse, responsibility for the abuse, work on the family of origin, flashbacks and memories, regression, trust, loss, getting in touch with feelings, anger, confrontation, forgiveness, living in the present: from victim to survivor. It is not possible to elaborate on their work in this chapter but the reader is referred to Hall and Lloyds' text along with Courtois (1988), Sanderson (1990) and Meiselman (1990).

Bookshops abound with texts on how to counsel adult victims of child sexual abuse. What is sometimes lost in the quagmire of specialist techniques is the core principle that adults who have been sexually abused in childhood are first and foremost human beings and their primary need in seeking help is to establish a caring and supportive relationship where they can feel safe enough to talk about and explore difficult feelings, thoughts and behaviours. Therapists and counsellors who work with this population do need training in the area of sexual abuse. They will inevitably encounter certain difficulties in this area of work which they would undoubtedly not experience with clients who have not had a sexual abuse history. They need continuing education and training in this area along with supervision to enable them to provide the best possible service to their clients. Nevertheless, they also need to keep the central focus on the individual client rather than the "sexual abuse label" with which clients come looking for help. The development of specialist training courses and specialist services can lead to a sense of de-skilling on the part of counsellors and therapists who do not have the opportunity to pursue the area of sexual abuse as a specialist area of work. This should not preclude counsellors and therapists from continuing to work with clients when they disclose sexual abuse in the context of a trusting relationship, provided they seek and receive the necessary training and supervision to enable them to continue their work.

SERVICES

The regional health boards around the country provide community services to adults who have been sexually abused, usually within their mental health programme. O'Doherty (1998) provides a list of contact numbers in her appendix and the *Directory for women who have suffered from domestic violence or the threat of violence* also lists health services which are appropriate for adults who have experienced sexual abuse in childhood (National Steering Committee and Department of Justice, Equality and Law Reform, 2000: see also Appendix 1 this volume). Although some psychiatric services require a referral to be made through a general practitioner, most psychology services accept self-referrals. Therapy is usually offered on an individual basis with groups being set up in response to demand in a particular area. The greatest advantage to groupwork with these clients is the reduction of isolation and stigmatisation experienced by participants which may facilitate communication about the abuse. Groupwork approaches may be directive with a specified agenda or process — orientated where the content of the work depends on what is happening for people on a week to week basis. There are particular complexities involved in planning groupwork for adults who have been sexually abused in childhood. The nature of the abuse is significant. Including clients of both intrafamilial and extrafamilial abuse will generate different issues which need to be addressed. Groupwork with an all-female group may vary significantly from an all-male group. Research suggests that focused educational work may be more helpful for all-male groups in the first instance while women may more easily engage in discussions about how they feel about their experiences. The gender of the offender is also significant. A woman who has been abused by a woman may find it difficult to feel identification with a group of women who have all been abused by men. The impact of sitting in a group of women may in itself be inhibiting rather than therapeutic in the first instance. Similar issues apply to men. Finally, the gender of the therapist will have its own impact on the group, whether male or female.

Within the specialist services such as the Rape Crisis Centres and LARAGH Counselling Service groupwork is more commonly found due to the availability of sufficient numbers of clients with similar needs. St. Louise's Unit (Our Lady of Lourdes Children's Hospital) also currently provides groupwork for parents of abused children who have themselves experienced sexual abuse in childhood in conjunction with LARAGH Counselling Service.

Couples therapy and psychosexual therapy may also be required. Sexual abuse often impacts on intimate relationships and couples may need help with dealing with difficulties that arise, particularly difficulties in sexual relationships. Also, clients may undergo considerable change during the course of therapy and this may in itself create difficulties in current relationships.

Many adult clients have multiple problems and therefore may need the involvement of other services such as mental health services, addiction counselling, child protection. Whilst it may be appropriate for an individual to attend one service only and focus on particular difficulties, other clients may need to attend various services simultaneously to enable them to engage in the work of addressing the impact of the sexual abuse. For a client who is addicted to drugs, it may be difficult to engage in therapy about their abuse experiences at an emotional level as the drugs can block their ability to explore feelings aroused by the discussions. These clients may also rely on drugs to cope with the emotions triggered in therapy. However, the difficulties associated with the abuse may well be the underlying cause of the addiction and therefore has to be addressed alongside the addiction. This is also the case for people experiencing severe mental health difficulties and who may require medication in order to help them cope with the feelings aroused by the abuse. Good inter-agency communication is essential when dealing with this group of clients.

IMPACT OF THE WORK ON THERAPISTS

Organisational Issues

When staff are working with clients who have been sexually abused they need to be cognisant of how the dynamics of sexual abuse can be mirrored or reflected within their own working group, in particular the dynamics of secrecy and feelings of being threatened or being abused. The secrecy inherent in the experience of sexual abuse may be replicated in the therapeutic relationship as in when a client binds a therapist to secrecy, even when to do so may endanger the client and/or others. An example of this is when a therapist unintentionally colludes with a client's belief that to maintain secrecy in relation to an abuser who may currently be abusing other children is in the client's best interests. Furniss (1991) has paid exceptional attention to how the syndrome of secrecy in child sexual abuse penetrates the multidisciplinary professions involved in working with clients with these difficulties. Furniss advocates challenging the secretive tendencies of the client, bringing the abuse "out into the open". When the therapist is able to discuss his/her work openly in supervision, this combats the mirroring referred to above.

Another dynamic is when the therapist can empathise too strongly with the client's feelings of being unprotected so that the therapist may feel vulnerable in discussing his/her work. Constructive criticism may be experienced as attacking rather than supportive, persecutory rather than stimulating. Therapists need support with these feelings and also clear guidelines as to their roles and responsibilities. It may sometimes be necessary to recruit an outside facilitator to help the staff group deal with how the sexual abuse dynamics are affecting the group of therapists.

Debriefing

It can be very distressing to hear the details of a client's experience of sexual abuse. A therapist may feel overwhelmed in their reaction to these details or alternatively may have emotional reactions such as anger or complete disconnection. The therapist may then respond to the client from this position, thus interfering with the client's own work. It is helpful to be able to discuss these reactions in supervision but also the therapist may require some debriefing time following the client sessions. This may present difficulties for therapists working in isolation and requires the therapist to develop support systems whereby they can avail of the opportunity to talk about his/her work.

Supervision

There are two aspects to supervision. Firstly, there is the therapeutic work itself, the quality of the work, what happens in the room between the client and the therapist, and secondly, there is the management of the work from an organisational standpoint. The first we refer to as *clinical supervision* and the latter as *case management supervision*. Clinical supervision can be operated on an individual basis or in a group setting. The therapist has the opportunity to explore the quality of his/her work along with its impact on the worker in a supportive relationship. It is best if in this case the supervisor is not responsible for the worker as a manager. Therapists usually seek supervision from a more experienced counsellor/therapist whose therapeutic orientation may match their own training. Group supervision may either take the form of a small group with one supervisor or a peer group with no identified leader.

Case management supervision, on the other hand, is conducted by the therapist's manager, usually in a group setting where therapists from other disciplines and/or therapeutic orientations share the responsibility for contributing to discussion. This forum addresses the monitoring of the work, the therapeutic contract, the most appropriate and best use of resources, sharing of skills and expertise in the group and record-keeping. Limitations on confidentiality can be usefully explored in this context.

Personal Therapy

The motivation to become a therapist can come from various sources. Therapists may be seeking to help others and share some of their own positive experiences of life or they may be motivated because of their own experiences of difficulties. Cecchin, Lone & Wendell (1994) have categorised this as the missionary therapist and the wounded therapist. It may be that therapists are motivated by both, which does not preclude them from being good therapists. However, personal issues can interfere with the ability of a therapist to remain neutral and objective. It is therefore necessary for therapists to explore their own personal issues in therapy so they do not unduly influence the client in the therapeutic process. In addition, it is helpful for the therapist to have the experience of being a client in therapy.

Therapists have reported difficulties in their own relationships due to the impact of their work — sexual difficulties, overprotectiveness of children; difficulties with trust in relation to men; sleeping difficulties; flashbacks, intrusive thoughts. This is referred to in the literature as vicarious traumatisation (Conte, 1999). It is therefore important for any therapist who is working with a number of clients who have been sexually abused to pay attention to the management of vicarious trauma: having a clear theoretical framework to inform one's work, setting clear boundaries in the therapy contract with the client (whether therapy contract is time-limited/open-ended, limits of confidentiality, agreed contact between therapist and client and whether any contact is acceptable outside the sessions), knowing oneself, one's vulnerabilities and strengths, and supervision. Conte (1999) stresses the importance of having a self-care plan whereby the therapist can nurture him/herself and ensure that other aspects of one's life are given the time and attention they require. An excellent textbook on this subject is Pearlman & Saakvitne's (1996) *Trauma and the Therapist.*

LIMITATIONS OF CONFIDENTIALITY

With the publication of *Children First* (Department of Health and Children, 1999) and recent debates about mandatory reporting, there is increasing pressure on all therapists to familiarise themselves with their reporting obligations and with how the social services and gardai operate when dealing with suspected cases of child sexual abuse. The current situation in

Ireland is that there is a professional obligation on therapists to report current concerns about children at risk of abuse. The *Child Abuse Guidelines* (1987) defines abuse and outlines indicators to assist professionals in determining the level of risk presented. These guidelines have been updated as *Children First* and are due to be implemented pending the training of professionals.

Therapists working independently may find themselves relying on their professional codes of ethics about confidentiality in the therapist/client relationship and discover that these are open to varying interpretations. In the absence of appropriate consultation, therapists may be vulnerable to engaging in poor professional practice despite their best intentions. As Furniss (1996) points out:

> Therapists who insist on working in therapeutic confidential isolation therefore also need to take full formal responsibility for child-protection and for prevention of possible further abuse (p. 109).

The Immunity from Prosecution Bill of 1998 will relieve anxiety relating to possible litigation for those who report suspected child abuse "in good faith" but does little to tackle the ethical issue of breaching confidentiality of the client-therapist relationship. The impact of mandatory reporting of retrospective reports of child sexual abuse made by adults presenting for counselling can have serious implications for both the mental health of adults and the protection of children potentially at risk of being abused (Blau, 1996; Blau & Hallahan, 1996; Blau & McElvaney, 1999). The LARAGH Counselling service has been operating a mandatory reporting policy in relation to adults' childhood sexual abuse disclosures as a result of legal advice to the Health Authority yet the Rape Crisis Centres, though receiving statutory funding, are not bound to the same reporting policies. The Child Abuse Commission has sought — and obtained — immunity from any obligations to report information obtained during the course of its investigations save when the person "reasonably believes that such disclosure is necessary in order to prevent an act or omission constituting a serious offence" (Government of Ireland, 2000, p. 20).

Another area of concern is when clients either disclose thoughts of self-harm, suicidal ideation or intent, or have indeed taken action in this regard, such as overdosing. It is important to have contact details of general practitioners, family members or significant others who may need to be contacted in the event that the client is in need of emergency support.

Thus, it is not possible in therapeutic work to offer complete confidentiality and this needs to be clarified at the outset of therapy.

INSTITUTIONAL ABUSE

Over the past ten years there has been increasing recognition of the experiences of abuse of children in institutions. Institutions in this context includes "a school, an industrial school, a reformatory school, an orphanage, a hospital, a children's home and any other place where children are cared for other than as members of their families" (Commission to Inquire into Child Abuse Act, 2000).

There are psychological dynamics which are distinctive to the experience of institutional abuse. Firstly, children who are placed in institutional care are an identified vulnerable group who are often in care due to difficulties around safety within their own families. The impact of being abused in an environment which is deemed to be safer and more caring than the child's home compounds the degree of confusion and damage to trust which is apparent in children who have been sexually abused outside an institutional context. Those in care are also more isolated, with less opportunity to disclose the abuse to trusted others. In many situations, children are not in the institution by choice and therefore feel powerless to complain. The level of powerlessness is exacerbated as institutions by their very nature are controlling and use the dynamics of power to ensure discipline and enforce acceptable behaviour. In many ways, for these children, there is no sense of control or autonomy. This reduces their ability to protect themselves and to seek help.

If the abuser is an employee of the institution, this person is often viewed by the child as representing the institution with the concomitant power that is invested by the institution. They may therefore believe that others within the institution know of the abuse and either condone it or deliberately abandon them to the abuse, therefore exacerbating their sense of betrayal. Often the sexual abuse does not occur in isolation but there may be physical and emotional abuse also. Although this is the case for all experiences of abuse, the public nature of the abuse in institutions — often in front of other children — can lead to a perception that the abuse was known and tolerated, thus removing the possibility of telling about it. Physical abuse was often experienced alongside sexual abuse in institutions because this was seen as an acceptable form of discipline. Survivors of abuse in institutions have described severe emotional and physical degradation which often occurred in full view of other children and/or staff, thus compounding the feeling of shame.

CHILD ABUSE COMMISSION

The Child Abuse Commission was established in May 1999 to inquire into abuse in institutions in Ireland. The focus of the commission covers the broad areas of abuse. The Commission has statutory functions, the purpose of which is to:

> listen to persons who have suffered abuse in childhood in institutions, telling of this abuse and making submissions; . . . conduct an enquiry into abuse of children in institutions since 1940 or earlier and where abuse occurred to find out why it occurred and who was responsible for it; . . . report directly to the public on the results of the enquiry and on the steps which should be taken now to deal with the continuing effects of abuse and to protect children in institutions from abuse now and in the future (Committee to Inquire into Child Abuse, 2000).

The events leading to the establishment of the Commission have led to an increase in the number of adults disclosing childhood sexual abuse (among other abuses) and seeking therapy. It is anticipated that referrals will continue to increase arising from the work of the Commission. For some the primary need is for their story to be heard and validated at a public level. For others, financial compensation and justice are issues which will need to be addressed in a comprehensive manner. This presents both legal and ethical dilemmas to the organisations who managed/funded these institutions, the government and to therapists involved with these clients. Therapists are being asked to provide reports based on their assessment of the psychological impact of the experience of abuse as part of civil legal proceedings. The changing role from "therapist" to "assessor" has its own psychological impact on the therapeutic relationship and on the client's view of themselves. "Assessors" offer professional opinions, something which "therapists" may be reluctant to do, depending on the stage in therapy and how this may influence the client's own opinions. Many therapists are reluctant to fulfil the "assessor" role, and although experienced therapists, may have little training in formal psychological assessment work. The legal system favours a particular style of investigative interviewing which is at variance with how information is obtained during the course of therapy. Therapists can therefore be cross-examined on their work and while found wanting from a legal perspective may have acted appropriately from a therapeutic perspective.

There are other dilemmas in preparing these types of reports. It is difficult to predict how effects of abuse may be manifested in the future, and what mediating factors may operate in an individual's future life which will help them cope with their difficulties. Reports which focus on the impact of the abuse may highlight the differences between people's coping strategies rather than how upsetting the experience of abuse was for the individual. Should the client who has more effective coping strategies and more supports from their family and friends receive less financial compensation than the client who does not develop effective ways of dealing with his/her psychological difficulties and has no one to lean on?

THE RECOVERED MEMORY DEBATE

There has been considerable controversy, both in research and practice, regarding the emergence of "recovered memories" or "false memories", the term used depending on the perspective taken, particularly when these memories are first discovered during the course of therapy. The accuracy of recollections may or may not be important during therapy. However, as Berliner and Briere (1999) point out, when therapy clients report being victims of a crime, this brings the therapeutic work into the legal arena where the accuracy of memories is paramount as memory may constitute the only evidence that exists regarding the occurrence of the crime. The British Psychological Society (1995) reviewed the research evidence concluding that: (1) Complete or partial memory loss is reported following psychological trauma, including child sexual abuse, which are sometimes fully or partially recovered after many years, both within and independent of therapy; and (2) Persuasion by an authority figure, such as a therapist, could lead to the retrieval of "memories" of events that never actually happened. Cognitive scientists and clinicians agree that both recovered and false memories occur, both in and out of therapy (for example, Briere, 1995; Lindsay & Briere, 1997; Read & Lindsay, 1997; Williams & Banyard, 1997). In more recent years, the debate has moved from questioning whether recovered memories are true or false to a debate as to the frequency of both. A lot of attention has been drawn to examining therapeutic techniques which are thought to influence introducing fabricated memories. Schooler (1999) suggests two main areas of research which are needed: Firstly, looking at the extent to which sexual abuse associated with recovered memory reports can be corroborated, and secondly, longitudinal studies of documented victims of various types of traumas to enable us to identify the specific situations, personality factors and mechanisms that may mediate forgetting, remembering and fluctuations in access to memories for trauma.

The unfortunate casualties of the lack of consensus in this area are the clients — both those who have recovered memories of abuse and those against whom accusations are made which are not substantiated.

The British Psychological Society (1995) advocates that therapists should be open to both "the emergence of memories of trauma which are not immediately available to the client's consciousness" and to "the dangers of suggestion"; avoid premature conclusions about the truth of a recovered memory; tolerate uncertainty and ambiguity; be alert to a range of possibilities including the possibility that the memory may be "literally true, metaphorically true or may derive from fantasy or dream material". The guidelines caution against the use of hypnosis, suggestion or leading questions when the therapist is seeking forensic evidence, and of diagnosing child sexual abuse on the basis of presenting symptoms alone.

DELAYS IN REPORTING AND LEGAL IMPLICATIONS

Despite the growing trend in reported sexual offences as noted in Gardai annual reports between 1988 and 1997, from 18 per cent of reported indictable crimes against the person in 1988 to 56 per cent in 1997 (Murphy, 1998), the rate of reporting both of adult sexual assaults and reports of retrospective child abuse are exceptionally low. The delay in reporting raises difficulties for the courts in both prosecuting such cases and in preparing defence for the accused. The Director of Public Prosecutions has been reluctant to prosecute such cases given the lack of evidence. Those cases which do proceed to the first stages of a criminal trial are often appealed to the High Court for Judicial Review proceedings to prohibit the trial from proceeding on the basis of unfair prejudice to the accused. Irish law recognises the right of an individual to a speedy trial (See Finlay C. J. in *State (O'Connell) v Fawsitt* (1985) 1R 362 at 378., Article 38. 1, Irish Constitution). The legal argument is that this right is contravened due to the delay in the victim of the assault coming forward to make a complaint. Psychologists have been involved in assisting the courts deliberate on this issue, in particular assessing the long-term impact of the alleged abuse and the extent to which the delay in reporting is associated with the effects of the abuse itself. Although the High Court has ruled against these prohibitions in several cases, an appeal to the Supreme Court has resulted in many of these judgements being overturned. Thus, after many months or even years of legal investigation and proceedings, the trial is prohibited from proceeding. The reasons given are primarily associated with the prejudice to the accused in terms of not being able to present an effective defence due to the passage of time since the crime is alleged to have been committed. In some cases, ill health or poor memory on the part of the accused, and the lack of availability of corroborative witnesses pertinent to the case, are cited as relevant issues. Unfortunately, these cases are not encouraging for adults who are considering, after many years of silence, to come forward and make formal complaints about individuals who have abused in the past and could well be continuing to abuse in the present.

In conclusion, therapy with adult clients who have been sexually abused in childhood is a much researched and documented area, with many valuable texts. However, it is important to be aware of the changing contexts and new developments in the field, both in terms of how this impacts on the client, the therapist, the therapeutic process and how sexual abuse is perceived in the society in which we live.

References

Berliner, L. & Briere, J. (1999). "Trauma, Memory, and Clinical Practice". In L. M. Williams & V. L. Banyard (Eds.) *Trauma and Memory* (pp. 19-29). Thousand Oaks, CA: Sage.

Boney-McCoy, S. & Finkelhor, D. (1995). "Psychosocial sequelae of violent victimization in a national youth sample". *Journal of Consulting and Clinical Psychology*, 63, 726-736.

Blau, I. (1996). "Ethical dilemmas in the reporting of child sexual abuse disclosed by adult survivors attending a counselling service". *Irish Journal of Psychology*, 17, 2, 126-143.

Blau, I. & Hallahan, E. (1996). "Adult Disclosure of C.S.A. prior to and during Counselling — A protective measure for children at risk". Presentation at 11th International Congress on Child Abuse and Neglect, Dublin.

Blau, I. & McElvaney, R. (1999). "Mandated reporting in an adult counselling service". Presentation at 9th Conference of European Association of Psychology and Law, Dublin.

Briere, J. (1992). *Child Abuse Trauma: Theory and Treatment of the Lasting Effects*. Newbury Park, CA: Sage.

Briere, J. (1995). "Child abuse, memory, and recall: A commentary". *Consciousness and Cognition*, 4, 83-87.

British Psychological Society (1995). *Recovered Memories*, Leicester: author.

Cecchin, G., Lone, G. & Wendell, R. (1994). *The Cybernetics of Prejudices in the Practice of Psychotherapy*. London: Karnac.

Commission to Inquire into Child Abuse (2000), Public Statement, June, Dublin,

Conte, J. (1999). "Vicarious Traumatization". Presentation at San Diego Conference on Responding to Child Maltreatment, San Diego, California.

Courtois, C. (1988). *Healing the Incest Wound*. New York: Norton.

Davidson, J.R.T. & Foa, E.B. (Eds.) (1993). *Post-traumatic Stress Disorder: DSM-IV and Beyond*. Washington, DC: American Psychiatric Press.

Department of Health (1987). *Child Abuse Guidelines*. Dublin: Department of Health.

Department of Health and Children. (1999). *Children First. National Guidelines for the Protection and Welfare of Children*. Dublin: DOHC.

Finlay, C.J. (1986). *State (O'Connell) v Fawsitt*, IR 362 at 378.

Furniss, T.(1991). *The Multiprofessional Handbook of Child Sexual Abuse*, London: Routledge.

Furniss, T. (1996). "Does Mandatory Reporting Help to Protect Children?" *Journal of Child Centred Practice,* 3, 101-116.

Government of Ireland (1937), *The Irish Constitution,* Dublin: Stationery Office.

Government of Ireland (2000) *Commission to Inquire into Child Abuse Act,* Dublin: Stationery Office.

Hall, L. & Lloyd, S. (1993). *Surviving Child Sexual Abuse.* London: Falmer Press.

Herman, J. (1992). *Trauma and Recovery: The Aftermath of Violence — From Domestic Abuse to Political Terror.* New York: Basic Books.

Kulka, R.A., Schlenger, W.E., Fairbank, J.A., Hough,R. L., Jordan, B.K., Marmar, C.R. & Weiss, D.S. (1990). *Trauma and the Vietnam War Generation.* New York: Brunner/Mazel.

Lindsay, D.S. & Briere, J. (1997). "The controversy regarding recovered memories of childhood sexual abuse: Pitfalls, bridges, and future directions". *Journal of Interpersonal Violence*, 12, 631-647.

Meiselman, K. (1990). *Resolving the Trauma of Incest.* San Francisco: Jossey-Bass.

Murphy, P. (1998). "Maximising Community Safety — The Treatment and Management of Imprisoned Sex Offenders", Paper presented at Irish Penal Reform Trust Conference, Dublin.

National Steering Committee on Violence Against Women and Department of Justice, Equality and Law Reform (2000). *National Directory for Women who have Experienced Violence or the Threat of Violence.* Dublin: author.

O'Doherty, I. (1998). *Stolen Childhood.* Dublin: Poolbeg.

Pearlman, L. A. & Saakvitne, K.W. (1995). *Trauma and the Therapist.* New York: Norton.

Read, J.D. & Lindsay, E.S. (Eds.) (1997). *Recollections of Trauma: Scientific Evidence and Clinical Practice.* New York: Plenum.

Sanderson, C. (1990). *Counselling Adult Survivors of Child Sexual Abuse.* London: Jessica Kingsley.

Schooler, J.W. (1999). "Seeking the Core: The Issues and Evidence Surrounding Recovered Accounts of Sexual Trauma". In L.M. Williams & V.L. Banyard (Eds.). *Trauma and Memory* (pp. 203-216), Thousand Oaks, CA: Sage.

Singer, M.I., Anglin, T.M., Song, L.Y. & Lunghofer, L. (1995). "Adolescents' exposure to violence and associated symptoms of psychological trauma". *Journal of the American Medical Association, 273,* 477-482.

Suedfeld, P. (1990). *Psychology and Torture.* New York: Hemisphere.

Weaver, T.L. & Clum, G.A. (1995). "Psychological distress associated with interpersonal violence: A meta-analysis". *Clinical Psychology Review,* 15,115-140.

Williams, L.M. & Banyard, V.L. (1997) "Perspectives on adult memories of childhood sexual abuse: A research review". In L. J. Dickstein, M.B. Riba & J. M Oldham (Eds.). *American Psychiatric Press Review of Psychiatry* (Vol. 16). Washington, DC: American Psychiatric Press.

Williams, L.M. & Banyard, V.L. (1999). *Trauma and Memory*. Thousand Oaks, CA: Sage.

Yule, W. & Williams, R. (1990). "Post-traumatic stress reactions in children". *Journal of Traumatic Stress*, 3, 279-295.

Chapter Five

Understanding and Treating Adult Perpetrators of Child Sexual Abuse

Olive Travers

The focus of this chapter is on the adult perpetrators of child sexual abuse. The myth that sex offenders are a homogeneous group is challenged and the different categories of offenders are outlined. Common characteristics of sex offenders and the factors which contribute to sexually abusive behaviour are examined. A case for treatment of sex offenders is made. Factors which contribute to successful treatment programmes, including the importance of the underlying ethos, are discussed. Finally, the inadequacies of our current system are highlighted and suggestions made as to how to rectify this.

Child sex offenders, more than any other criminal group, provoke strong feelings of revulsion among both the general public and professionals. They are despised, reviled and viewed as essentially evil. It is right and proper that the sexual violation of a child by an adult should be viewed as grievously wrong and inexcusable. It is also true that moral outrage, however justified, does not contribute to the wellbeing of current victims or the protection of future potential victims. The amount of publicity given to a small number of horrific high-profile cases (for example, the "West of Ireland Farmer" and Brendan Smyth) has contributed to the public demonising of sex offenders. There have also been the horrific reports of the sadistic physical and sexual abuse of children in state run institutions by persons in positions of power and influence. This media coverage has resulted in the belief that sex offenders are a homogenous group of dangerous criminals rather than a heterogeneous population who vary greatly in terms of degrees of dangerousness, insight and openness to rehabilitation and remorse. The move from individualisation to classification within the court system as described by O'Malley (1999) has also contributed to this erroneous belief. In the past all offenders were treated as individuals and sentencing took account of the offender's history, personality, problems, strengths and weaknesses. In recent years, however, people are classified solely on the basis of the offences for which they are convicted. Everyone convicted or suspected, therefore, of child abuse is now routinely branded as a paedophile. The courts are now expected to select a punishment that fits the label (paedophile) rather than the individual (O'Malley, 1999). In this way all sex offenders are wrongly tarred with the one brush and this obscures the need to treat offenders as individuals and, where appropriate, to find more creative ways of responding to proven abuse than the current response of "anger and desire for revenge" (Hassal & Wood, 1996). Classifying a whole group of people solely on the basis of offences they have committed also serves a socially complacent agenda (O'Malley, 1999). It enables us to distance ourselves from sex offenders and allows a "them" and "us" comfort zone.

WHO ARE THE SEX OFFENDERS?

Some facts about sex offenders are as follows:

- The vast majority are male (80-95 per cent) (Finklehor, 1986). However, there is increasing evidence that the number of female abusers has been underestimated (Briggs, 1995; Saradjian, 1996).

- One-third of all sexual abuse is perpetrated by adolescents under the age of 18 years (O'Reilly, this volume).

- Eighty to ninety-five per cent of child sex abuse is perpetrated by someone known to the victim: 50 per cent by a family member; 50 per cent by others — teachers, religious and youth leaders (Safer Society Foundation, 1995). In Ireland, 2 per cent of the population of clergy have been convicted of sexual abuse of children.

The majority of men who sexually abuse children are heterosexual. The common use of the term paedophile to refer to all men who sexually abuse children is very misleading. Paedophiles are individuals who have a primary sexual preference and sexual arousal to children (Wyre, 1987). The paedophile can also be described as being "fixated" in his sexual preference for children, that is, "recurrent, intense sexually arousing fantasies, urges or behaviours involving sexual activity with a prepubescent child or children" (DSM-IV, 1994, American Psychiatric Association). Paedophiles can be subdivided into three main groups:

- **Moral Conflict Paedophile**. This abuser has a compulsive sexual preference for children. He is, however, aware of the wrongness of his sexually abusive activities and he will feel guilty in relation to it. He is very amenable to treatment to assist him in gaining control over his sexually deviant behaviour.

- **Social Conflict Paedophile**. This abuser sees nothing wrong with sexual activity with children and argues that it is society's attitude which is wrong. He has no feelings of guilt and believes that his sexual activity with children is a normal part of a loving relationship. Social conflict paedophiles see themselves as part of a persecuted sexual subculture. They use the Internet and join clubs which provide them with a focus for their sexual perversions. They are unlikely to benefit from treatment as their cognitive distortions are so strong. However, the extent to which intervention at an early stage may be successful in challenging their distorted thinking needs more research. Legal sanctions such as the prosecution in their home countries of those who go on "sex tourism trips" is certainly needed to modify their behaviour.

- **Sociopathic Offenders**. While these abusers are included under the paedophile heading they are, in fact, not strictly paedophiles. Some may have an exclusive preference for sex with children but many do have age-appropriate sexual preferences. These abusers do not identify at all with their victim who is seen only as an object for use as a means of sexual gratification. They are frequently violent and punitive and have no moral constraints about their crimes. They will sometimes use abduction and murder to avoid detection. They are highly dangerous and, as they are essentially amoral, not amenable to treatment. However, these socio-pathic offenders form a tiny minority of all abusers but they are given the most publicity and universally inspire horror and revulsion.

However, while the sociopathic abuser and the moral and social conflict abusers obtain most publicity, the majority of children are not abused by fixated paedophiles but by heterosexual men. These "non-fixated" abusers can be subdivided into (1) transitional offenders and (2) regressed or compensatory of-fenders (Wallis, 1995).

1. The **transitional offender** does have the capacity to be-come sexually aroused by adult females. However, he lacks the ability and social skills to form age-appropriate rela-tionships. He turns to children to meet his intimacy and sex-ual needs and his sexual abuse of children is usually his only sexual experience.

2. The **regressed** or **compensatory offender**. This abuser does have sexual relationships with adults. However, at dif-ferent times in his life and for different reasons, he turns to children to meet his sexual and intimacy needs. He is usu-ally married and may abuse within his own family. He is the classic incest offender.

Faller (1990) classified men who sexually abuse children into three major types: interfamilial (including incest); extrafamilial (but known to the victim) and strangers. However, all of the above classification schemes for offenders have been shown to be unreliable and need to be viewed as approximate (Fischer & Mair, 1998). For example, seven per cent of child abusers also sexually assault adult victims (Elliott et al., 1995). One-third of incest abusers sexually abuse both their own and other people's children. Transitional and regressed offenders can also sometimes be true paedophiles and comprehensive assessment of all abusers is necessary. All perpetrators can, however, be divided into those who have a deviant pattern of sexual arousal in that they are only sexually attracted to children and those others who are heterosexual and who do not have a deviant pattern of arousal but who tend to convert non-sexual problems into sexual behaviour (Salter, 1988).

Other researchers have classified sex offenders on the basis of the levels and types of denials used by them in order to justify their abusive behaviour and excuse themselves from responsibility (Salter, 1988; Kennedy & Grubin, 1992). DeVolder (1998) in a study of 86 untreated sex offenders in Arbour Hill Prison in Dublin found four recognisable patterns of denial amongst an Irish sex offender population. These were similar to the four different groups identified by Kennedy and Grubin (1992) in research on convicted sex offenders in Britain on their patterns of denial. In the Irish study the following groups were identified:

- Group 1 was composed of men who admitted their offence and accepted that their action brought some degree of harm to their victim. However, they were most likely to attribute their actions to a drunken or enraged state, denying any deviant sexual preference. They had a tendency to blame the offence on the victim or other third parties whom they feel contributed to the offence taking place. This group corresponds to Kennedy's "internaliser" group, that is, men who were most likely to admit fully to the offence and to accept that it harmed their victim but who blamed an abnormal mental state and/or third parties. As well as their internal style of attribution, this group displayed high levels of distress.

- Group 2 had an external style of attribution and tended to blame the victim and/or third parties. They denied harming the victim (most often an adult woman) and were dissatisfied with the way the legal system dealt with their offence, taking on a persecutory tone when speaking of the police or courts. They were least likely to admit to the offence they were

charged with. This group correspond to Kennedy's "exter-
naliser" group.

- Group 3 contained the highest proportion of offenders of
  children under the age of 16 of both sexes. Offenders in this
  group accept that they have a deviant sexual preference
  and are the most motivated to obtain treatment specifically
  aimed at their deviant behaviour. They are characterised by
  a combination of ready admission and acceptance of harm
  to the victim along with the acceptance of sole responsibility. This group, while equivalent to Kennedy's "rationaliser"
  group, differ significantly in that they acknowledge that
  their behaviour was harmful to their victims. In contrast,
  Kennedy's group denied causing harm to their victims,
  claiming rather to have helped them. Kennedy's group cor-
  responded much more to the "social conflict" paedophile.

- Group 4 are termed the "absolute deniers" and composed
  mostly of offenders against children. This group denied they
  had even committed a crime and, thus, were the least likely
  to feel they could benefit from treatment. A minority were
  willing to accept treatment for other problems such as alcohol or substance abuse. In Kennedy's study of UK offenders,
  this group contained the highest proportion of men from
  ethnic minorities.

In the Irish study, the four recognisable patterns of denial were
found to be related to personal characteristics, that is, personality, lifetime psychiatric history, child sexual abuse, physical
abuse in childhood and psychosexual characteristics (De
Volder, 1998). The identification of these patterns of denial and
the factors most likely to be associated with these patterns are
of particular value in devising therapeutic programmes. In the
past, offenders presenting with a high level of denial have been
excluded from treatment programmes on the basis that denial
is seen to indicate that the offender does not consider his behaviour to be a problem that he wants to overcome
(O'Donoghue and Letourneau, 1993). There has, however, been
concern about the fact that offenders who deny their offences
remain untreated and can be viewed as having a higher risk of

recidivism (McGrath, 1991). In response to this, clinicians who have devised programmes to help convicted offenders to admit to their offences have shown encouraging results. Marshall (1994) reduced the number of "deniers" from 31 per cent to 2 per cent in his programme while Barbaree (1991) reduced the number of "deniers" from 22 per cent to 3 per cent. Similarly, O'Donoghue and Letourneau (1993) reduce the "deniers" in their programme from 17 per cent to 4 per cent. These results emphasise the value of clinicians working with sex offenders who are in "denial", rather than letting the potentially most dangerous offenders remain untreated (De Volder, 1998).

CHARACTERISTICS OF SEX OFFENDERS

Marshall and Barbaree (1990) put forward a theoretical framework in which they identify a number of factors that are influential in the aetiology and maintenance of deviant sexual behaviour. There is a strong link between childhood abuse and subsequent sexual offending and this may also reflect the interaction of a number of other causative factors as not all of those who have been subject to abuse and neglect become abusive (Finkelhor, 1996). However, research indicates that the majority of offenders grew up in families where there were disruptions in parent/child relations and where violence, abuse and neglect were common (Barbaree, Marshall & McCormick, 1998). These experiences result in a failure to develop the skills and capacities necessary to establish intimate adult relationships (Marshall, 1989). This failure to meet one's intimacy needs leads to the experience of emotional loneliness, and this type of loneliness has been shown to predict the aggressive, self-serving behaviour evident in the sexual abuse of children (Barbaree et al., 1998). Therefore, as a result of poor childhood attachment with their parents, sex offenders grow up ill-equipped to meet the demands of adult social and sexual relationships. They also lack self-confidence and are unable to experience the empathy necessary to share fully the emotional issues relevant to adult partners. They have also been found to be low in self-esteem as it manifests in social interactions (Marshall, 1993). There is evidence that the capacity of the offender to benefit from treatment is impeded by low self-esteem and that assisting offenders to improve their self-confidence has been shown to increase the effectiveness of treatment programmes (Marshall et al., 1996). Research done with over 800 offenders in Australia indicated that sex offenders are less socially competent than non-offenders. Non-fixated offenders perceive themselves as powerless (Briggs, 1995). These men have very traditional views about the roles of men and woman. They see themselves failing in their male role and also feel that they are unable to develop and maintain relationships with women. Their inability to live up to gender role stereotypes results in their feelings of self-doubt and over-dependence. Their sexual offending is usually triggered by some form of real or imagined threat to their dependence. Their victims are usually female children onto whom they transfer their dependence needs. Many offenders, therefore, retreat from problematic adult relationships to seek emotional and sexual fulfilment in a sexual relationship with a child. They project adult needs and expectations onto their victims and the children are expected to forsake childhood and become pseudo-adults. It is a minority of sex offenders, therefore, whose behaviour can be understood in sexual terms alone. Other factors such as the need for control, emotional insecurity or feelings of inadequacy outweigh the former.

FACTORS WHICH CONTRIBUTE TO SEXUALLY ABUSIVE BEHAVIOUR

It is not enough to know the individual characteristics and life history of the individual offender. All men who are sexually attracted to children do not sexually abuse them. Neither do all men with poor emotional detachment, poor self-esteem and intimacy deficits abuse children. Finkelhor (1983) identified four preconditions for the sexual abuse of a child to occur:

1. The offender has the motivation to abuse, that is, an emotional need to relate intimately with someone is coupled with a sexual interest in children which leads to abuse.

2. The offender overcomes his own internal inhibitions by using cognitive distortions or through substance abuse.

3. The offender overcomes external inhibitions such as the supervision of the child by others.

4. The offender overcomes the resistance of the children by building up trust, using blackmail or physical force.

In addition to Finkelhor's four preconditions, we also need to understand the factors which promote a sexual assault cycle. The abuse cycle can be summarised as follows (Wolf, 1984):

- The adult experiences sexual arousal in relation to a child.

- He uses the recall of this experience as a content of his sexual fantasy which results in masturbation.

- He continues to do this, often for many months, and the fantasy involving sexual activity with the child becomes his only source of sexual arousal.

- He targets a child and focuses on creating the conditions in which he can act out his fantasy.

- He grooms the child.

- He abuses the child.

- He experiences fear and guilt afterwards and thinks "I'll never do this again".

- He uses distorted thinking to make himself feel better about what he has done, for example, "it was only horse-play".

- The child does not tell and his anxiety recedes.

- He starts to use the recall of the abuse of the child as a basis of his sexual fantasy and masturbation.

- He will distort and repress the nature of the abuse to allow him to do this, for example, "she did not tell, she must have enjoyed it".

- Above all, he will engage in denial, that is, an inability to accept the sexual behaviour he indulged in as harmful to the victim, is not desired by her and is, in fact, criminal and coercive.

All of our understanding of the individual characteristics and psychological functioning of the offender and of the cycles of abuse needs to be placed within a wider understanding of society's role in creating a climate conducive to individual aggression. The sexual abuse of children needs to be viewed as just one aspect of the many inequalities and abuses of power which permeate our society (Keenan, 1999). Keenan highlights the need for sexual abuse to be viewed within the context of the social constructions of masculinity, male sexuality and the family and issues of inequality and oppression. Feminist researchers have documented how women and children have traditionally been expected to endure high levels of abuse (Herman and Hirschman, 1998). Bentovim (1998) is a proponent of the systemic family therapy approach as a way of acknowledging the complexities of the relationships within a family in which sexual abuse occurs. This approach does not mean that the sexually abusive behaviour is not the sole responsibility of the abuser. It rather acknowledges that issues which involve the individual also extend to the family and the wider social context.

THE CASE FOR TREATMENT

The case for providing treatment for sex offenders is based on the belief that it contributes to the protection of children and community safety. The use of the term "treatment" is felt by many practitioners to not accurately reflect the nature of intervention with sex offenders. There is a risk that the term treatment implies the possibility of "cure" while the emphasis of all work done with sex offenders is rather on "control" of their deviant sexual behaviour. Practitioners working with sex offenders see their work more in terms of re-education and training and management. Treatment is viewed as being tough for offenders rather than a soft option, with the insistence on offenders facing up to and taking responsibility for their crimes.

There is ample evidence that treatment works. Hanson & Bussiere (1996) found that the overall recidivism rate in a sample of 23,393 treated sex offenders was 13.4 per cent (18.9 per cent were rapists, 12.7 per cent child abusers). There was a median follow-up of their behaviour of four years. These rates are much lower than those of the general prison population and would be even lower if account was taken of the small number of perpetrators who have a very high rate of offending (Sturgeon et al, 1979). Marshall & Barbaree (1988) found that treated offenders had less reconvictions than non-treated offenders, both at two-year follow-up (5.5. per cent) and (12.5 per cent) respectively, and four-year follow-up (25 per cent) and (64 per cent) respectively. Deviant sexual preference, criminal lifestyle and dropping out of treatment were the biggest risk factors to re-offending. In the UK the STEP study (Sex Offender Treatment and Evaluation Project) (Beckett, Beech, Fisher and Fordham, 1994) evaluated six representative community-based treatment programmes for sex offenders, together with the Gracewell Clinic, a specialist residential treatment programme for child abusers. Short-term group work, averaging 54 hours of treatment, successfully treated 62 per cent of offenders entering treatment with low deviancy profiles, compared with only 42 per cent of men who started treatment with a highly deviant profile. However, long-term therapy, averaging 462 hours of treatment, increased the successful treatment of low deviancy men from 62 per cent to 80 per cent and highly deviant men from 42 per cent to 60 per cent. In an evaluation of prison sex offender treatment programmes in Britain (Beech, Fisher, Beckett & Scott-Fordham, 1998) it was found that 67 per cent of offenders attending programmes showed a significant positive treatment effect. Browne, Fordham and Middleton (1998) found that 81 per cent of sex offenders attending a community treatment programme showed some improvement and all of those completing the programme (63 per cent) showed improvement in one or more of the treatment targets. In an Irish community treatment programme run by the North Western Health Board and the Probation and Welfare Service, a 10-year follow-up of the approximately 100 men who had attended the programme indicated a 3 per cent reoffending rate. An in-depth follow-up of 16 of these men (Travers & Moriarty, 1998) indicated that incest offenders were at least risk of reoffending as the majority had been reintegrated back into their families and had benefited from the resulting family monitoring and support. Their sexual and intimacy needs were also being met within the family context. The extra-familial offenders were experiencing more difficulties in meeting their sexual and intimacy needs, which was a cause for concern. Research indicated that it is a lack of intimacy and a failure to develop a capacity for intimacy that contributes to the development of sexual offending (Marshall, 1993; Garrick, Marshall & Thornton, 1996). The extra-familial offenders had, however, successfully taken on board the relapse prevention aspects of the programme, in particular the need to avoid contact with children.

It is, therefore, evident from this research that treatment of all convicted sex offenders will contribute significantly to the reduction of child sexual abuse. However, Murphy (1998) outlines the inadequacy of what is currently happening within the Irish prison system. Out of four prisons holding the majority of the 250 imprisoned sex offenders, only one (Arbour Hill) has the resources to provide a sex offender treatment programme. The programme there has been running successfully since 1994 but offers an intake of only ten places. A programme is planned for the Curragh Prison, the main institution catering for sex offenders, in the near future. However, even the provision of the much needed treatment within the prison system will remain inadequate without follow-up treatment in the community to maintain positive changes in attitude and behaviour (Murphy, 1998). To date, community-based treatment programmes are not widely available within this country. There is one rural programme provided since 1985 by the North Western Health Board and the Probation & Welfare Service in the North West and one Dublin-based programme provided at the Granada Institute as part of the St. John of God Services. The Department of Justice, Equality and Law Reform Strategy Statement 1998-2000 announced the establishment of the first government-supported community-based programme for sex offenders under the aegis of the Probation & Welfare Service. This programme is to cater for those sex offenders processed through the criminal justice system and placed on statutory supervision under the Probation & Welfare Service. There are, at present, approximately 100 such offenders in this category. However, to date, a lack of resources has meant that this programme has not, in fact, materialised. The Sex Offenders' Bill (1999) makes provision for the post-release supervision of sex offenders in the community but the absence of the back-up of community programmes will reduce the effectiveness of this welcome measure.

Other advantages of community-based treatment programmes include:

- They provide a therapeutic option for the majority of sex offenders who never reach the courts. Eighty-eight per cent of the offenders attending the community-based treatment programme in the North Western Health Board Area had no legal sanctions on referral. Sixty-nine per cent of the offenders attending a community-based treatment programme in Northern Ireland had no legal sanctions on referral (Leonard, 1998).

- Community programmes enable those offenders who are awaiting the often very lengthy processing of their cases through the criminal justice system to avail of treatment. Twelve per cent of the offenders attending the community-based treatment programme in the North Western Health Board Area attended on this basis. The offender may have selfish reasons for engaging in treatment but this is sufficient to engage him in a challenging process in which he will discover how to live a life that is not abusive (Walsh, 1998).

- It is acknowledged that, while treatment in prison is essential for incarcerated offenders, prison is an unsuitable environment in which to facilitate change. In the prison environment, sex offenders are not exposed in any realistic way to the kinds of stresses, temptations or opportunities which present in the community which may lead them to re-offend on release (Murphy, 1998). Much of the work which needs to be done with offenders to ensure that they will not re-offend can be done more effectively through a community-based approach (Walsh, 1998).

- Community-based programmes facilitate the involvement of the offender's family and significant others in his treatment. This is essential in order to effectively assess how well the offender is acquiring the attitudes, perceptions and behaviours which will enable him to meet his needs in non-abusive ways. Responsible family members are able to monitor the offender's progress and play an active role in his relapse prevention programme. The fact that 68 per cent of the offenders attending the community treatment programme in the North Western Health Board Area had either direct or indirect contact with children and that 55 per cent of the offenders attending a community treatment programme in the Western Health and Social Services Board of Northern Ireland had either direct or indirect contact with children, and many lived in family situations, highlights the importance of this (Leonard, 1998).

• The provision of alternatives to custodial sentences may encourage more victims of sexual abuse to disclose their abuse. Marshall (1998) found that almost 100 per cent of a sample of children who had disclosed sexual abuse reported that they would not do so again. Among their reasons was the hostility towards them for getting the abuser into trouble and removing him from where he was needed.

The success of any community-based programme is dependent upon a number of factors. Competent clinical assessment of each individual offender is essential. The community's right to safety is the primary issue and only those offenders assessed as being in the low to moderate risk should be considered eligible. McGrath (1992) highlights five factors relevant to any risk assessment process:

1. Offence type. Quincy (1995) found that abusers of unrelated boys had a higher recidivism rate than those who abused unrelated girls.

2. Multiple paraphilias.

3. Degree of force used. The more violence the abuser uses in his sexual attacks the more difficult he is to treat.

4. Criminal lifestyle. Sex offenders with prior sexual conviction pose a higher risk of reoffending. Offenders who have a history of non-sexual crime are also unsuitable for community treatment. Patterns of antisocial behaviour such as the

need for stimulation or parasitic lifestyle, poor behaviour controls, impulsivity and irresponsibility are also viewed as negative indicators for inclusion in community programmes (Walsh, 1998).

5. Treatment for alcohol or substance abuse is also a prerequisite for acceptance onto a community-based programme.

In 1992 the British Home Office commissioned a research project to evaluate the impact of community-based treatment programmes on sex offenders. Beckett et al. (1994) developed a Sex Offenders' Assessment Pack (SOAP) to measure both the personality characteristics and "offence specific" characteristics of child abusers both before and after treatment. In addition to evaluating the impact of treatment on child abusers, this assessment pack also provides useful information in determining risk assessment. The assessment measures fall into three broad categories:

1. Offence specific, that is, measures of empathy, cognitive distortions and justification for offending

2. Personality measures, that is, measures of self-esteem, assertiveness, general empathy, locus of control and emotional loneliness

3. Faking and social desirability — such measures include sex offenders' general propensity to present themselves in socially desirable ways and to deny sexual drives and interests.

Most treatment programmes for sex offenders employ a cognitive behavioural approach with a relapse-prevention component. Core themes covered in treatment programmes include:

- Offence cycle, including role of fantasy, in offending

- Cognitive distortion

- Victim empathy

- Sexuality

- Self-esteem, social skills, anger management, assertiveness.

Walsh (1998) identifies the main tasks facing the offender in a treatment programme:

1. The uncovering and acknowledgement of the pattern of abuse perpetrated

2. The identification of the factors which create the conditions under which the perpetrator abuses and continues to abuse

3. The development of some understanding of the impact on the victim of the abuse and a fundamental change and attitude to and feeling for those abused

4. The commitment to a process whereby the abuser can avoid situations which may increase the risk of re-offending.

A combination of individual treatment, group treatment and family work is necessary to enable the offender to achieve these tasks. It is important that the clinicians know the function of the abusive behaviour for the individual offender. An understanding of the specific "pay-off" for the offender, whether it be outright sexual pleasure, the acting out of anger and revenge, or the opportunistic actions of someone who lacks social skills will determine the content of the individual's treatment programme (Walsh, 1998).

In addition to programme content, the ethos underlying treatment programmes is an essential element in ensuring success. Barker and Morgan (1993) found that in successful programmes offenders were treated as individuals and felt that they were not viewed as men without hope of changing. A context needs to be set in treatment of working together to protect children. The recognition of the whole person in treatment rather than acceptance of society's view of the one-dimensional monster is crucial. It motivates the offender to change his behaviour, rather than to respond to the experience of being shamed in an angry, blaming way. The individual offender's capacity to become a caring, protective, non-abusing adult needs to be acknowledged. Tanner (1999) includes the need for sex offenders, regardless of the nature of their crimes, to be treated with respect and dignity by all members of the treatment team, in his guiding principles to working with sexual offenders.

CONCLUSIONS — THE WAY FORWARD

The provision of treatment programmes for sex offenders both in prison and in the community are just one of the initiatives necessary to reduce the risk of sexual victimisation of children. In recent years, the government implemented a number of other measures to increase the protection of children (see Chapter 2, this volume). While treatment for sex offenders alone is not a sufficient response to protecting children, the treatment facilities and procedures in this country remain in their infancy. Kelly (1998) in his review of effective treatment strategies in the USA and Canada stresses the need for any response to sex offenders to have a clear protocol for inter-agency co-operation to ensure quality services and to establish community safeguards which will not fail. The slow progression of over-lapping treatment stages, typical in the USA and Canada, highlight the gross inadequacy of what is currently happening in this country. In the former regions, there is a highly structured exit sequence from inpatient treatment to transition groups to outpatient groups to self-help groups. For example, in Canadian prisons 90 per cent of sex offenders participate in a treatment programme prior to release, compared to 15 per cent in Ireland. There is also mandatory treatment and supervision for sex offenders released from prison while, to date, in this country sex offenders are denied access to temporary release, making it impossible to provide such a service (Murphy, 1998). There is, in this country, a lack of options for dealing with convicted sex offenders compared to the more flexible approach in other countries, with options ranging from prison sentences with mandatory treatment and post-release treatment monitoring to non-custodial sentences with supervision and treatment options. In addition to the government initiatives in Britain, Browne and Lynch (1998) make recommendations to further reduce the risk of sexual assault which are also applicable in Ireland. These include "additional legislation to deal with the majority of alleged sex offenders who are not convicted 'beyond all reasonable doubt' and are, therefore, not covered by the Sex Offenders Act". Here, as in Britain, a large number of sex offenders are known to statutory health board child protection services but there is no way of mandating them to receive treatment in the absence of criminal charges brought against them. In 1998 only 18 cases of incest were dealt with by the criminal justice system, a tiny fraction of the 598 cases of incest known to the health boards and gardai. Health boards have to deal with serious child protection issues in relation to the re-integration of families where incest has occurred, yet the North Western Health Board, together with the Probation & Welfare Service, is the only health board in the country to provide a community-based treatment programme for adult sex offenders. This is an integral aspect of its child protection policies. At present, other than within this one health board area, there is no wide-spread integration of the legal and statutory systems to enable effective treatment, combined with supervision of offenders in the community, to reduce the risk of recidivism.

There is a strong "business case" why both the Probation & Welfare Service and health boards should support the development of inter-agency sex offender treatment programmes (Beckett and Goodman, 1994). The health services already deal, both directly and indirectly, with the consequences of sexual abuse. Adults who have been sexually abused as children present, directly or indirectly, to a variety of mental health services (Browne and Finkelhor, 1986). A disproportionate number of young people referred to child and adolescent health services have been sexually abused (Fredrich et al., 1986; Herman, 1981; Reich and Guttierres, 1979).

Successful treatment programmes would also reduce the work done by social work departments supervising families where an untreated sex offender returns from prison. The optimistic outcomes of treatment effectiveness outlined earlier in this chapter point to the value of regarding treatment programmes as an integral aspect of child protection policies.

The setting up of an Irish branch of the British National Organisation for the Treatment of Offenders (NOTA) in 1999 is an important step towards bringing together practitioners in the field, to both develop and update their knowledge and skills and to influence government policy, which will contribute to the necessary integration of the legal and statutory systems.

In this country we have much laudable concern about sexual violence against children, but what we also need is the will to provide the necessary resources to implement effective preventative measures.

References

American Psychiatric Association (1994, 4th edition). *Diagnostic and Statistical Manual of Mental Disorders*. Washington, DC: APA.

Barbaree, M.E. (1991). "Denial and Minimisation among Sex Offenders: Assessment and treatment outcome". *Forum on Corrections Research*, 3, 330-333.

Barbaree, M.E., Marshall, W.L., & McCormack, J. (1998). "The development of deviant sexual behaviour among adolescents and its implications for prevention and treatment". *Irish Journal of Psychology*, 19(1), 1-31.

Barker, M. & Morgan, R. (1993). *Sex offenders: A framework for the evaluation of community-based treatment*. London: HMSO.

Beckett, R.C., Beech, A., Fisher, D. & Fordham, A.S. (1994). *Community-based Treatment for Sex Offenders: An Evaluation of Seven Treatment Programmes*. London: Home Office Publications.

Beckett, R.C. (1998). "Community Treatment in the United Kingdom". In Marshall, W., Fernandez, Y., Hudson, S., & Ward, T. (Eds.). *Source Book of Treatment Programmes for Sexual Offenders*. New York: Plenum Press

Beckett, R.C. & Goodman, P. (1994). *Business Cases for the Thames Valley Sex Offender Project*. Oxford Forensic Service, Fair Mile Hospital, Oxon, England.

Beech, A., Fisher, D., Beckett, R. & Scott-Fordham, A. (1998). *An Evaluation of the Prison Sex Offender Treatment Programme*, Home Office Research, Development and Statistics Directorate. Research Findings No. 79.

Bentovim, A. (1998). "The trauma organised system of working with family violence". In C. Cordess & M. Cox. (Eds.). *Forensic Psychotherapy: Crime, Psychodynamics and the Offender Patient. Vol. 11*. London: Jessica Kingsley.

Briggs, F. (1995). *From Victim to Offender: How Child Sexual Abuse Victims become Offenders.* Sydney: Allen & Unwin.

Browne, A. & Finkelhor, D. (1986). "Impact of child sexual abuse: A review of the research". *Psychological Bulletin*, 99, 66-67.

Browne, K.D., Foreman, L. & Middleton, D. (1998). "Predicting treatment drop out in sex offenders". *Child Abuse Review* 7, 402-419.

Browne, K. & Lynch, M.A. (1998). "Protecting Children from Sex Offenders". *Child Abuse Review*, 7, 369-378.

Cotter, A. (1998). "Managing sex offenders in the community — A strategy for societal safety in the treatment of sex offenders". Proceedings of Irish Penal Reform Trust Conference, Dublin.

De Volder, J. (1998). The Assessment of Denial in Sex Offenders: Masters of Psychological Science (research) thesis. University College, Dublin.

Elliot, M., Browne, K.D. & Kilcoyne, J. (1995). "Child Sexual Abuse Prevention: What Offenders Tell Us". *Child Abuse and Neglect* 19, 579-594.

Faller, K.C. (1990). *Understanding Child Sexual Maltreatment.* Beverly Hills: Sage.

Finkelhor, D. & Arajis, S. (1983). *Explanations of Paedophilia: A Four-Track Model.* University of New Hampshire Family Violence Research Program.

Finkelhor, D. (1996). "Long-term effects of sexual abuse". Paper presented at the 11th International Congress of the International Society for the Prevention of Child Abuse and Neglect (ISPCAN), Dublin.

Fisher, D. & Mair, G. (1998). "A review of classification systems for sex offenders". *Home Office Research and Statistics Directorate Research Findings*, 78.

Fredrich, W.N., Urquiza, A.J. & Beillke, R. (1986). "Behaviour problems in sexually abused young children". *Journal of Paediatric Psychology*, 11, 47-57.

Garlick, Y., Marshall, W.L. & Thornton, T. (1996). "Intimacy Deficits and Attribution of Blame Among Sex Offenders". *Legal and Criminology*, 1, 251-258.

Hanson, K.R. & Bussiere, M.T. (1996). "Predicting Relapse: A Meta-analysis of Sexual Offender Recidivism". *Journal of Consulting and Clinical Psychology*, 66 (2).

Hassal, I. & Wood, B. (1996). "Facing up to child abuse and neglect". Paper presented at ISPCAN 11th International Congress, Dublin.

Herman, J. L. & Hirschmann, L. (1981). *Father-Daughter Incest*. London & Cambridge MA: Harvard University Press.

Keenan, M. (1999). "Child Sexual Abuse — The Web of Human Suffering". In *Child Sexual Abuse: The Irish Experience so far and the way forward*. Papers and reports from a conference sponsored by the National Conference of Priests of Ireland.

Kelly, J. (1998). "An international perspective on establishing community safe-guards for sex offender treatment". In *The Treatment of Sex Offenders*. Proceedings of an Irish Penal Reform Trust Conference, Dublin.

Kennedy, M. & Grubin, D. (1992). "Patterns of denial in sex offenders". *Psychological Medicine*, 22, 191-196.

Leonard, M. (1998). Western Health and Social Services Board, N. Ireland, Statistical Analysis of the Programme for Prevention of Sexual Abuse Client Group. Thesis submission for M.Sc. Advanced Social Work, Queen's University, Belfast.

Marshall, W.L. (1989). "Intimacy, Loneliness and Sexual Offenders". *Behaviour Research and Therapy*, 27, 491-503.

Marshall, W.L. (1993). "The role of attachment, intimacy and loneliness in the etiology and maintenance of sexual offending". *Sexual and Marital Therapy*, 8, 109-121.

Marshall, W.L. (1994). "Treatment Effects on Denial and Minimisation in Incarcerated Sex Offenders". *Journal of Behaviour, Research and Therapy*, 32(5), 559-564.

Marshall, W. L. (1998). Information presented at the Association for the treatment of sexual abusers annual research and treatment conference: discussed in Tanner, J. (1999). *New Frontiers in Sex Offender Treatment*. Irish Penal Reform Trust.

Marshall, W.L. & Barbaree, M.E. (1988). "The long-term evaluation of a behavioural treatment programme for child molesters". *Behaviour Research and Therapy*, 26(6), 499-511.

Marshall, W.L. & Barbaree, M.E. (1990). "An integrated theory of the etiology of sexual offending". In W.L. Marshall, D. R. Laws & M.E. Barbaree (Eds). *Handbook of Sexual Assault: Issues, Theories and Treatment of the Offender*. New York: Plenum Press.

Marshall, W.L., Anderson, D. & Champagne, F. (1996). "Self-esteem and its relationship to sexual offending". *Psychology, Crime and Law*, 3, 81-106.

Murphy, P. (1998). "Maximising community safety: The treatment and management of imprisoned sex offenders" in *The Treatment of Sex Offenders*. Proceedings of an Irish Penal Reform Trust Conference, Dublin.

McGrath, R. (1992). "Five Critical Questions: Assessing Sex Offender Risk". *APPA Perspectives* 16(3), 6-9.

McGrath, R.J. (1991). "Sex Offender Risk Assessment and Disposition Planning". *International Journal of Offender Therapy*, 35(4), 328-350.

O'Donohue, W. & Letourneau, E. (1993). "A Brief Group Treatment for the Modification of Denial in Child Sexual Abusers: Outcome and Follow-up". *Child Abuse and Neglect*, 17, 299-304.

O'Malley, T. (1999). Responding to Sexual Abuse: reconciling justice and humanity in child sexual abuse. The Irish experience so far and the way forward. Papers and reports from a conference sponsored by the National Conference of Priests of Ireland.

Quincy, V. (1995). "Predicting Sexual Offences". In T. Campbell (Ed.) *Assessing Dangerousness: Violence by Sexual Offenders and Child Abusers*. Newbury Park, CA: Sage.

Reich, J.W. & Gutierres, S.C. (1979). "Escape/aggression incidence in sexually abused juvenile delinquents". *Criminal Justice and Behaviour*, 6, 239-243.

Salter, A. (1988). *Treating Child Sex Offenders and Their Victims: A Practical Guide*. Newbury Park, CA: Sage.

Saradjian, J.C. (1996). *Women Who Sexually Abuse Children: From Research to Clinical Practice*. Sussex: Wiley.

Sturgeon, M., Taylor, J., Goldman, R., Hunter, M. & Webster, D. (1979). *Report on Mentally Disordered Sex Offenders Released from Atascadero State Hospital*. Atascadero, CA: Atascadero State Hospital.

Tanner, J. (1999). *New Frontiers in Sex Offender Treatment.* Irish Penal Reform Trust.

The Safer Society Foundation Inc. (1995). *Sexual Abuse.* Vermont: Brandon.

Travers, O. & Moriarty A. (1998). "Ten Years On: An evaluation of a community-based treatment programme for sex offenders". Unpublished paper presented at the Psychological Society of Ireland Annual Conference, Kilkenny.

Wallis, K. (1995). "Perspectives of child molesters". In F. Briggs (Ed.) *From Victim to Offender: How Child Sexual Abuse Victims become Offenders.* Sydney: Allen & Unwin.

Walsh, P. (1998). "Prison is not Enough! The Role of Community-based Treatment Programmes in the Treatment of Sex Offenders". Proceedings of an Irish Penal Reform Trust Conference, Dublin.

Wolf, S.C. (1984). "A multi-factor model of deviant sexuality". Paper presented at Third International Conference on Victimology, Lisbon.

Wyre, R. (1987). *Working with Sex Abuse: Understanding Sex Offending.* Oxford: Perry Publications.

Chapter Six

Adolescents Who Sexually Abuse Others

Gary O'Reilly[1]

INTRODUCTION

Sexually abusive behaviour committed by adolescents is a significant but often hidden problem in our society. This chapter provides an introduction to what we know about juvenile males who sexually abuse others and describes current approaches used in assessment and intervention with this population. Throughout the chapter material is organised around three themes. These are (a) supporting the discussion with research evidence, (b) framing the material within an Irish context, and (c) given that the primary focus of this chapter concerns adolescents an attempt is made to present information within a developmental framework.

THE AGE DISTRIBUTION OF PERPETRATORS OF SEXUAL ABUSE IN IRELAND

Evidence from two comprehensive and reliable studies of confirmed cases of child sexual abuse conducted in the Eastern Health Board Region and in Northern Ireland has supplied us

---

[1] This chapter was the basis for a keynote address at an European Commission sponsored conference on sharing models of good practice in the prevention of the sexual victimisation of children and adults — ACCESS 2000, Birmingham, May 10–12, 2000.

with important information on the age distribution of perpetrators of child sexual abuse (McKeown, Gilligan, Brannick, McGuane, & Riordan, 1989; The Research Team, 1990). These studies are respectively based on 512 and 408 *confirmed* cases of child sexual abuse occurring in a one-year time frame and reveal that in 36 per cent of cases the perpetrator is under 20 years of age, and in 21 per cent of cases the perpetrator is under 15 years of age:

Table 6.1: *Age Distribution of Perpetrators of Child Sexual Abuse in Ireland*

Age	Eastern Health Board Study	Age	Northern Ireland Study
15 Years and Under	21% of cases	15 Years and Under	20.5% of cases
16-20 Years	16% of cases	16-19 Years	16.2% of cases
21-35 Years	24% of cases	20-39 Years	34.4% of cases
36-45 Years	17% of cases	40-59 Years	18.5% of cases
46-66 Years	9% of cases	Over 60 Years	11% of cases

This surprisingly high proportion of sexually abusive behaviour by children and adolescents is not a uniquely Irish phenomenon and is further confirmed by a variety of sources in the UK and North America (Vizard, Monck & Misch, 1995; Barbaree, Hudson & Seto, 1993). The extent of sexually abusive behaviour by adolescents and children has prompted many professionals and health care providers to recognise the importance of developing services for young people who abuse others. The rationale of these services is to prevent further sexual abuse by working with children and adolescents who can be considered to be at risk of engaging in sexual abuse in the future. Given the space available, the present chapter will present information on what we know about the developmental experiences and behaviour of male adolescents who sexually abuse others and will outline some of the approaches currently popular in assessment and intervention. Readers who are interested in a discussion of prepubescent children who engage in sexually abusive behaviour are referred to two excellent books on this topic by Toni Cavanagh Johnson (1999) and Sharon Araji (1997) which are listed in the reference section of this chapter.

DEVELOPMENT PRIOR TO THE ONSET OF SEXUALLY ABUSIVE BEHAVIOUR

At present we have available to us two key sources of information on the early development of adolescent males who engage in sexually abusive behaviour. These are the theoretical formulations of clinicians and researchers experienced in this field, and a limited number of empirical studies. It is to each of these two sources that we now briefly turn our attention.

The Barbaree, Marshall and McCormick Model

Barbaree, Marshall and McCormick (1998) outline one of a number of important models of the development of sexual offending behaviour, (see Figure 6.1 below). In their most recent formulation of their model they emphasise the role played by growing up in an abusive family to the development of sexually abusive behaviour. Barbaree, Marshall, and McCormick are concerned with describing this particular developmental pathway as it leads into sexual offending for some individuals. Their approach should not be confused with erroneous conclusions such as "all people from abusive family backgrounds are at risk of sexual offending" or "all adolescent offenders come from abusive family backgrounds".

Figure 6.1: Model of the Development of Sexually Deviant Behaviour (Barbaree, Marshall & McCormick (1998))

Abusive Family Experience.
* Disrupttion in attachment experiences with primary care-givers
* Parents present but emotionally unavailable
* Children adopt the strategy of attracting parental attention through disruptive demanding behaviour
* Alcohol/substance abuse if present severely limits parents capacity to give appropriate feedback to their children
* Children fail to learn appropriate interpersonal and intimacy skills within the context of a bonded relationship
* Aggressive, coercive, and manipulative strategies for interpersonal relationship management are modeled and reinforced
* Child adopts coercive, aggressive and manipulative strategies if they prove to provide some success for coping with the family environment.

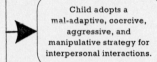

Child adopts a mal-adaptive, coercive, aggressive, and manipulative strategy for interpersonal interactions.

Failure of "coercive" strategy when applied to relationships outside of home.

Outcome of the Failure of theCoercive Strategy
* Child fails to form stable and satisfying relationships with peers and other adults outside of the immediate family system.
* The Child's social and intimacy skills are not given a developmental pathway that allows their potential to unfold.
* Failure to establish successful relationships outside the family leads to a negative self-image and a reduction in self-confidence, further blocking the potential for interpersonal development.

Intermediate Outcome of the Abusive Family Experience - A Syndrome of Social Disability.
1. An inability to establish and maintain intimate relationships
2. Low self-esteem
3. Diverse antisocial and criminal attitudes and behaviours
4. Lack of empathy
5. Cognitive distortions that support and justify criminal behaviour.

Additional Factors in the Aetiology of Deviant Sexual Behaviour.
* Being the victim of sexual, physical, or emotional abuse
* Inherited temperamental factors predisposing impulsiveness

Puberty and the failure to establish relationships that appropriately meet the emerging need for the development of an intimate and sexual quality to some relationships

Personal Outcome
* Feelings of exclusion from experience of intimate relationships.
* Feeling powerless to establish healthy relationships through appropriate interaction.
* Concept of self as masculine is negatively effected.
* Feelings of anger and resentment directed towards girls and women.

Employment of "Coercive" Strategy and Emergence of Sexually Deviant Behaviour
* Desired sexual contact achieved through employment of "coercive" strategy that was learnt within the abusive family.
* Sexual contact achieved by force, or with younger, more vulnerable person.
* Memories of sexual contact become elaborated in-corporating fantasies
* Memories and fantasies are reinforced.
* Reinforced memories and fantasies promote urge to act out sexually.
* Progressive desensitisation to and development of cognitive distortions concerning fear of being caught and impact of sexual assault on victims.

Barbaree, Marshall, and McCormick outline a view that families characterised by physical, emotional and/or sexual abuse are developmental environments that limit a child's experience of healthy interpersonal relationships while simultaneously promoting a style of relating to others that is characterised by co-erciveness. This double-sided coin of family experience limits a child's development of healthy relationship skills and concurrently teaches a child that they best way to get others to respond to you is through coercive behaviour. A child with limited healthy relationships skills and a tendency to be coercive in his behaviour is ill-equipped to meet the challenge posed by environments outside the family such as school and the successful establishment of relationships with peers. A child in this situation is unlikely to form stable and satisfying relationships with peers, teachers and other adults who find their aggressive and coercive relationship style to be unappealing. This further impedes the development of pro-social skills. Ultimately this developmental pathway may lead to what Barbaree, Marshall and McCormick call the intermediate outcome of the abusive family experience which they characterise as a "syndrome of social disability". They describe the five main features of the syndrome of social disability as follows:

1. An inability to establish and maintain intimate relationships

2. Low self-esteem

3. Diverse anti-social and criminal attitudes and behaviours

4. A lack of empathy

5. Distorted thinking that supports and justifies criminal behaviour.

A young person whose development brings him to a point where these characteristics have a relevance in describing his relationships and behaviour is at a disadvantage in facing the many challenges heralded by the onset of puberty. In particular he may find it very difficult during adolescence to successfully develop appropriate relationships that have a more intimate and sexual quality with suitable age-equivalent partners. This may lead a young person to feel that he is powerless in establishing healthy relationships, and is emotionally isolated. This may promote strong feelings of anger and resentment. For some these become directed at the object of desire; intimate contact with others based upon sexual attraction. A young person in this situation may fall back on the aggressive, manipulative and coercive strategy learnt from negotiating relationships with important figures in the abusive family environment. Such a young person may seek sex either forcefully or with younger, more vulnerable children. These inappropriate sexual contacts may become reinforced through fantasy and masturbation, thus promoting an orientation towards coercive and/or paedophilic sexual behaviour.

In summary, Barbaree, Marshall and McCormick see the following as the key causal factors in the development of sexually abusive behaviour:

1. Disruption in relationships with attachment figures (parents)

2. Experiences of sexual, physical and/or emotional abuse as a child

3. Dysfunctional family relationships including parental reinforcement of coercive, disruptive and aggressive behaviour

4. Inherent temperamental factors that predispose impulsiveness

5. Repeated failure to successfully relate to peers

6. The development of a syndrome of social disability

7. The application of a coercive relationship strategy to achieve sexual contact with others

8. The reinforcement of inappropriate sexual contact through fantasy and masturbation.

Research Evidence Concerning Pre-offence Development

There is a limited but growing body of research available to aid our understanding of the development of adolescents who engage in sexually abusive behaviour. As can be seen below the general trend of the available research supports and further refines the Barbaree, Marshall and McCormick model. O'Reilly, Sheridan, Carr, Cherry, Donohoe, McGrath, Phelan, Tallon and O'Reilly (1998), and Sheridan, McKeown, Cherry, Donohoe, McGrath, O'Reilly, Phelan, and Tallon (1998) provide the only currently available Irish research studies on adolescents who sexually abuse. O'Reilly et al. (1998) compared 23 sexually abusive adolescents referred to a community-based treatment programme in Dublin with a group of non-offending adolescents who were matched for age, sex and socio-economic status. Supporting the Barbaree, Marshall and McCormick model this study confirms important differences in the developmental experiences of adolescents who engage in sexually abusive behaviour. When compared to non-offending peers adolescents who sexually abuse others are (a) more likely to have been the victim of physical abuse, (b) more likely to come from families where parents have separated, (c) more likely to have experienced specific reading difficulties, (d) more likely to have significant school-based behavioural problems, and (e) more likely to have been expelled from school. O'Reilly and colleagues (1998) also report the following abuse histories for the adolescents who engaged in sexually abusive behaviour: 21 per cent had been sexually abused, 65 per cent were physically abused, and 87 per cent had been subject to emotional abuse. O'Reilly et al.'s study also indicated that those adolescents judged by their therapists as still being at high risk of sexually re-offending post-treatment could be distinguished from low risk adolescents by their independently rated self-report of the levels of care they perceived in their relationships with their parents. High risk adolescents reported lower levels of maternal and paternal care. This study indicates that prior to engaging in sexually abusive behaviour young people who sexually assault others have been subject to life experiences that set them on a different developmental trajectory. For a fuller description of empirical studies on adolescents who sexually abuse others interested readers are referred to the above studies and to review articles by Davis and Leitenberg (1987); Vizard, Monck and Misch (1995) and Boyd, Hagan and Cho (2000).

THE SERIOUS NATURE OF ASSAULTIVE BEHAVIOUR BY JUVENILE ABUSERS

It is clear from our discussion up to this point that, on their own, the life experiences prior to offending of many young people who sexually abuse put them in a category that for most people would suggest the appropriateness of therapeutic intervention. In determining the characteristics of a fitting intervention we need to balance our empathy for their developmental experiences with an understanding of the seriousness of their sexually abusive behaviour. O'Reilly (1996) and O'Reilly et al. (1998) provide the following information on the sexually abusive behaviour of the 23 adolescent abusers attending a community-based treatment programme discussed above. These 23 young people had an average age at the time of their first known offence of 14.2 years. Their average age at the time they began treatment was 15.5 years. Despite their youthfulness only 6 (26 per cent) had only one known offence while the remaining 17 (74 per cent) had perpetrated between 3-50+ assaults. In total they had perpetrated sexual assaults on 41 children and adults. Only 13 (56 per cent) of the juvenile abusers had just one victim while 10 (44 per cent) had more than one victim. The serious nature of their abusive behaviour is further underlined by the range of sexual assaultive behaviour from fondling to penetrative acts. Of the total number of people victimised 26 (63 per cent) were under 10 years of age. The gender ratio of victims was 3.1 females: 1 male. Abuse was both familial (29, 71 per cent) and extrafamilial (10, 24 per cent). The most frequent location where the abuse took place was in the victim's home and 15 (65 per cent) adolescent abusers were acting as babysitters at the time of their offence. The above findings are summarised in Table 6.2 below.

Table 6.2: Findings on the Nature of Sexual Assaults by 23 Adolescents in Ireland (O'Reilly et al., 1998)

Variable	Value
Average age at the time of first offence	14.2 years
Average age when entering treatment	15.5 years
Only one known offence	6 (26 per cent)
Between 3 and 50+ offences	17 (74 per cent)
Young offenders with only one victim	13 (56 per cent)
Young offenders with more than one victim	10 (44 per cent)
Total number of people victimised	41
People victimised under 10 years of age	26 (63 per cent)
Gender ratio of people victimised	3.1 females : 1 male
Intra-familial abuse	29(71 per cent)
Extra-familial abuse	10 (24 per cent)
Young offenders acting as babysitters at time of offence	15 (65 per cent)

THE STRUCTURE OF ASSESSMENT AND INTERVENTION SERVICES

The underlying philosophy of assessment and intervention services for young people who engage in sexually abusive behaviour is to prevent future sexual victimisation of children and adults by working with those who have been involved in this behaviour in the past. At present there are four programmes in the Republic of Ireland and three in Northern Ireland whose remit is to work therapeutically with this population. To operate effectively, programmes usually endeavour to develop a multi-disciplinary and multi-agency structure. Given the many needs of these adolescents successful programmes require the co-operation of services that often run independently of each other such as community care services, child and adolescent psychiatry services, residential child care services, gardaí, probation and welfare services, the judicial system, educational psychology services, schools and vocational training services (see Figure 6.2). A commonly employed strategy in Ireland is that each or some of these agencies release members of staff from a variety of disciplines for part of their working week to come together to offer assessment and intervention for young people who engage in sexually abusive behaviour. In what follows we will outline some of the approaches that inform the clinical practice of those involved in this work.

Figure 6.2: Services that Need to Co-operate to Provide an Effective Service for Adolescents Who Sexually Abuse

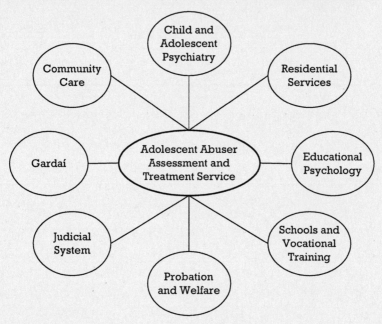

CHARACTERISTICS OF A GOOD ASSESSMENT

Assessment represents a pivotal point in successfully working with a young abuser and his family. Consequently it is important to give some consideration to what constitutes a good assessment. A good assessment incorporates the following features:

1. It allows for the fact that the young person and his family can be at various points along a continuum from complete denial to acknowledgement of sexually abusive behaviour.

2. It is guided by clear theoretical models and research findings.

3. It incorporates strategies to motivate engagement in assessment and intervention.

4. It conveys to the young person and his family that the crises and dilemmas they face are understood by the assessment team.

5. It offers hope when appropriate.

6. It assumes that most juvenile abusers will not be motivated to disclose full details of their offending behaviour during the assessment.

7. It incorporates strategies for the detection of faking.

8. It has access to third party information such as victim statements to gardaí and/or social services.

9. It incorporates psychological testing as an integral part of the assessment process.

10. It attempts a formulation of the strengths and weaknesses of the young person and his family that can use to rebuild their lives in an abuse-free way.

11. It formulates a considered opinion of the degree of future risk of re-offending posed by the young person.

12. It concludes with feedback to the young person and his family on the formulation and treatment plan reached through multi-disciplinary team discussion.

13. It concludes with a contract for intervention if this is the recommendation of the assessment team.

14. It has access to a mechanism to ensure mandated attendance at assessment and intervention if the young person and his family decline the offer of voluntary assistance.

15. It shares appropriate information from the assessment with the child protection network.

CLINICAL ASSESSMENT

Clinical assessment usually takes a number of appointments to complete and incorporates meetings with the young person and key members of his family or care network. Below are listed the main areas usually covered during an assessment:

- A comprehensive developmental history from pregnancy to the present day (incorporating what we know from the literature on the pre-offence development of young people who sexually abuse)

- Family history

- Family attitude to the abusive behaviour

- Family attitude to assessment and treatment

- School-related experiences

- Past and current capacity for making and maintaining friendships

- History of delinquent or conduct disordered behaviour

- Psychosexual development

- Antecedents, behaviours and consequences of the sexually abusive behaviour

- Understanding of the perspective of the child or adult who was sexually assaulted

- Distorted ways of thinking that support sexually abusive behaviour

- Attitude towards assessment and intervention

- Current access to children.

Psychological testing is a central part of the assessment process. At present most treatment programmes in Ireland use a battery of psychological tests that are currently being developed specifically for this population known as the Adolescent Sex Offender Assessment Pack (ASOAP) (Beckett, 1997). The ASOAP tests cover three broad areas of psychological functioning: (1) personality functioning related to sexually abusive behaviour, (2) attitudes and behaviours related to deviant sexuality and the young person's sexual assault, and (3) providing dishonest and inaccurate information during the assessment. Using the ASOAP allows the young person's psychological test profile to be incorporated into the formulation based on the clinical assessment and included in feedback. These tests can also be re-administered after treatment as part of an evaluation of treatment outcome. Further details on assessment can be found in Sheerin and O'Reilly (2000a).

THE STRUCTURE OF INTERVENTION

Intervention for adolescents who have engaged in sexually abusive behaviour is a lengthy process and is usually based on cognitive behavioural and relapse prevention models. Most intervention programmes in Ireland operate using a group therapy structure. Whether or not group rather than individual therapy is more effective is as yet an unanswered empirical question as no-one has compared each approach in a controlled trial. However, a group therapy approach has a number of features which differentiate it from individual therapy that may help explain its relative popularity. These are (1) a group approach can allow for a greater number of clients to be seen, (2) offering group therapy means that staff will be able to co-work, which allows staff to support one another and helps prevent burn-out while working with a difficult client population, (3) group therapy allows adolescents to benefit from feedback from one another and not just from their therapists; this works particularly well if intervention is offered in a "rolling group" format which is made up of those at beginning and advanced stages of therapy, and (4) therapy groups can be used to promote the emergence of healthy social skills in interactions with peers and adults.

On average a young person will attend a community-based intervention programme once a week for roughly one year to eighteen months. During this time they will work their way through a series of modules around which most programmes are structured. Typically these modules include the following:

- Understanding the rules of the group

- Giving an initial account of his abusive behaviour

- Understanding and improving his motivation to change his sexually abusive behaviour

- Understanding and changing his distorted thinking about his sexually abusive behaviour

- Understanding and taking responsibility for his sexually abusive behaviour

- Developing victim awareness

- Outlining his life story

- Relationships and sexuality education

- Positive life skills development; anger management, social skills and problem solving

- Developing a relapse prevention plan.

Further details on intervention can be found in Sheerin and O'Reilly (2000b).

THE PROCESS OF INTERVENTION

The above description gives a sense of the task-focused orientation adopted in structuring intervention for juvenile abusers. However, equal consideration needs to be given to the process of treatment. An essential part of the therapeutic process is delicately balancing appropriately breaking down denial and minimisation of responsibility for abusive behaviour without the young person being subjected to feelings of self-derogation that will result in him adopting a defensive position that will impede progress in therapy. Many people expect that in order to break down denial and minimisation we need to adopt a confrontational style. However, a confrontational style is more likely to be counterproductive as it produces a defensive response from clients thus blocking progress. Instead it is more effective to cultivate a therapeutic experience with the following four attributes:

1. *Where a distinction is made between a person's behaviour and their underlying personality.* When a young person acknowledges engaging in something as damaging to others as sexual abuse he must confront the negative impact that his actions have had on those he has assaulted. This appropriate step has deep negative implications for the young person's self-concept and, unfortunately, experiencing a negative self-image is often an important feature of the emotional, cognitive and behavioural cycle which leads to offending (Lane, 1997). Consequently, if during treatment we aim to help young offenders to abandon denial and minimisation and realistically acknowledge their abusive behaviour and its impact on abuse survivors we must be sure that in doing so we are not in fact increasing their risk of re-offending by further undermining their self-concept. One possible solution to this therapeutic dilemma is to explicitly make a distinction between a person's behaviour and his underlying personality. Working with a young person in treatment to co-construct a perception of their sexually abusive *behaviour* as distinct from their underlying *personality* allows treatment to proceed by appropriately rejecting the abusive behaviour while exploring personal strengths the young person may have that can be capitalised upon to prevent relapse.

2. *A non-collusive collaborative style* rather than a confrontational style should be promoted from first contact with the client. In adopting this style the therapist presents the client with the idea that they will be working together to attempt to fully understand his development to the point where he engaged in sexually abusive behaviour, with the aim of using this understanding to help him develop skills that he can use to choose to avoid being abusive in the future. By twinning a collaborative venture to understand the young person and his behaviour with the aim of preventing abuse in the future the therapist gradually builds a situation where difficult questions can be asked and difficult realities can be faced without forcing the young person to adopt a defensive and uncooperative position.

3. *The adoption of therapist features demonstrated by research to have a positive impact on treatment outcome* also contributes to breaking down denial and minimisation without undermining progress towards an abuse-free lifestyle for the young person. Marshall, Anderson, and Fernandez (1999) describe the following therapist features as being reliably identified as positively linked with successful treatment outcome:

- Empathic

- Non-collusive

- Respectful

- Appropriately self-disclosing

- Warm and friendly

- Appropriate use of humour

- Sincere and genuine

- Communicates clearly

- Rewarding and encouraging

- Encourages active participation

- Directive and reflective

- Encourages pro-social attitudes

- Confident

- Asks open-ended questions

- Interested

- Deals with frustration and difficulties

- Non-confrontational challenging

- Spends appropriate time on issues.

4. *The inclusion of a holistic life development focus in conjunction with offence specific treatment tasks.* Young people who engage in sexually abusive behaviour often present with a range of emotional, behavioural and vocational difficulties

that may play a maintaining role in their offending behaviour. Consequently it is important that these are tackled either during treatment or as an adjunct to treatment. For example, areas that may require attention are enuresis, conduct problems, attention deficit difficulties, bullying behaviour, communication problems, depression, educational and vocational drop-out. In tackling these areas we are attempting to return the young person to a life-development pathway that is more normative and consequently supports an abuse-free lifestyle for the future.

PARENTS' SUPPORT GROUPS

Most programmes also run a parallel group for parents. They attempt to help families come to terms with their child's sexually abusive behaviour, to begin to tackle family factors that may have had a role in precipitating and maintaining abusive behaviour, and to help family members become a proactive and constructive part of the young person's network of people who will form their relapse prevention support system.

POST-OFFENCE DEVELOPMENT

At present we quite simply do not know how to predict the post-offence developmental pathways of young people who abuse and how these might or might not be influenced by therapeutic intervention. Becker and Kaplan (1998) theorise three untested potential outcome pathways following sexually abusive behaviour. These are:

- *A dead end pathway*, where the young person discontinues his sexually abusive behaviour in the face of negative consequences and, perhaps, therapeutic intervention

- *A delinquency pathway,* where the young person may continue to be involved in sexual assaults in the context of the commission of other non-sexual crimes

- *A deviant sexual interest pathway,* where the adolescent commits further sexual crimes and develops a paraphilic arousal pattern. This group is likely to be made up of those adolescents who found their sexually assaultive behaviour very pleasurable, experienced no or minimal consequences in relation to the commission of their sexual crimes, experienced reinforcement of their deviant sexual behaviour through fantasy and masturbation, and continue to have deficiencies in their ability to relate to age appropriate peers.

At present we also do not have any methodologically sound studies that inform us of the re-offence rate of treated juveniles compared with untreated juveniles with sexually abusive behaviour. In reality these studies are practically and ethically very difficult to conduct as they are long-term (2-20 years) pieces of research requiring control groups of untreated adolescents and access to police records and sophisticated psychological testing. However, some interesting sources of data do exist. Abel, Mittelman and Becker (1985) investigated a group of 240 untreated adult sex offenders who began their sexual offending behaviour prior to age 18. These adolescents who continued to offend as adults had an average of 580 attempted or completed sexual offences. In contrast, Alexander (1999) reports that from a sample of 875 treated adolescents with sexually abusive behaviours against both children and adults the rate of re-offence was just 7.5 per cent. These studies illustrate the considerable potential for both an escalation and an extinction of sexually abusive behaviour by young people.

FUTURE DIRECTIONS

It is unrealistic to think that at present we can successfully understand and intervene with all young people who engage in sexually abusive behaviour. However, we are beginning to sufficiently understand their development and current psychological functioning to initiate the process of constructing effective assessment and intervention services to meet their therapeutic needs and work towards the primary goal of preventing other children and adults from being subjected to sexual victimisation in the future. Hopefully this chapter has illustrated that attempting these goals is possible. Our success in reaching them will be determined by the quality of the services we develop, their integration within the overall child protection and judicial systems, and our commitment to methodologically sound research.

References

Abel, G., Mittelman, M. S. & Becker, J. B. (1985). "Sex offenders: Results of assessment and recommendations for treatment". In H. Ben-Aaron, S. Hacker & C. Webster (Eds.), *Clinical Criminology: Current Concepts.* Toronto: M & M Graphics.

Alexander, M. A. (1999). "Sexual offender treatment revisited". *Sexual Abuse, A Journal of Research and Treatment*, April. Vol. 11(2).

Araji, S. (1997). *Sexually Aggressive Children: Coming to Understand Them.* London, Sage Publications.

Barbaree, H. E., Hudson, S. E. & Seto, M. C. (1993). "Sexual assault in society: The role of the juvenile offender". In H. E. Barbaree, W. L. Marshall, & S. M. Hudson (Eds.), *The Juvenile Sex Offender.* New York: Guilford Press.

Barbaree, H. E., Marshall, W. L. & McCormick, J. (1998). "The development of deviant sexual behaviour among adolescents and its implications for prevention and treatment". In G. O'Reilly and A. Carr (Eds.), *Understanding, Assessing, and Treating Juvenile and Adult Sex Offenders, A Special Issue of The Irish Journal of Psychology*, Vol. 19 (1).

Becker, J. & Kaplan, M. S. (1988). "The assessment of adolescent sexual offenders". *Advances in Behavioural Assessment of Children and Families*, 4, 97-114.

Beckett, Richard (1997). *The Adolescent Sex Offender Assessment Pack (ASOAP).* Unpublished Manual. UK, The Oxford Forensic Psychology Service.

Boyd, N., Hagan, M. & Cho, M. E. (2000). "Characteristics of Adolescent Sex Offenders: A Review of the Research". *Aggression and Violent Behaviour,* Vol. 5 (2), 137-146.

Cavanagh Johnson, T. (1999). *Understanding Your Child's Sexual Behaviour: What's Natural and Healthy.* California, New Harbinger Publications.

Lane, S. (1997). "The Sexual Abuse Cycle". In G. Ryan & S. Lane, (Eds.). *Juvenile Sexual Offending. Causes, Consequences, and Correction*, (2nd edition). San Francisco: Josey-Bass.

Marshall, W. L., Anderson, D & Fernandez, Y. (1999). "Therapeutic processes and client self esteem". *Cognitive Behavioural Treatment of Sexual Offenders*. New York: John Wiley & Sons.

McKeown, K., Gilligan, R., Brannick, T., McGuane, B. & Riordan, S. (1989). "Child Sexual Abuse in the Eastern Health Board Area", Ireland, 1988: *Volume 1: A Statistical Analysis of All Suspected and Confirmed Child Sexual Abuse Cases Known to the Community Care Teams in the Eastern Health Board and Open at Any Time in 1988*, Unpublished Report, Dublin: Department of Health.

O'Reilly, Gary (1996). A Psychological Investigation of the Characteristics of Adolescent Perpetrators of Child Sexual Abuse. Unpublished M. Psych. Sc. Thesis, Department of Psychology, University College Dublin.

O'Reilly, G. & Carr, A. (in press). "Theoretical models of sexually abusive behaviour". In G. O'Reilly, W. Marshall, R. Beckett, & A. Carr (Eds.) (In press). *The Handbook of Clinical Intervention with Juvenile Sexual Offenders*, London: Routledge.

O'Reilly, G., Sheridan, A., Carr, A., Cherry, J., Donohoe, E., McGrath, K., Phelan, S., Tallon, M. & O'Reilly, K. (1998). "A descriptive study of adolescent sexual offenders in an Irish community based treatment programme". In G. O'Reilly and A. Carr (Eds.), *Understanding, Assessing, and Treating Juvenile and Adult Sex Offenders, A Special Issue of The Irish Journal of Psychology,* Vol. 19 (1).

Research Team, The (1990). *Child Sexual Abuse in Northern Ireland: A Research Study of Incidence*. Northern Ireland: Greystone Press.

Sheerin, D, & O'Reilly, G. (2000a). "Treatment of adolescent sexual offenders — Part 1: Assessment and treatment approaches". *Modern Medicine* Vol. 30 (3), 49-54.

Sheerin, D. & O'Reilly, G. (2000b). "Treatment of adolescent sexual offenders — Part 2: Group therapy". *Modern Medicine* Vol. 30 (4), 35-41.

Sheridan, A., McKeown, K., Cherry, J., Donohoe, E., McGrath, K., O'Reilly, K., Phelan, S. & Tallon, M. (1998). "Perspectives on treatment outcome in adolescent sexual offending: A study of a community based treatment programme". In O'Reilly, Gary, and Carr, Alan (Eds.), *Understanding, Assessing, and Treating Juvenile and Adult Sex Offenders, A Special Issue of The Irish Journal of Psychology*, Vol. 19 (1).

Vizard, E., Monck, E. & Misch, P. (1995). "Child and adolescent sex abuse perpetrators: A review of the research literature". *Journal of Child Psychology and Psychiatry*, 36, 731-756.

Chapter Seven

Child Sexual Abuse Victims and the Legal Process

Geoffrey Shannon

INTRODUCTION

The term "child sexual abuse" is a relatively recent addition to legal and social discourse. It is defined in the Department of Health guidelines entitled *Children First: National Guidelines for the Protection and Welfare of Children* as occurring "when a child is used by another person for his or her gratification or sexual arousal, or that of others" (1999, 6).[1] Prosecutions for the sexual abuse of children have risen significantly in recent years. This may not necessarily signpost an increase in the incidence of child sexual abuse but rather a more frequent reporting of the offence. Cases of sexual abuse of children are very difficult to prove. The prosecution is frequently left with little other than the victim's testimony. Indeed, the conduct of child sexual abuse cases reflects the current uncertainty attaching to the law in this area. In this chapter it is proposed to address the law and trial procedures relating to child sexual abuse. We shall examine the removal of a child into care where there are allegations of child sexual abuse, the processing of such cases, the rules of law and evidence that apply in the

---

[1] Department of Health (1999) *Children First: National Guidelines for the Protection and Welfare of Children.* Dublin: Government Publications.

hearing of such cases, the impact of international law and recent statutory developments.

REMOVING CHILDREN INTO CARE

The general welfare of the child is a matter of concern not only to the family of which it is a member but also to society at large. It is no longer accepted that the State should defer to the autonomy of the family in all matters relating to children. There are clearly defined circumstances in which the State is not merely entitled, but obliged to intervene with a view to safeguarding children from harm, even from within their own families.[2] Such intervention is regulated by the Child Care Act, 1991.

Care Proceedings

Part IV of the Child Care Act, 1991 allows for the making of various orders designed to protect a child in the medium to long term who is believed to be in danger, whether currently or in the past. In particular, part IV empowers the health board in whose functional area a child resides or is found to make an application for a care or supervision order (as it sees fit) where it forms the view that there is reasonable cause to believe that the child has been sexually abused.

The two key orders that may be made in this situation are as follows:

- *Care Order* — this allows a child to be committed to the care of the health board. For these purposes the child may be removed from the care of their parents or other custodians.

- *Supervision Order* — this allows a child, while remaining in the custody of their parents or other custodian, to be visited periodically by the health board.

Only a health board may apply for such orders to be made.

There is an international obligation, imposed by Article 3 of the European Convention of Human Rights, to protect children from harm and ill treatment. In *Z. and Ors v. U.K.* (a case now

---

[2] One such circumstance is where allegations of child sexual abuse arise.

before the European Court of Human Rights) the Commission on Human Rights held that a local authority has a positive duty to see that measures are taken to protect a child at risk.[3] The Commission noted, in particular, the local authority's failure to assign a senior social worker or guardian *ad litem* in respect of the child at the centre of that case, more of which later.

Standard of Proof

In cases of child sexual abuse, applications by health boards to remove children from the custody of their parents are generally contested by the civil standard of proof on the balance of probability. That said, the court is always alert to the inalienable rights of parents in relation to their children under Articles 41 and 42 of the Constitution. Indeed, most recently in the *North Western Health Board v. HW and CW McCracken J.* held as follows:

> Quite clearly the welfare of the child is not the only matter to be considered under S.3 of the Act [of 1991], and the rights of the parents and the position of the family unit is clearly both recognised and emphasised in subsection (2) (b) and (c) of that section. Article 41.1 places the family in a very special position as being the natural primary and fundamental unit group of society. It also provides that the family possess rights which are antecedent and superior to all positive law . . . There have been a number of cases which have spoken of a hierarchy of rights under the Constitution, but the wording of Article 41.1 certainly would appear to place the rights of the family in relation to their children, very high up in this hierarchy.[4]

Procedural Safeguards

The case of *State (D. & D.) v. Groake*[5] set down certain procedural safeguards which should apply in cases where allegations

---

[3] No. 29392/95, Comm. Rep. 10.9.99.

[4] Unreported, High Court, October 27, 2000, at pp. 12-13.

[5] [1990] 1 IR 305.

of child sexual abuse are made. In that case the supreme court stated that the court deciding such issues, must have before it basic evidence from which a conclusion of child sexual abuse has been drawn. The lawyers acting for the parents are entitled to have, in sufficient time for the trial, reports or summaries of the evidence which is to be given, and an examination of any video recording made.[6] Where anatomically correct dolls have been used a demonstration of the precise use and the expert witness's belief in the meaning of the use by the child should be given. In the later case of *M.Q. v. Glesson*[7] Barr J. held that in abuse cases, the complaint should be put to the alleged abuser in the course of the investigations and he/she should be given an opportunity of responding to the allegation.

In cases where information is not made available to the lawyer acting for the alleged abuser, it is now possible to seek discovery in the District Court pursuant to the District Court (Discovery of Documents) Rules 1998.[8] The case of *W.W. (A Minor) v. P.B.*[9] should be noted wherein Barr J. held that material was *prima facie* discoverable if it came into existence prior to the date when the plaintiff first consulted a solicitor about his allegations.

Provision of Reports to Parents Defending Allegations of Child Sexual Abuse

Failure to consult or provide a parent with adequate information regarding their children in care constitutes a violation of Article 8 of the European Convention on Human Rights, save where it is justified under Article 8(2). In *McMichael v. UK* the European Court stated that a parent's lack of access to reports or documents affected participation in the decision-making process and may breach Article 8.[10] The denial of such information also raises an issue under Article 6 which guarantees the right to a

---

[6] No. 28945/ 95, *T.P. and K.M. v. UK*, Comm. Rep. 10.9.99.

[7] Unreported, High Court, February 13, 1997.

[8] S.I. No. 285 of 1999.

[9] Unreported, High Court, March 18, 1999.

[10] [1995] 20 EHRR 205.

"fair and public hearing". Such a fair hearing necessarily involves access to reports or documents, save where they may be detrimental to the interests of the child. The Commission recently in *T.P. and K.M. v. the UK* expressed the view that parents, defending serious allegations regarding children, should be provided with full information as to their factual basis.[11] The European Court has yet to issue its judgment on the matter.

Delay in Care Proceedings

Delays in care proceedings may fall foul of either Article 6 or Article 8 of the Convention. Alternatively, as was the case in *W. v. U.K.,* the delay may result in a violation of both provisions.[12] A review of the jurisprudence of the European Court of Human Rights reveals that national authorities must display special diligence in expediting proceedings. Indeed, exceptional diligence is required where the maxim "justice delayed is justice denied" is fully applicable. This might arise where custody and access proceedings are initiated by parents of children in the care of health boards as such proceedings are decisive for the parents' future relations with their children and have a "particular quality of irreversibility".[13] The current delay in the procurement and completion of Section 20 reports[14] and the difficulties encountered in retaining guardian *ad litem*s must surely fall to be considered under this heading.

---

[11] No. 28945/ 95, *T.P. and K.M. v. UK*, Comm. Rep. 10.9.99.

[12] [1987] 10 EHRR 29 at p.65.

[13] For example, because of claims of sexual abuse against them.

[14] In the course of private family law proceedings a court can order a report under section 20 of the Child Care Act, 1991 where it believes that in order to adequately protect the children in a case a care order or supervision order may need to be made. Specifically, the court can of its own motion or on the application of any person adjourn private family law proceedings and direct the health board to undertake an investigation of the child's circumstances and the court may also give directions as to the care and custody of the child or may make a supervision order pending the outcome.

Access to Children in Care Consequent upon Child Sexual Abuse

Article 8 of the European Convention on Human Rights guarantees parents and children access to each other when a care order is in place as a result of proceedings concerning child sexual abuse allegations. Access is the right of the child rather than that of the parents. This has long been the case in England where Wrangham J. in *M. v. M.* stated that access by a parent should not be denied to the child except where the interests of the child so required.[15] Up until the 1990s in this jurisdiction the Supreme Court seemed to view access as a right of the parents as opposed to a basic right of the child.[16]

It was not until the High Court judgment of Carroll J. in the case of *M.D. v. G.D.* that the tenor of the language in access cases assumed a child focus.[17] In that case Carroll J. held, *inter alia*, that the welfare of the child is paramount and that it is the right of the child with which the court is concerned not the right of the adult. This view has been expressed by the European Court of Human Rights in the case of *Hendriks v. Netherlands*[18], *W. v. U.K.*[19], *R. v. U.K.*[20], *O. v. U.K.*[21], *H. v. U.K.*[22], *McMichael v. U.K.*[23] and *Olsson v. Sweden*[24]. It also now forms part of Article 9(3) of the 1989 UN Convention on the Rights of the Child which provides for:

> the right of the child who is separated from one or both parents to maintain public relations and direct contact with both

---

[15] [1973] 2 All ER 81 (Fam. D).

[16] See *State (D&D) v. G* [1990] ILRM 10 and *State (F) v. Superintendent* (B) Garda Station [1990] ILRM 243.

[17] High Court, 30 July 1992.

[18] (1983) 5 EHRR 223.

[19] (1988) 10 EHRR 29.

[20] (1988) 10 EHRR 74.

[21] (1988) 10 EHRR 82.

[22] (1988) 10 EHRR 95.

[23] Application No. 16,424/90.

[24] (1988) 11 EHRR 259.

parents on a regular basis, except if it is contrary to the child's best interests.

Section 37 of the Child Care Act, 1991 concerns access to children in care. This section specifically provides for parents and persons acting *in loco parentis* to be allowed access.

There is, in addition, a positive duty on the health board to facilitate access between the parent and child.[25] For example, in *Olsson v. Sweden* the Court noted that there was a positive obligation on each State to take appropriate measures to facilitate reunion between children and their parents.[26] In that case, three children from one family (the Olssons) had been placed in foster care with different foster parents living a considerable distance from each other and from the parents of the children. As a result of the geographical distance between them, contact between the children themselves and between the parents and the children was made virtually impossible. This, the Human Rights Court concluded, constituted a breach of Article 8 of the Convention, the State having failed to make adequate provision for intra-familial contact. The administrative difficulties (such as the apparent shortage of appropriate foster families) asserted in defence by the State were deemed not to be of sufficient weight to prevent a ruling against it. Little guidance is given, however, as to what is an acceptable distance by which children and their parents can be separated.

Supervised Access

It is, indeed, exceptionally uncommon for an application of access to be refused. Where it is felt that unsupervised access may, for whatever reason, be unwise it is the standard practice of the Court to grant access subject to the condition that it be supervised. In *O'D. v. O'D. (C.) & Others*, for instance, the High Court granted supervised access to the father where there was a reasonable suspicion that he might have sexually abused his child, Geoghegan J. pointing out that the primary matter to be considered by the court in determining access rights to a child was the

---

[25] See *Eriksson v. Sweden* (1989) 12 EHRR 200.

[26] (1988) 11 EHRR 259.

welfare of the child.[27] Indeed, supervised access is an important facility in situations involving allegations of child sexual abuse. Investigation and validation of such allegations take considerable time. Facilities for supervised access by the parent "under suspicion" are practically non-existent. Only a health board may apply for a supervision order under section 19.

From a child welfare perspective, a supervision order facilitates continuity in that it enables a child to be monitored in their own home without the child having to be taken into care. The Law Society of Ireland's Law Reform Committee in its report on domestic violence highlighted the important role of court orders providing supervised access.[28] The Probation and Welfare Services should be given a dominant role in supervised access arrangements and should be allocated adequate resources to fulfil this role.

HELPING THE CHILD VICTIM TO GIVE EVIDENCE

A court can be an intimidating place even for a worldly adult. For a child sexual abuse victim it must be especially so. A key concern must be to avoid the process causing additional trauma for the children involved. Several commentators have referred to the stress involved in testifying in open court as a "revictimisation" or secondary victimisation. A child already scarred by the subject matter of the proceedings may be further traumatised by the process of testifying in court. In addition to preventing trauma there is also a further concern of a more judicial nature. The court will also be concerned to ensure that a child giving evidence will be able to give as full, accurate and coherent an account of their experiences as possible. A belief that this is not always possible added to the fear of further traumatising the child often results in the courts failing to hear the evidence of children. The prevailing wisdom, it seems, has been that the benefit of hearing the child's evidence is generally

---

[27] [1994] 3 Fam. L.J. 81. See also *H. v. H. and C.* [1989] 3 All ER 740 and *Re B (A Minor) (Contact: Stepfather's Hostility)* [1997] 2 FLR 579.

[28] Law Society of Ireland Law Reform Committee, *Domestic Violence: The case for reform*, (Law Society of Ireland: Dublin, 1999).

outweighed by the danger of the child incurring "secondary trauma" as a result of being exposed to the formal questioning of legal personnel.

That children have a right to have their evidence or their views and concerns heard in cases that determine their future safety or welfare is no longer questionable given our obligations under the 1989 United Nations Convention on the Rights of the Child. A child's testimony is of central importance in cases concerning sexual abuse, even more so than other types of child maltreatment litigation, because of the fact that there may be no other corroborating evidence, and as the case load in this area increases so will the pressure to facilitate child witnesses.

In this regard some advances have been made. Statutory reform has allowed the family courts to reduce to a minimum the formality involved in a family case. Great efforts have been made to alleviate unnecessary formality, for instance by prohibiting the wearing of wigs and gowns by either judges or legal representatives in family proceedings in the Circuit Family and High Courts. This is a worthy gesture designed to normalise the atmosphere of the court in such cases. It was effected by section 33 of the Judicial Separation and Family Law Reform Act, 1989, which further requires that all such proceedings be as informal as is possible in all the circumstances. It is worth noting, in addition, that the personal kindness and concern of judges and legal personnel alike frequently comes to the fore in such stressful circumstances. The courts must be careful, however, not to throw caution to the winds — such informality as is permitted must be consistent with the administration of justice and must be without prejudice to the rights of the parties.

Procedural changes have also allowed the child to be seated in the well of the court along with the judge, counsel and solicitors and to be accompanied by a friend or relative, willing and able to support the child if needs be. Amplification equipment has been installed in some courts to facilitate greater ease of communication. Occasionally, an interpreter may be appointed to clarify or explain certain questions being asked of, or answers being made by, the child.

Furthermore, several innovative methods have been formulated to enable a child's voice to be heard in the judicial process, in some cases without requiring the child to be present in court.

Hearsay Evidence

The rule against hearsay states that a statement initially made outside court by any person may not be repeated in court. There are indeed many exceptions to this rule but the basic thrust is described succinctly by Cross as follows:

> A statement other than one made by a person while giving oral evidence in the proceedings is inadmissible as evidence of the fact stated.[29]

The rationale behind this may simply be that what a person says is not always good evidence of what they in fact do. Nonetheless, enforced to its full extent, it is obvious that such a rule would cause great hardship. In the context of child law proceedings, and particularly where such proceedings relate to child sexual abuse allegations, it may prevent evidence being given by a person who has interviewed a child as to the content of that interview. Thus, short of presenting the child as a witness, such evidence could not be admitted. In recent times in family law proceedings, however, the rule has been eroded considerably.

In the context of public child law cases the inclusion of hearsay evidence is permitted, albeit at the discretion of the court. The Supreme Court affirmed this proposition in *Southern Health Board v. C.H.*[30] In effect, this case dealt with the admissibility of a videotape interview with the child, and the purpose for which the court could view the interview. Was the video recording the hearsay evidence of the child or was it part of the expert testimony? The court determined that the video tape interview was part of the expert testimony to be given by the social worker.

Section 23 of the Children Act, 1997 furthermore permits the inclusion of hearsay evidence of any fact in all proceedings relating to the welfare of a child, public or private. The legislation also applies in cases relating to any person who has a mental

---

[29] Cross, *Evidence* (London: Butterworth's, 1974) at 6.

[30] [1996] 1 IR 219.

disability to such an extent that independent living is not feasible. However, in all cases to which section 23 relates, several conditions apply. These conditions are listed in section 23 of the Children Act, 1997.

Section 24 of the Children Act, 1997 contains provisions regarding the weight to be given to the hearsay evidence under Section 23, with regard to all the circumstances from which inferences as to its accuracy or otherwise can be drawn, and a list of other considerations in section 24(2).

Section 25 of the Children Act, 1997 allows evidence regarding the credibility of the child to be admitted, notwithstanding the fact that the child is not, strictly speaking, a witness.

Section 26 of the Children Act, 1997 provides that where a document is admissible in proceedings permitting hearsay evidence, it may be given in evidence by producing an authenticated copy (including a faxed copy) of it.

Hearsay evidence has recently been held to be admissible in wardship proceedings when the judge is satisfied of the necessity for so doing and that the evidence is reliable. In the case of the *Eastern Health Board v. M.K. and M.K.* the judges of the Supreme Court recognised the changes introduced in the Children Act, 1997.[31] Indeed, the law applied by the Supreme Court bears a resemblance to the statutory approach, and thus this decision is relevant to the interpretation of the Act, a factor considered by Barron J. in his judgment. He noted that the real difference would not be in the admission of hearsay evidence, but in the ability of the courts to give direct weight to such statements.

Video Link Evidence

Stress experienced by children during the trial process is of concern because firstly, child witnesses should be protected from trauma caused by the legal process itself and secondly, it interferes with the child's ability to give a coherent, complete and credible testimony which will facilitate justice. Minimising stress suffered by young children in open court will encourage

---

[31] Unreported, Supreme Court, January 29, 1999 (S.C. Nos. 65 & 67 of 1996).

future reporting, lessen the need for plea bargaining (in order to avoid a child witness having to testify), and minimise the possibility of a case collapsing due to a child's inability to recount the traumatic details and go through the cross-examination process.

Video link systems enable the evidence of a child to be broadcast live in court during the trial from a separate room. This facility is now available in Dublin courts and it is hoped that this alternative will significantly reduce the level of stress involved.

The first live television/video link evidence was permitted in criminal cases by virtue of section 12 of the Criminal Evidence Act, 1992. Section 13 of the 1992 Act allows for the giving of evidence through an intermediary where evidence is being given through a television link, so long as the court is satisfied that such is required having regard to the witness's age or mental condition. The intermediary must be a person who, in the opinion of the court, is competent to act as such.

The videotaping of children's evidence for tendering at a trial was facilitated by section 15 of the Criminal Evidence Act, 1992. However, by section 15(2), this can only be done in circumstances where a particular witness is available for cross-examination and the court is content that it will not result in unfairness to the accused. Section 15 1(b) of the 1992 Act is worthy of particular note as it provides that in the case of a child under 14 years of age, video recordings of any statement by a victim of an offence is admissible where the statement is made to a member of the Garda Siochana or to "any other person who is competent" for that purpose. In relation to the second situation, this provision would seem to facilitate the admissibility of video recordings made between a child sexual abuse victim and a child psychologist in a child sexual abuse assessment unit. Section 15(1)(b), however, is also curtailed by section 15(2) which provides that a video recording will not be admitted in evidence if the trial judge takes the view that it should be excluded, particularly if he considers that its admission would "result in unfairness to the accused".

Section 16 of the 1992 Act empowers the court to transfer proceedings to a Circuit or District Court District which has the necessary technical facilities for enabling evidence to be given through a television link or by means of video recording.

The provisions introduced by the 1992 Act for easing the trauma of children giving evidence by providing television links have always been open to challenge on constitutional grounds. While welcome and necessary these provisions represented a major departure in the conduct of courtroom proceedings. The Supreme Court in the case of *Donnelly v. Ireland*[32] upheld the constitutionality of this facility, affirming the approach of the High Court in the earlier case of *White v. Ireland.*[33] It concluded that an accused person in Ireland had no constitutional right to have a witness to give evidence in his presence or to "confront" him. Hamilton CJ stated:

> [A]n accused person's right to a fair trial is adequately protected and vindicated. Such right does not include the right in all circumstances to require that that the evidence be given in his physical presence and consequently there is no such constitutional right. [34]

The fact that the video link provisions were upheld is to be welcomed. That said, there appears to be some limits placed upon the use of television links. In particular, the Supreme Court was clear that the use was not a breach of fair procedures in the case presented as there were sufficient other safeguards, including the giving of evidence on oath.

The Children Act, 1997 extends the use of video link evidence to civil proceedings concerning the welfare of a child.[35] Part III of the 1997 Act allows the giving of evidence by children through television link in civil proceedings concerning the welfare of a child. Section 21 of the Act allows for the Court to permit the giving of evidence in private law cases by means of a live television link. While such evidence will be broadcast live there is also a further requirement that it be video-

---

[32] [1998] 1 IR 321.

[33] [1995] 2 IR 268.

[34] [1998] 1 ILRM at 413.

[35] The relevant part of the Act, part III, came into force on 1 January 1999.

recorded (presumably for the further perusal of the judge and, where necessary, of any appellate court).

One remarkable feature is that such evidence may be made from outside the State. However, any material statement made during the proceedings by a child giving evidence outside the State will be treated as if made within the State. Thus where the child makes a statement that he or she knows to be false or does not believe to be true, that child will be guilty of perjury or of an offence under section 28 of the Children Act, 1997 as if such offence had been committed in Ireland.

A standard procedure associated with court proceedings is that of identification in open court. Where a person is mentioned, particularly in connection with an allegation of wrongdoing, a court may require the person mentioned to be identified by the speaker in open court. This would of course undermine the efficacy of section 21 of the 1997 Act and to this end it is possible for a child to forego this requirement. If the child gives evidence by television link, as contemplated by section 21, that they knew a person before the commencement of the proceedings, it will not be necessary for the child to identify such person in open court. This obviates the trauma often associated with court proceedings where alleged wrongdoers and their victims are thrown together in open court.

A further safeguard is contained in section 22 of the 1997 Act. This allows evidence, given by means of a television link, to be conveyed through an intermediary. This may be done provided that the court is satisfied that, having regard to the age and mental condition of the child, evidence should be gathered through such an intermediary.[36] The benefit of this approach is that it enables questions to be put to the child in language that they understand. Indeed the Act requires as much.[37] This is particularly important in a case concerning allegations of child sexual abuse. The Court must also be satisfied that the intermediary is competent to perform such a task.[38] It

---

[36] Section 22(1).

[37] Section 22(2).

[38] Section 22(3).

may not be sufficient that the intermediary be experienced as a social worker *per se*.[39] In some cases at least, more specific experience with children may be required.

A key fear may be that the interposition of an intermediary will blunt the opportunity for robust cross-examination of witnesses. All parties are still, of course, entitled to put questions to the child but only indirectly. The Supreme Court considered the use of the television link and intermediary in child law proceedings in *Eastern Health Board v. M.K. and M.K.*[40] While critical of the handling of the particular interview, the remarks of the Supreme Court were generally favourable to video link evidence, as two judges noted that one could see the conduct of the interview and thus be in a better position to judge its veracity. Interestingly, the Supreme Court classified the videotape interview as simply back-up material to the testimony of the social worker in the same way a doctor might rely upon a medical report.

In light of the decision in *Donnelly v. Ireland*, it is indeed unlikely that the new provisions in the Children Act, 1997 will face constitutional difficulties.[41] That said, caution is still required. The latter mentioned case underlines the particular need to ensure that such procedures as are followed do not prejudice the right of all concerned to natural justice, in particular to challenge the veracity of evidence delivered by television link.

The main practical concern surrounding these innovations, however, is one of resources. Few Irish courts have adequate facilities to carry out a remote television link. Indeed, until recently there was only one room in the Four Courts complex that facilitated evidence to be given in this manner. The commencement of Part III of the Children Act, 1997 (in January 1999) could only have compounded these shortcomings. With this in mind section 27 of the Act allows the court, where it lacks such facilities, to transfer proceedings to a Circuit or District Court building that has adequate facilities (although this can only put further pressure on already limited resources).

---

[39] See the dicta of Hamilton C.J. in *Eastern Health Board v. M.K. and M.K.* Unreported, Supreme Court, January 29, 1999.

[40] *Ibid.*

[41] *Ibid.*

Unsworn Evidence and Corroboration

Section 26 of the Criminal Evidence Act, 1992 allows a child under fourteen years of age to give evidence otherwise than by oath or affirmation once certain conditions specified in section 26 are satisfied. In private law cases the general requirement that a person giving evidence before a court must do so under oath or on affirmation is removed where the provisions of section 28 of the Children Act, 1997 are satisfied. Section 28 applies to all civil proceedings and not just to those contemplated by the Act itself. It permits the court to accept the evidence of a child under the age of 14 years, even where such evidence is given otherwise than on oath or affirmation. The provisions also apply to any person, regardless of age, who has a mental disability.[42] Such evidence as is given in both public and private cases may be taken as corroborating other evidence, whether the latter is sworn or unsworn.

There are, however, certain important conditions. The court must be satisfied that the child is able to give an intelligible account of all relevant events to justify the reception of the evidence and understands the duty of speaking the truth. It is further stipulated that, the absence of an oath notwithstanding, a child who gives evidence knowing it to be false or not believing it to be true shall be guilty of an offence. Such person shall, on conviction, be treated as if guilty of perjury and sentenced accordingly.

The Use of Anatomically Correct Dolls

In many cases, especially those involving alleged sexual abuse, a child may lack the language necessary to describe their experiences. An innovative solution to the problem of the child's limited vocabulary is the use of anatomically correct dolls. These enable a child to convey to the court, by gesture rather than words, the nature of their experiences. For instance, a child allegedly the victim of sexual abuse can point to the places where they have been touched, thus obviating the need to mention what to the child may be embarrassing words. This

---

[42] See also section 20(b).

was first used in the criminal case of *D.P.P. v. J.T.*[43] While this case involved the alleged sexual abuse of a person who was mentally disabled, it is submitted that the Court's decision is equally applicable to civil cases involving minors.

SEPARATE REPRESENTATION FOR CHILDREN IN CHILD SEXUAL ABUSE PROCEEDINGS

Evidence Gathered by Means of Social Report

Despite the strictures of the adversarial approach, it has been the frequent practice of the courts to request section 20 reports in respect of children who are the subject of child sexual abuse proceedings. These reports allow the court to order the making of an investigation with a view to determining whether a care order or supervision order is appropriate in relation to a child who is the subject of the proceedings. The court may order such investigation of its own motion or following the request of any party to the proceedings. As a condition precedent to such an order, it must appear to the court that it may be appropriate to make such an order, although the court obviously need not have made up its mind on this point. If it comes to such a conclusion it may order the health board in whose functional area the child resides to undertake an investigation of the child's circumstances.

Following such an order proceedings will be adjourned pending the publication of the results of the investigation. In the interim, the court may make such orders regarding the child(ren)'s care and custody as appear proper, including a supervision order. During the adjournment, the health board will be obliged to investigate the child's circumstances. In doing so it must consider in particular whether it should apply for a care order or supervision order in respect of a child, provide services or assistance for the benefit of a child or their family or take any other appropriate action in relation to the child. Once made, such report must be delivered in writing to the court. If the health board, having completed its investigation, decides

---

[43] 3 Frewen 141.

not to proceed to obtain a care or supervision order, it must inform the court of its reasons for so deciding and of any service or assistance that it has provided or intends for the child or their family. It is also required to appraise the court of any action that it has taken or intends to take in respect of the child. It is possible, in addition, for the court to call the person making the report to give evidence before it.

Social reports allow evidence relating to the child's welfare to be collected without necessarily requiring the child to appear in court. This task was originally performed by the probation and welfare service on an informal basis although since 1996 such reports have generally been made by social workers, the former maintaining that they lacked the resources to continue doing so adequately. There seems to be a view that such reports give a voice to the child and thereby satisfy the Irish State's obligations under Article 12 of the 1989 UN Convention on the Rights of the Child. This is not entirely accurate as social reports may (and sometimes do) tend to approach the circumstances of the family from the perspective of the adults as they relate to their children rather than focusing on the children's interests in and of themselves. Great care is needed then to ensure that the ultimate purpose of the proceedings — to secure the welfare of the child — is not obscured or diluted.

Independent Representation for Children:
The Guardian *Ad Litem*

Traditionally, common lawyers have been wary of innovations such as the guardian *ad litem*. The common law system of adjudication is typified by an adversarial approach to judicial proceedings. The net effect of this perspective is that the parties are viewed as competing against each other for the court's favour. The judge, furthermore, is limited in the inquiries they may initiate. In the classical adversarial model, it is the legal representatives of the parties rather than the court that dictates the direction and tenor of the proceedings. This is in sharp contrast to the more inquisitorial system operated in the civil law jurisdictions of continental Europe, a system that, with respect, lends itself much more readily to the type of proceedings being discussed here.

Of particular concern at this juncture is the fate of the child in the adversarial model of proceedings. The latter perspective tends to view a custody application, for instance, as a struggle between competing parents with the child being the sought-after "prize". This jars with what is, after all, the overriding concern of the court in such cases — the requirement that the welfare of the child is paramount, taking precedence over all other considerations and interests.[44] It seems strange then that at least until recently very little consideration was given to the proposition that the child him or herself should be represented in court.

Recent innovations have, however, tended to exhibit a will for reform in this regard. One such innovation was the introduction on a statutory basis of the guardian *ad litem* in public law cases. The guardian *ad litem* is effectively an independent representative appointed by the court to represent the child's personal and legal interests in proceedings. Such a representative is particularly important for the child sexual abuse victim.

The concept of a *guardian ad litem* and independent representation for children is an entirely new development in Ireland. It was first given legislative effect in public law cases under the Child Care Act 1991, Sections 25 and 26 thereof. Sections 25 and 26 of the Child Care Act 1991 were implemented in Ireland in October 1995. Section 26 of the Child Care Act 1991 deals with the appointment of a *guardian ad litem* and it simply states as follows:

> If in any proceedings under Part IV or Part VI the child to whom the proceedings relate is not a party, the court, if it is satisfied that it is necessary in the interests of the child and in the interests of justice to do so, can appoint a *guardian ad litem* for the child.

That is the extent of the guidelines provided. The section is deficient in terms of assisting practitioners and judges alike in

---

[44] See section 3 of the Guardianship of Infants Act, 1964.

determining who should be appointed a guardian or what qualifications, if any, that person should have. The dearth of detail in relation to the *guardian ad litem* continues when considering the role of the *guardian ad litem*, the duties of the guardian and the powers, if any, of the guardian. There is clearly an urgent need for guidance or specification relating to the role or function of the *guardian ad litem* in public law proceedings in Ireland.

The law as it stands is nothing more than chaotic. It falls well short of what is required and what the State have agreed to sign up for, having ratified the 1989 UN Convention on the Rights of the Child and having signed the 1995 European Convention on the Exercise of Children's Rights.

It cannot be asserted by the State that sections 25 and 26 of the Child Care Act, 1991 discharge our obligations under the UN Convention on the Rights of the Child or the European Convention on the Exercise of Children's Rights. The duty of the author of the report pursuant to these sections is to report to the court, but there is no duty to give a voice to the child's wishes. The author is in the role of an expert witness to assist the court.

There is a critical difference between the role of an expert witness and the role of the *guardian ad litem*. The duty of an expert witness is to report to the court on a set of facts which have presented themselves to that court, to gather information and to make recommendations in relation to proceedings before the court. While the expert witness may interview the child/children who are caught up in a custody or access dispute, it is not their role to explore their wishes, to present them to the court or to ensure that those wishes are the courts' primary concern, nor has the expert witness any control over the proceedings. They are simply asked to submit the report. Often times the report prepared is never seen by the judge as the proceedings may settle before the matter comes on for hearing. These provisions go someway towards improving the management of family law disputes. However, they are significantly short of what is necessary.

INTERNATIONAL LAW: STATE INTERVENTION AND SEPARATE REPRESENTATION OF THE CHILD AT RISK

UN Convention on the Rights of the Child 1989

The UN Convention on the Rights of the Child, adopted by the UN General assembly in November 1989, details an extensive list of rights to which all children are entitled. Article 19(1) of the Convention mandates Member States to protect the child from:

> all forms of physical and mental violence, injury or abuse, neglect or negligent treatment, maltreatment or exploitation, including sexual abuse, while in the care of parent(s), legal guardian(s) or other person who has care of the child.

The primary foothold for separate representation of children in child sexual abuse cases in international child law can be found in the United Nations Convention on the Rights of the Child 1989, Article 12 of which provides that:

> 1. State parties shall assure to the child who is capable of forming his or her own views the right to express those views freely in all matters affecting the child, the views of the child being given due weight in accordance with the age and maturity of the child.
>
> 2. For this purpose, the child shall in particular be provided the opportunity to be heard in any judicial and administrative proceedings affecting the child, either directly, or through a representative or an appropriate body, in a manner consistent with the procedural rules of national law.

In line with the overriding principles of Irish child law, the welfare of the child is deemed to be of crucial importance. Article 3 of the Convention underlines this preference, noting that:

> 1. In all actions concerning children, whether undertaken by public or private social welfare institutions, courts of law, administrative authorities or legislative bodies, the best interests of the child shall be a primary consideration.

While this article demands only that the children's interests be "a" primary consideration, not "the" primary consideration, it must also be read alongside the series of explicit rights which the Convention protects. The 1989 UN Convention on the Rights of the Child gives recognition to children's rights in its widest sense and is soundly based on a defensible concept of children's rights. The law in Ireland, however, falls short of such a concept.

European Convention on the Exercise of Children's Rights 1996

Ireland has signed the European Convention on the Exercise of Children's Rights 1996. In some respects, it is of more limited application than its 1989 counterpart. It focuses predominantly on procedural rather than substantive rights, the emphasis being on such matters as the right of children to participation in, and information about cases that concern their welfare. For example, Article 5 of the 1996 Convention provides:

> Parties shall consider granting children additional procedural rights in relation to proceedings before a judicial authority offering them, in particular:
>
> a. the right to apply to be assisted by an appropriate person of their choice in order to help them express their views;
>
> b. the right to apply themselves, or through other persons or bodies, for the appointment of a separate representative, in appropriate cases a lawyer;
>
> c. the right to appoint their own representative;
>
> d. the right to exercise some or all of the rights of parties to such proceedings.

Clearly, the foregoing provisions are aimed primarily at children of sufficient age and maturity to understand the matters under scrutiny. That said, in appropriate cases, a child should have a person to help the expression of his or her views. The absence of a facility for children in this jurisdiction to articulate their views,, where a case is settled in advance of the hearing, needs to be addressed. It is a serious problem, particularly where the legal representative believes that the child is at risk.

The European Convention on Human Rights

Of special significance in discussing our international obligations are the relevant provisions of the European Convention on Human Rights and Fundamental Freedoms, the incorporation of which into Irish law is to be by way of statute. It will then be possible to take proceedings in the Irish courts alleging a breach of the Convention. There is little doubt that inconsistencies will arise between, on the one hand, Irish child law and practice and, on the other, the standards required by the Convention. That said, the significance of this development has been overstated in the arena of Irish child law. The indirect or interpretative mode of incorporation preserves the domestic primacy of the Constitution. Consequently, Article 41 of the Constitution will continue to act as an impediment to the effective implementation of children's legal entitlements under the Convention. In summary, incorporation of the Convention at sub-constitutional level will ensure that child rights remain subordinate to parental rights.[45]

One cannot avoid noting the enormous potential of the Convention to protect and promote rights for the individual members of the family. Article 8 of the European Convention on Human Rights, for example, guarantees as a basic right to every individual the right to respect for private and family life, home and correspondence. Paragraph 2 of the provision states that there shall be no interference with that right unless it is shown to be in accordance with law, has an aim or aims that is or are legitimate and is "necessary in a democratic society". Accordingly, the European Convention on Human Rights has as a core principle the protection of individual rights from arbitrary interference by the State. As a result, where the state intervenes, such as where a child is taken into care because of child sexual abuse allegations, family members are entitled to challenge that order under Article 8 of the Convention. Consideration will then be given as to whether the order is in accordance with law, has an aim or aims that is or are legitimate and is "necessary in

---

[45] If there is a conflict between a provision of the Constitution and of the Convention, the Constitution will prevail.

a democratic society". It is clear from the ruling in *Marckx v. Belgium* that the Convention draws no distinction between the marital and non-martial family when interpreting "respect . . . for family life", as enshrined in Article 8 of the Convention.[46]

The Convention also has certain ramifications for the question of separate representation of children in Court proceedings. A State's positive obligation under Article 8 includes guaranteeing the procedural safeguards. These include the right to a fair trial.[47] While this obligation mirrors a State's explicit duties under Article 6, it is also part of the procedural safeguards inherent in Article 8.

There is clearly an inextricable relationship between the rights expressly guaranteed under Article 6 and the inherent safeguards of Article 8. This relationship can be seen in the child's right to participate in legal proceedings. Indeed, the provision of separate and impartial representation to children is essential in public law proceedings given the potential far-reaching consequences that follow from the granting of orders in this area. This approach was adopted by the European Court in criminal proceedings in its recent *T* and *V* judgments[48] and is likely to be the approach of the Court in civil proceedings involving children. The provision for the separate representation of children in Ireland is chaotic. The guardian *ad litem* provision, as previously stated, was introduced in public law cases in section 26 of the Child Care Act, 1991. However, the infrastructure to give effect to this provision has yet to be put in place. Accordingly, there are significant variations as to the operation of this provision throughout the country. It is only a matter of time before the State will face a challenge in the European Court of Human Rights on this issue for failing to offer adequate protection of children's rights.

The European Convention on Human Rights Bill, 2001, issued on 12 April 2001, will give effect at sub-constitutional level to the European Convention on Human Rights and Fundamental

---

[46] Series A No. 31, para. 31.

[47] *V. v. U.K.*, European Court of Human Rights, December 16, 1999 (Appl. No. 24888/94).

[48] *T. v. U.K., V. v. U.K.*, December 16, 1999 (Appl No. 24888/94).

Freedoms.[49] It is likely to come into force at the end of 2001 or early in the new year.

RECENT DEVELOPMENTS

Protections for Persons Reporting Child Abuse Act, 1998

Allegations of child sexual abuse take a considerable length of time to complete and the procedures set out in *Guidelines on Procedures for the Identification, Investigation and Management of Child Abuse* all take time.[50] In addition, once the allegation has been made the gardai are notified in accordance with the *Guidelines on the Notification of Suspected Cases of Child Abuse between Health Boards and Gardai*.[51] Ultimately, if the allegations transpire to be "unfounded" or not established there is very little which the "wronged party" can do from a practical point of view. It should be noted that the effects of an unfounded or malicious complaint may prove irreversible. Indeed, the feeling of stigmatisation and paranoia may never leave a family. Barr J. in *M.Q. v. Gleeson* identified the consequences of unfounded complaints in the following terms:

> A health board ought always to remember that such complaints, if unfounded, have of their nature a potential for great injustice and harm, not only to the person complained of but also to the particular child or children sought to be protected and others in the family in question. A false complaint of child abuse, if incorrectly interpreted by a health board could involve the destruction of a family unit by wrongfully having the children it comprises taken into care. It may also destroy or seriously damage a good relationship between husband and wife or long-standing partners.[52]

---

[49] No. 26 of 2001.

[50] See Department of Health Guidelines Revised, 1997.

[51] Department of Health, 1995. See criticisms of the application of the 1995 guidelines in a study commissioned by the Mid-Western Health Board, entitled "Keeping Children Safe – Child Abuse, Child Protection and the Promotion of Welfare" (Mid-Western Health Board, 2001).

[52] Unreported, High Court, February 13, 1997 at p.21.

The Protections for Persons Reporting Child Abuse Act, 1998 protects those who report their opinion that a child has been abused, once the report is made to "an appropriate person".[53] The Act defines these as members of the Garda Siochana or designated officers of a health board.

The operative section is section 3(1) which provides that a reporter "shall not be liable in damages in respect of the communication" of their opinion that a child is or has been abused. The immunity is contingent upon the person acting reasonably and in good faith in forming the opinion and in communicating it. This is a test which the courts have long been familiar with. Such a test, however, runs the risk of giving "a licence to prurient members of the general public to cast stones at their neighbours with impunity".[54]

Parents who make false allegations can, however, expect serious censure. In the case of *S v. S* the Supreme Court upheld the award of custody of three children to the husband in a case where the High Court Judge had considered that the wife had attempted to make false and bogus allegations against the husband of improper sexual behaviour.[55] That said, the higher standard prescribed by the Law Reform Commission in its Report on Child Sexual Abuse would perhaps have been preferable:

> We recommend that express statutory immunity from legal
> proceedings should be given to any person who *bona fide*
> and with due care reports a suspicion of child sexual abuse
> to the appropriate authority.[56]

Given the seriousness of any allegations involved it may be that this higher standard is necessary. Despite creating the offence of false reporting in section 5, which is committed where a person makes a statement knowing it to be false, the law must protect against the "busybody" as much as a malicious reporter.

---

[53] No. 49 of 1998.

[54] LRC 32 — 1990, p. 6.

[55] [1992] ILRM 733.

[56] LRC 1990, p. 11.

In this regard a constitutional balance between the rights to a good name and fair procedures on the one hand and those relating to the protection of children on the other must be maintained. One may want to err on the child's side but to overweigh the balance is a mistake. Also, over-reporting does not assist the health boards. Resources are limited enough without being diverted to investigate spurious claims. On the whole, however, this Act is a necessary complement to existing child care provisions. It remains to be seen how it will interact with any mandatory reporting regime that may be introduced.

Child Sexual Abuse Guidelines

Increasing concern about child sexual abuse led to the issue by the Minister for Health in 1978 of the first guidelines to help professionals isolate, identify, investigate and treat child abuse. Revised guidelines have been issued intermittently in the intervening period, the most recent in September of 1999. These guidelines, under the name of "Children First: National Guidelines for the Protection and Welfare of Children", were drawn up by a Working Group established in February 1998.

While the guidelines are designed to be applicable to everybody, they are especially directed at practitioners in child protection and welfare and members of An Garda Síochana. The aim is to assist people in identifying and reporting child abuse, primarily to a health board. The guidelines profess to be informed by the principles underlying the Child Care Act, 1991 and the 1989 UN Convention on the Rights of the Child, specifically that the child's welfare is paramount, but also to have regard to the needs of families and to the child's wishes. In some ways the guidelines could be seen as an enactment of article 19 of the Convention, whereby parties are to take appropriate measures to protect children. At the time the guidelines were launched, it was planned to put them on a statutory basis, something that may well amount to mandatory reporting by the backdoor.

The guidelines cover child abuse, which has been given a wide meaning. There are four kinds specified in the report: neglect, emotional abuse, physical abuse and sexual abuse. The indicators and symptoms of each are well described in plain language. A three-stage guide for the recognition of abuse is set out. Firstly, to consider the possibility of abuse, including looking for signs of distress and behavioural problems. The second stage is looking for signs of abuse. It is explained that these can be physical, behavioural or developmental, and some indicators are listed. Finally, there is the recording of information. It is stressed that as much detail as possible should be recorded of the abuse.

The grounding principle in reporting suspected abuse is the well-being of the child. It is stressed that the report should be made without delay to the health board. The health board must treat all reports seriously and evaluate the complaint. The decision taken must strike a balance between protecting the child and avoiding unnecessary intervention. It is specified that anonymous reports can be investigated, depending on the content and circumstances. The procedures to be followed by the health board thereafter are also set out, as are procedures for co-operation with the Gardai.

In summary, the guidelines are child-centred and have attempted to deal as comprehensively as possible with the most important elements of child protection work. That said, they are not legally binding and are therefore of limited legal value in that professionals dealing with children are not obliged to enforce them.

Mandatory Reporting

The Law Reform Commission[57] and Kilkenny Incest Report[58] recommended the introduction of mandatory reporting for certain persons, such as psychologists, doctors, psychiatrists, social workers, health board workers, teachers and probation officers. The Government has not yet introduced legislation to implement this recommendation. Proposals on the mandatory reporting of instances of the sexual abuse of children are, however, soon to be published in a white paper.

---

[57] LRC 32 — 1990, Chap. 1.

[58] *Kilkenny Incest Investigation; Report presented to Minister for Health by South Eastern Health Board* Pl. 9812 (Dublin, 1993).

Mandatory reporting laws will not solve the problem of under-reporting child sexual abuse and should not be seen as a panacea. There are arguments in favour and against mandatory reporting laws. For example, it is difficult for professionals to build and foster a confidential relationship with their patients/clients when it is known to all parties that the professional will be required under law to report suspected abuse to the relevant authorities.

Commission to Inquire into Child Abuse Act, 2000

The Commission to Inquire into Child Abuse Act, 2000 has four main functions: to afford an opportunity to persons who have suffered abuse in childhood institutions during the relevant period to tell their stories to a committee; to investigate the abuse of children in childhood institutions in order to determine the causes, nature, circumstances and extent of such abuse; to determine the extent to which childhood institutions, management and regulatory authorities had responsibility for the abuse; and to produce and publish a report. The "relevant period" is determined as being from and including 1940 (or such earlier year as the commission may determine) up to and including the year 1999 and such later year (if any) as the commission may determine.

The institutions referred to include industrial schools, orphanages, reformatories, children's homes, hospitals and any other places where children are cared for other than as members of their families. The Commission to Inquire into Child Abuse had its first public sitting on 29 June 2000. Its chairwoman is Mrs. Justice Mary Laffoy.

Statute of Limitations (Amendment) Act, 2000

The Statute of Limitations (Amendment) Act, 2000 became law on 21 June 2000. Its central provision is section 2, which extends the concept of disability contained in the Statute of Limitations, 1957 to accommodate circumstances of childhood sexual abuse. The extension of disability to include victims of childhood sexual abuse clearly excludes all of those victims who were physically or mentally abused while in care. It is probable that the vast majority of victims will not benefit from this statute as the matter of physical and mental abuse has not been addressed. An action under Section 2 of the Statute of Limitations Act, 2000 must be brought not later that 21 June 2001. Any such action is subject to the conditions detailed in subsection (3) of that section. Section 3 of the Act addresses the issue of delay and retains the power of a court "to dismiss an action on the ground of there being such delay between the accrual of the cause of action and the bringing of the action as, in the interests of justice, would warrant its dismissal".

Delay

Delay between the alleged incident(s) of abuse and the making of a complaint by the victim of that abuse can create serious difficulties for both the person seeking redress and the person seeking to defend themselves from such allegations. However, delay is frequently explained either by the exercise of dominion by the alleged perpetrator over the complainant, or the repression or suppression of the alleged abuse as a consequence of dominance and the abuse itself. In particular, where power imbalance is found to characterise the relationship between the alleged perpetrator and the victim the courts have been unwilling to hold that such delay of itself and without more can justify prohibiting a trial.[59] A relevant and instructive case is *Stephen Mitchell v. D.P.P.* wherein McGuinness J. emphasised the importance of the concept of dominion in permitting prosecutions to proceed after lapses of time.[60]

Recently, the Supreme Court has consistently stated that the right of the alleged wrongdoer to fair procedures is superior to the community's right to prosecute.[61] In fact, the Supreme Court

---

[59] See *D. v. D.P.P.* [1994] 2 IR 465, *Z. v. D.P.P.* [1994] 2 IR 496, *Hogan v. President of the Circuit Court* [1994] 2 IR 513, *G. v. D.P.P.* [1994] 1 IR 374, *B. v. D.P.P.* [1997] 2 ILRM 118 and *M. M. O'H v. D.P.P.* Unreported, High Court, 25 March 1999 (O'Sullivan J).

[60] Unreported, High Court, 20 December 2000. See also *B. v. D.P.P.* [1997]1 IR 140.

[61] Per Denham J. in *D. v. DPP* [1994] 2 IR 474. See also *P.C. v. D.P.P.* [1999] 2 IR 25.

has granted orders preventing the further prosecution of a number of cases alleging child sexual abuse on the grounds of delay.[62] Two of the cases concerned a teacher facing five charges of indecent assault against a former boy pupil between 1982 and 1983, and a man facing charges of rape, indecent assault and buggery of a girl aged between seven and nine between 1979 and 1980.

The first case concerned a teacher facing five charges of indecent assault against a former pupil, alleged to have taken place between 1 January 1982 and 31 December 1983, when the pupil was aged 11 and 12. The accused teacher held that his right to a fair trial was prejudiced due to excessive delay and submitted that he was specifically prejudiced because he could not prove definitively, due to the passage of time, his recollection that the room where the alleged abuse took place could not have been locked at the time.

The High Court held that there was evidence of specific prejudice due to delay and that the accused had established, as a matter of probability, that there was a real and serious risk of an unfair trial. A five judge Supreme Court unanimously upheld the High Court decision. Keane C. J. stated that where a conflict arose, the public interest in ensuring that anyone charged with a criminal offence received a fair trail must take precedence over the community's right to prosecute. Denham J. cautioned, however, that a prohibition would occur only where there was a real and serious risk of an unfair trial and would be an exception, not the rule.

In the second case, the Supreme Court again granted an order restraining the further prosecution of a man for rape, indecent assault and buggery of a girl arising from an incident between 1 June 1979 and 30 September 1980. The Court found that there was evidence of specific prejudice and that the applicant had established, as a matter of probability, that there was a serious risk of an unfair trial. In particular, the accused claimed that three months before the offence was alleged to have oc-

---

[62] See *J.L. v. D.P.P.* unreported, Supreme Court, July 6, 2000 and *O'Connor v. D.P.P.* unreported, Supreme Court, July 6, 2000. See also *O'C. v. D.P.P.* unreported, Supreme Court, July 6, 2000.

curred, he had moved out of the caravan where it was said to have happened. However, due to the lapse of time, he could not locate the person to whom he had sold the caravan or people who could confirm that he was living at another location at the time of the alleged offence. McGuinness J, summarised the position in the following manner:

> [R]elying in particular on the matter of the whereabouts of the caravan, it seems to me that the applicant has established on the balance of probabilities that his defence in any trial held after so long a lapse of time would be seriously prejudiced and that there is a real and serious risk that his trial would be unfair.[63]

Particular attention should be drawn to the judgments of Hardiman J. He stated that the courts had allowed prosecutions of child sexual abuse cases to proceed after significant lapses of time because the courts recognised such cases were in a special category and that children need to be protected against sexual abuse.[64] Significantly, Hardiman J. noted that the courts had operated on the assumption that complaints of abuse were true. He expressed grave reservations in relation to that assumption but deferred discussion of it until it was raised in an appropriate case:

> I have outlined my grave reservations in relation to the assumption of the truth of the complaint. I leave to one side, unless and until these matters are raised in an appropriate case, all question of the propriety of that assumption and of the necessity to make it.[65]

Hardiman J. also stressed the need for caution by the courts when it came to assessing psychological evidence in sexual abuse cases. He identified the psychological effects which the court would regard as potentially excusing gross delay in

---

[63] *J.L. v. D.P.P.* unreported, Supreme Court, 6 July, 2000 at p. 24.

[64] See *G. v. D.P.P.* [1994] 1 IR 347, *B. v. D.P.P.* [1997] 3 IR 140, *P.C. v. D.P.P.* [1999] 2 IR 25 and *D.P.P v. J.O'C.* unreported, Supreme Court, May 19, 2000.

[65] *J.L. v. D.P.P.* unreported, Supreme Court, 6 July, 2000 at p. 3. See also judgment in *D.P.P. v. J.O'C.* unreported, Supreme Court, May 19, 2000.

making a complaint of abuse as (1) dominance, particularly if the accused and complainant were closely related or associated and (2) repression or suppression of the alleged abuse. Hardiman J. also stated that the defendant in a child sexual abuse case was entitled to the benefit of the presumption of innocence. Indeed, Denham J. in *B. v. D.P.P.* cautioned that:

> the fact that the offence was of a sexual nature was not itself a factor which would justify the court in disregarding the delay, however inordinate, and allowing the trial to proceed.[66]

Keane C.J. adopted a similar approach in *J.L. v. D.P.P.* stating as follows:

> Given the presumption of innocence to which, at this stage of the enquiry, the applicant is entitled, I am satisfied that he has discharged the onus which rested on him of establishing as a matter of probability that there is a real and serious risk of an unfair trial which cannot be avoided by the giving of directions or rulings by the trial judge.[67]

The Sexual Offenders Act, 2001

Legislation to control sex offenders after the expiration of their punishment was signed into law on June 30, 2001 in the form of the Sexual Offenders Act, 2001. The approach adopted is similar to that in place in the United Kingdom for a number of years. This Act, drafted in January of 2000, provides for the post-release monitoring of convicted sex offenders; post-related supervision of sex offenders; and Garda powers to preclude sex offenders from doing anything the court considers necessary for the purpose of protecting the public from serious harm. The Act also makes it an offence for a convicted sex offender to apply for or assume a job with children and provides legal representation for victims of rape where the defence seeks to adduce

---

[66] [1997] 3 IR 140.

[67] Unreported, Supreme Court, July 6, 2000 at p.5. See also *P.C. v. D.P.P.* [1999] 2 IR 25.

evidence of their prior sexual history. "Sex offenders" are defined in part 5 of the Act as persons convicted after the commencement of the Act, of an offence for which the court deems the appropriate punishment to be imprisonment.

Part 2 of the Sexual Offenders Act provides for certain notification requirements that must be complied with by persons convicted of a sexual offence to facilitate the compilation of a register of sex offenders. The requirement only applies to those convicted after the coming into force of the Act and those previously convicted but still awaiting or serving a sentence for such an offence. Consequently, the immediate value of the register may not become apparent for a number of years. Part 2 provides that a convicted sex offender will have 10 days to notify the Gardaí of his address when he leaves prison. In particular, under section 9 of the Act a convicted sex offender must notify the Gardaí of his name and home address, any other address within the State at which he resides for a period of 10 days in any 12 months, and any change of name or address, within 10 days of such change. Offenders are also required to notify the Gardaí if they leave the state for a continuous period of 10 days or more at a time.

Under section 15, a new civil order, a "sex offender order" may be sought from the court *ex parte* by a Garda not below the rank of Chief Superintendent, where a person has been convicted at home or abroad of a sexual offence. The threshold for the granting of such an order is that the court is satisfied, on the balance of probabilities, that the person has acted on one or more occasions as to give reasonable grounds for believing that an order is necessary to protect the public from serious harm. The order prohibits the sex offender from doing any thing the court considers necessary for the protection of the public from serious harm. A sex offender order may remain in force for 5 years, or longer if the court directs, and breach of the order attracts a maximum penalty of five years imprisonment.

Section 25 of the Act provides that sex offenders must notify any prospective employer of their conviction, if applying for any position, whether paid or unpaid, that would require unsupervised access to children as a necessary and regular feature.

In the neighbouring jurisdiction, an offence of applying for work with children has been enacted in the Criminal Justice and Court Services Act, 2000. It is more elaborate and comprehensive than the Irish equivalent provision. The 2001 Act also applies to persons convicted of sex offences outside the state whether the offender was resident in the state at the time or not.

The provisions of the Sexual Offenders Act, 2001 are in line with the Sex Offenders Act, 1997 in the neighbouring jurisdiction, where sex offenders are required to give their address to the police within 14 days of being freed from prison. The penalty for a breach of the domestic provision is a fine of up to £1,500, a jail sentence of 12 months or both.

The Act is silent as to the use to be made of the register and, in particular, to whom information gathered by gardai as part of the registration process will be released. The Minister for Justice, Equality and Law Reform, John O'Donoghue, stated that:

> ... information will only be disclosed to other persons in the most exceptional circumstances in order to prevent an immediate risk of crime or to alert members of the public to an apprehended danger and then only on a strict need to know basis.[68]

A significant shortcoming in the Act is a lack of emphasis on medical help and re-integration of offenders into the community. At present, the rehabilitation of sex offenders while in custody is hopelessly inadequate. In fact, of the 103 sex offenders released in 1999, a mere eleven received sex therapy treatment.[69] The Act does little to improve the situation and must be criticised for its failure to make provision for increased treatment places for sex offenders.

The Child Trafficking and Pornography Act, 1998

Recent years have seen a significant increase in the trafficking of children and child pornography. The Child Trafficking and Pornography Act, 1998, which became law on 29 June 1998, is

---

[68] Dáil Debates, 6 April, 2000.

[69] See *Irish Times*, 13 April 2000.

therefore a timely piece of legislation. By criminalising the pro-
duction, distribution and possession of child pornography, this
Act provides a valuable protection against the pernicious activities of paedophiles. Of particular importance is the interpretation
section of the Act which specifically includes the following:

> (a) any visual representation —

>> (i) that shows or, in the case of a document, relates to a
>> person who is or is depicted as being a child and who is
>> engaged in or is depicted as being engaged in explicit
>> sexual activity,

>> (ii) that shows or, in the case of a document, relates to a
>> person who is or is depicted as being a child and who is
>> engaged in or is depicted as witnessing any such activ-
>> ity by any person or persons, or

>> (iii) whose dominant characteristics is the depiction for a
>> sexual purpose, of the genital or anal region of a child,

> (b) any visual or audio representation that advocates, en-
> courages or counsels any sexual activity with children which
> is an offence under any enactment, or

> (c) any visual representation or description or information
> relating to, a child that indicates or implies that the child is
> available to be used for the purpose of sexual exploitation
> within the meaning of section 3,

> irrespective of how or through what medium the represen-
> tation, description or information has been produced,
> transmitted or conveyed and, without prejudice to the gen-
> erality of the foregoing, includes any representation, de-
> scription or other electronic or mechanical means . . .

In summary, the Act protects children in three ways. First, it
protects against the trafficking of children for the purpose of
their sexual exploitation. Secondly, it protects children from
being used and thereby sexualised and abused in the making
of child pornography. Finally, it criminalises the possession of
child pornography.

New offences introduced by the Act include child trafficking and taking a child for sexual exploitation,[70] permitting a child to be used for pornography,[71] producing and distributing child pornography,[72] and the possession of child pornography.[73] A formidable obstacle in prosecuting child pornographers is the means by which the age of the victim (defined as a person under 17 years of age) can be proved for the purposes of the Act. This problem is circumvented by section 2(3) of the Child Trafficking and Pornography Act, 1998 which provides that:

> In any proceedings for an offence under section 3, 4, 5 or 6 a person shall be deemed, unless the contrary is proved, to be or have been a child or to be or have been depicted or represented as a child, at any time if the person appears to the court to be or have been a child, or to be or have been so depicted or represented at the time.

In essence, the Child Trafficking and Pornography Act, 1998 is part of a series of legislative initiatives designed to protect children against sexual abuse and exploitation.

THE CONSTITUTION

Section 3 of the Guardianship of Infants Act, 1964 makes it abundantly clear that in considering an application relating to the guardianship, custody or upbringing of a child, the court must have regard for the welfare of the child. This, the section states, is the "the first and paramount consideration". The Supreme Court, however, have determined that the welfare of the child must, unless there are exceptional circumstances or other overriding factors, be considered to be best served by its remaining as part of the marital family. This was dictated, the court considered in a number of cases, by the constitutional preference for the marital family exhibited in Article 41 of the Constitution and the requirement therein that it be protected

---

[70] Section 3.

[71] Section 4.

[72] Section 5.

[73] Section 6.

from attack.[74] Article 41 of the Constitution protects the family based on marriage only. The rights guaranteed by this Article do not belong to individual members of the family but rather to the family unit as a whole. Its lacks a child focus and fails to recognise the child as a juristic person with individual rights to which separate representation must be given. This is largely due to the principle of parental autonomy created by that Article. Consequently, Article 41 establishes a private realm of family life which the State can enter only in the exceptional circumstances mentioned in Articles 42.5 of the Constitution. Article 42 provides as follows:

> 1. The State acknowledges that the primary and natural educator of the child is the Family and guarantees to respect the inalienable right and duty of parents to provide, according to their means, for the religious and moral, intellectual, physical and social education of their children. . . .

> 5. In exceptional cases, where the parents for physical or moral reasons fail in their duty towards their children, the State as guardian of the common good, by appropriate means shall endeavour to supply the place of the parents, but always with due regard for the natural and imprescriptible rights of the child.

Clearly, this Article provides that only in *exceptional cases*, where parents, for *physical* or *moral* reasons, fail in their duty towards their children, can the State as guardian of the common good endeavour to supply the place of the parents. We see therefore an uneasy compromise between, on the one hand, the provisions of Articles 41 and 42 of the Constitution and, on the other, the welfare principle outlined in section 3 of the Guardian of Infants Act 1964. In recent years, the Supreme Court has reiterated the primacy test by emphasising the welfare of the child, rather than the interests of its parents. In *Southern Health Board v. C.H.*[75] O'Flaherty J. observed, in a case concerning the

---

[74] See, for example, *Re J.H. (An Infant)* [1985] IR 375.

[75] [1996] 1 IR 219

admissibility of a video-taped interview containing allegations of paternal abuse, that:

> . . . it is easy to comprehend that the child's welfare must always be of far graver concern to the court. We must, as judges, always harken to the constitutional command which mandates, as prime consideration, the interests of the child in any legal proceedings.[76]

While the ethos of the more recent case law is decidedly child-centred, the constitutional fiction that a child is always best served by a ruling that promotes the interests of its married parents must be removed in favour of a perspective that looks solely to the child's own best interests. If this more child-centred tendency is followed, it will displace one of the enduring ironies of the earlier Supreme Court case of *K.C. and A.C. v An Bord Úchtála*[77], that is that, under it, the welfare of the non-marital child was arguably accorded more respect than that of the marital child. It is therefore recommended that Article 41 of the Constitution be amended to contain a provision respecting the precedence of the 'best interests test'.

One of the significant conclusions of the Constitution Review Group was that Article 41 of the Constitution be amended by the insertion of express children's rights. In particular, it recommended the inclusion of the:

> judicially construed unenumerated rights of children in a coherent manner, particularly those rights which are not guaranteed elsewhere and are particular to children.[78]

In the earlier Kilkenny Incest Investigation report the investigations team, chaired by Mrs Catherine McGuinness SC (now Mrs Justice Catherine McGuinness of the Supreme Court), also proposed that Article 41 of the Constitution be amended to include a charter of children's rights. It stated that:

---

[76] *ibid* at 238.

[77] [1985] ILRM 302.

[78] *Report of the Constitution Review Group,* Dublin: Government Publications, 1996, p. 319.

While we accept that the courts have on many occasions stressed that children are possessed of constitutional rights we are some what concerned that the 'natural and imprescriptible rights of the child' are specifically referred to in only one subarticle (Article 42.5) and then only in the context of the State supplying the place of parents who have failed in their duty. We feel that the very high emphasis on the rights of the family in the Constitution may consciously or unconsciously be interpreted as giving a higher value to the rights of the parents than to the rights of the children. We believe that the Constitution should contain a specific and overt declaration of the rights of born children. We therefore recommend that consideration be given by the Government to the amendment of Articles 41 and 42 of the Constitution so as to include a statement of the constitutional rights of children. We do not ourselves feel confident to put forward a particular wording and we suggest that study might be made of international documents such as the United Nations Convention on the Rights of the Child.[79]

The Constitution should be amended to ensure that the right of children to have their welfare protected is given the paramountcy it deserves. Such a reform would bring much needed clarity to the present situation regarding the principle and place of the child at the centre of Irish child law proceedings.

LEGAL REFORM

It is regrettable in view of the large number of cases concerning claims of child sexual abuse recently before the courts that there has been no move to introduce a general offence of child sexual abuse. Indeed, in order to comply fully with the terms of article 19(1) of the 1989 United Nations Convention on the Rights of the Child, Ireland should introduce such an offence. The Law Reform Commission in its *Report on Child Sexual Abuse* recommended that an offence of "child sexual abuse" be introduced.[80] It recommended the definition of child sexual abuse

---

[79] *Kilkenny Incest Investigation Report*, Dublin: Government Publications, 1993, p. 96.

[80] LRC 32 — 1990.

propounded by the Western Australia Task Force in its 1987 Report for that purpose:

> (i) intentional touching of the body of a child for the purpose of the sexual gratification of the child or the person;
>
> (ii) intentional masturbation in the presence of the child;
>
> (iii) intentional exposure of the sexual organs of a person or any other sexual act intentionally performed in the presence of the child for the purpose of sexual arousal or gratification of the older person or as an expression of aggression, threat or intimidation towards the child; and
>
> (iv) sexual exploitation, which includes permitting, encouraging or requiring a child to solicit for or to engage in prostitution or other sexual act as referred to above with the accused or any other person, persons, animal or thing or engaging in the recording (on video-tape, film, audio tape, or other temporary or permanent material), posing, modelling or performing of any act involving the exhibition of a child's body for the purpose of sexual gratification of an audience or for the purpose of any other sexual act . . .[81]

Such a change is timely, since prosecutors currently must rely on offences such as incest, unlawful carnal knowledge and sexual assault, which lack the flexibility necessary to cover all forms of sexual abuse to which children are subjected.

One of the greatest shortcomings in modern child care protection legislation has been the requirement that, before a health board can intervene to provide therapeutic or protective services, there must be a finding by the court that the child is in need of protection. Family support therefore ranks as a poor third to child protection and alternative care in the battle for resources. The focus is on supplanting parents rather than supporting the role of parents. This stands in contrast to the situation which exists internationally where the main thrust of child care objectives has been developing preventative services to combat child abuse. In fact, as far back as 1976 in the Canadian

---

[81] *Ibid.*

jurisdiction the preventative approach was outlined and endorsed in the case of *Kingston v. Reeves* in the following terms:

> Perhaps the most important recent development in the
> child-care field has been the growing commitment to pre-
> vention work, to family rehabilitation rather than removal
> from the home. It is recognised that children should be
> permanently removed from the home only when the factors
> which have produced an environment of risk to the physical
> or mental health of the child cannot be ameliorated by help
> given to that child and those who care for him or her.[82]

The traditional grounds of when a child is found to be in need of
protection continue to find favour in Ireland.[83] Little attention is
given to a situation where a child is being emotionally abused
or is alleged to be in a substantial risk situation. One statute that
has taken on board the substantial risk situation and the notion
of emotional abuse is the Alberta Child Welfare Act, 1984. Section 1 stipulates:

> (2) [F]or the purposes of this Act, a child is in need of pro-
> tective services if there are reasonable and probable
> grounds to believe that the survival, security or develop-
> ment of the child is endangered because of any of the fol-
> lowing: . . .
>
>> (f) the child has been *emotionally*[84] injured by the
>> guardian of the child;
>>
>> (g) the guardian of the child is unable or unwilling to
>> protect the child from emotional injury; . . .
>
> (3) for the purposes of this Act,
>
>> (a) a child is *emotionally*[85] injured
>>
>>> (i) if there is substantial and observable impairment of
>>> the child's mental or emotional functioning that is evi-
>>> denced by a mental or behavioural disorder, includ-

---

[82] *Reports of Family Law,* Vol. 23,391(Ont. Prov. Ct), p.393.

[83] I refer here to the tangible physical and sexual abuse grounds.

[84] This is the writer's emphasis.

[85] This is the writer's emphasis.

ing anxiety, depression, withdrawal, aggression or delayed development, and

(ii) there are reasonable and probable grounds to believe that the *emotional*[86] injury is the result of

(A) rejection,

(B) deprivation of affection or cognitive stimulation,

(C) exposure to domestic violence or severe domestic disharmony,

(D) inappropriate criticism, threats, humiliation, accusations or expectations of or towards the child, or

(E) the mental or emotional condition of the guardian of the child or chronic alcohol or drug abuse by anyone living in the same residence as the child.

The Irish legislature should put in place a preventative and protective provision similar to that enacted in Alberta. The aforementioned suggestion can be implemented without removing the child from the home. This can be achieved through supervision, which is an important preventative mechanism and can take a variety of forms: attendance by parents at counselling, treatment for alcoholism, and medical or psychiatric attention, with reports to be made of future assessments planned.

The establishment of Regional Family Courts[87] and judicial training in child law matters are also urgently needed to eliminate judicial inconsistencies in applying child law provisions in public law cases and in dealing with evidential requirements.

CONCLUSION

In conclusion, the legislative provisions for the protection of children are primarily for the children themselves and the entitlement accrues to them as of right, not as some kind of dispensation.

---

[86] This is the writer's emphasis.

[87] This was considered in the Denham report where it was viewed as a long-term solution. The model postulated involves 15 regional centres operating as a division of the Circuit Court.

The last decade has seen a heartening development of interest in the victim of child sexual abuse. Attitudes have become more sensitive to children subjected to such abuse and more conscious of children's disadvantaged position vis-à-vis adults. The 1989 United Nations Convention on the Rights of the Child, ratified by Ireland without reservation on 21 September 1992, gives a firm base for a charter of children's rights. Recent legislative innovations have, in aggregate, resulted in enhanced decision making for children at risk in the Irish courts. They have also managed to further children's rights and have facilitated greater co-operation between lawyers and child care experts.

While the menu of issues and unresolved problems which emerge from an examination of recent legislation introduced in Ireland to protect the victim of child sexual abuse can seem overwhelming, there has been nonetheless a notable movement towards child-centred legislation. The realisation of a vibrant and flourishing child-centred statutory system will necessitate discarding the shackles of the Irish adult-centred past. This can only be achieved by ensuring that children are given the capability of being heard in all judicial and administrative proceedings affecting them, either directly or through a representative, having regard to their age and understanding. Reform is therefore needed, and as Lord Atkin stated:

> When the ghosts of the past stand in the path of justice clanking their mediaeval chains the proper course . . . is to pass through them undeterred.[88]

---

[88] *United Australia Ltd. v. Barclays Bank Ltd.* [1920] AII ER 29.

* The law and practice alluded to in this chapter are stated as at July 2001.

Chapter Eight

From Delusion to Ambition: Creating a New Agenda for Children in Ireland

Owen Keenan

INTRODUCTION

The publication of this book will hopefully represent a significant and influential contribution to policy, provision and practice in relation to child sexual abuse in Ireland. Nevertheless, an effective and sustained response to the horror of sexual abuse must take a broad perspective which considers it in the context of the child and childhood in contemporary Ireland. And, in particular, of how that context is either likely to, or how one might hope it might, change in the future.

Before we can engage with any confidence in predictions for the future, it is necessary to identify performance to date and trends or developments that might influence future direction. This chapter, therefore, will combine a critical review of our past performance with an analysis of our current provision for children in Ireland, suggesting that we have collectively failed children while deluding ourselves that ours was the most wonderful society in which to be a child. The particular failures of our system for protecting our most vulnerable child-citizens will be identified while asserting that these are essentially failures of our society rather than — narrowly — of the child protection system. On the contrary, it will be suggested that this has been bestowed in several respects with tasks, responsibilities and expectations that are both unrealistic and unreasonable and have not been adequately supported or resourced.

Nevertheless we are at a critical point in the development of Ireland's policy response to the needs of children which may prove a watershed. The external pressure to meet our responsibilities under the United Nations Convention on the Rights of the Child, a maturing acceptance of our past inadequacies, the unprecedented availability of resources, and an increasingly strategic and ambitious political agenda have combined to create this opportunity. But it will not be realised without sustained, ambitious and determined action.

DELUSION AND FAILURE

If sexual abuse may be described as the end of innocence for the child, perhaps the past decade might be seen as the end of innocence — or, perhaps more accurately, of delusion — on the part of a society that previously indulged in romanticised notions of happy, safe, innocent and loved children. These have given way, over the past decade, to a realisation that the reality was not so rosy. From the poverty recounted in *Angela's Ashes,* the abuse depicted in *Dear Daughter* and *States of Fear* to revelations about "illegitimate" children being sent for adoption to the United States, we have been confronted not only with the sins of past generations but with the acknowledgement that, even today, we are not doing so well. In a decade that has featured a litany of child abuse scandals — including the Kilkenny Incest Case, "Kelly", the McColgan family, Fr. Brendan Smyth, Donal Dunne, Fr. Sean Fortune, amongst many others — we have also come to realise that Ireland is not, nor has been, a good place in which to be a vulnerable child. Ireland has a crumbling care system which has had to send very troubled and vulnerable young people to facilities abroad for treatment while others have been accommodated in unsuitable facilities on the direction of the High Court as a last resort, a growing youth homeless population, a consistently poor record on child poverty compared with other European Union member states, significant numbers of young people being exploited in prostitution, the worst level of pre-school provision in Europe and only minimal parental leave arrangements. One could go on.

Why should this reality be so divorced from our aspirations and assumptions?

This writer described child care in 1991 as "the most neglected area of public policy since the foundation of the State".[1] That was arguably true then, less so today, but we continue to struggle with the legacy of successive governments' neglect of children over the first seventy years of independence. A considerable deficit to date in our provision for children has been the absence of a vision to underpin and guide our efforts. How should children be provided for in Ireland? What are the particular tasks of our various agencies for children and what are our expectations of them? What is the fit between these responsibilities and expectations and the position of children in our society? What, ultimately, are we trying to achieve and how will we know when it has been achieved? Is there a consensus on this?

In the absence of a vision we appear to have stumbled blindly towards a set of vague objectives that have been neither clearly identified nor agreed. This has led to much of the unevenness of provision and dissatisfaction with outcomes. There have been wide disparities of ambition and expectation, which perhaps reflect differences of values and commitment. This has resulted in some parts of our child care system being satisfied if it is keeping up with demand for service, while others appear to be constantly critical and wedded to an ideal of provision and protection for children which far exceeds the reality on the ground.

These differences relate not only to the parts of the system represented by these views, but suggest a conflict of values. Much of the criticism aimed at the current level of provision in recent years has been based on its shortcomings relative to international standards of what is acceptable, never mind best practice. One can understand and sympathise with the reactions of committed, hardworking and sorely pressed professionals in the statutory services who have a vital role in the sys-

---

[1] Keenan O., *A Window on Irish Children*, Barnardos Annual Conference, October 1991 (unpublished)

tem yet feel under constant attack from children's rights advocates. It is perhaps their misfortune to have to represent and defend actions within a system that has been lacking, not only in
vision, but in a commitment to the rights of children that would
demand and drive the attainment of the highest standards.

In fact much of the inadequacy of our State's intervention on
behalf of children derives from a view of children as vulnerable
objects to be protected, rather than as subjects with rights to be
vindicated; as "adults in waiting" rather than as citizens in their
own right; as not being capable of expressing their needs nor
articulating what is in their best interests. In short, the way we
have responded to children has been both narrow and minimalist. We have many examples of this, not least perhaps the
immense time it took to finally pass and subsequently enact the
Child Care Act, 1991, a piece of legislation which, for all its
positive features, now looks very out of date in several critical
respects — fundamentally, the fact that its remit is confined to
children "who are not receiving adequate care and protection"[2]
rather than all children, the exclusion of any form of regulation
of childminding, and so on. Its important provision for the appointment of guardians *ad litem* (see Chapter 7, this volume) for
children involved in legal proceedings were not in the original
Bill but added by amendment in the Oireachtas. They were effectively disowned by the Department of Health and the health
boards for several years subsequently and, in some cases, to
this day. In many respects it is because of this minimalist approach that the range of support services to children and families experiencing inadequate care and protection was not provided as comprehensively as was required while the provision
of therapeutic interventions has also been seriously deficient. It
should, however, be acknowledged that, in the intervening
years since the 1991 legislation was enacted, significant steps
have been taken to provide a more comprehensive framework
of services to both prevent situations of children requiring care
and protection and a better, if still seriously inadequate, range
of therapeutic services for children and their families.

---

[2] Child Care Act, 1991, Part 11, Section 3.

However, much of this development has been reactive rather than visionary. Much of it indeed has been driven by media interest and exposure of system failure. In 1991 an extra £1 million was provided from the National Lottery to fund the implementation of the new legislation. Neither, in spite of the quarter of a century gestation period of this State's first legislation on the care of vulnerable children,[3] was it going to be implemented with urgency. Rather, it was announced, this was to take seven years. In 1992 a sum of £2 million was provided, again from National Lottery funds. No additional funding was provided in the Government's Budget for 1993. Where were the values, passion and vision to drive progressive developments for children of which Ireland could be proud?

Not for the first time, events took a hand. Media interest in the case that was to become known as the Kilkenny Incest Case led to the establishment of an inquiry[4] and the subsequent provision of an additional £35 million over three years. This represented an increase of mammoth proportions given what had gone before but it was accompanied by neither an assessment of the adequacy of existing provision and analysis of what was needed, nor indeed of its objectives in terms of improved services. In the event it funded a disparate series of service developments, some of which were necessary and strategic, but many of which represented more of the same — that is, services and models that already existed though they had not necessarily been demonstrated to be effective. This reflected a lack of clarity in the identification of ultimate goals and an absence of strategy in making the most effective investment of these significantly increased resources. Furthermore, the increased funding was seen as effectively a once-off, soon to be completed, additional investment rather than marking the beginning of a much needed and overdue resourcing of the child care system. Indeed, by late 1996 senior health board managers were expressing the view that investment in childcare

---

[3] See, for example, Keenan O., "Child Welfare", in Robins, Joseph (ed.) *Reflections on Health — Commemorating Fifty Years of The Department of Health 1947–1997* Department of Health, Dublin, 1997.

[4] McGuinness, C., *Report of the Kilkenny Incest Investigation*, Dublin 1993.

services had now come to an end and it was time to focus on the resourcing of other need groups, for example, of services for the elderly.

Whatever this may suggest about the development of services for our older citizens, it reveals a quite depressing view of the service needs of our youngest and equally vulnerable citizens. It also suggests a view of one service target group having to compete with the equally legitimate needs of another. While realistically this is always the case in terms of allocating resources, it would be reassuring to know that those charged with making these choices have at least a reasonable appreciation of the full extent of the needs of these respective groups relative to current levels of provision and a vision of what might ultimately constitute a reasonably satisfactory level of service. Otherwise, pragmatism monopolises and the most glaring inadequacy can be rationalised.

CHILDREN'S RIGHTS AS A CATALYST FOR CHANGE

Never has this been more evident than in Ireland's report to the United Nations Committee on the Rights of the Child[5] and, in particular, the subsequent appearance before the Committee in Geneva in January 1998. For those few children's rights activists present it was a riveting watershed in the treatment of children's affairs by Irish Governments. For example, the pragmatic proposal to raise the age of criminal responsibility to ten years initially and, subsequently, when resources would allow, to twelve years was rejected by the Committee. The vindication of children's rights could not wait for the Government to allocate the necessary resources, it said. Children's rights are absolute and universal, the Government has ratified the UN Convention on the Rights of the Child, now it must demonstrate its commitment in implementing it. Likewise, the State's development of policy and services on a "case by case" basis was also rejected by the Committee. Children's rights demand that Ireland should have a clear national strategy for children. Chil-

---

[5] Department of Foreign Affairs, United Nations Convention on the Rights of the Child: First National Report of Ireland, Dublin, 1996.

dren must be consulted. So, too, must non-governmental activists for children. And the State must support and enable all children to exercise their rights.

This has very significant implications for Government action affecting children, particularly those who are vulnerable. It is no longer acceptable to withhold support measures to children until they are "in need of care and protection". A rights-based strategy demands a more proactive approach, identifying and addressing the conditions likely to prevent a child achieving his/her full potential. An "acceptable" level of child poverty, for example, cannot coexist with a commitment to children's rights. This is important because too often inadequacies have been accommodated as inevitabilities. Children's rights dictate that determined action be taken, over as long a period as necessary, to eradicate any barrier to their vindication.

There is an important message here too for the range and orientation of services to support children and their families. In the past the rights and responsibilities of families have been celebrated but often with the effect of leaving them to their own devices, without the supports and resources that can enable them to provide positive experiences for their children. A minimalist approach then comes into play when the family situation has broken down or when the family is adjudged to be incapable of providing adequately for its children. A visionary, proactive, rights-based approach on the other hand requires that a comprehensive and flexible range of support services — including, for example, a spectrum from financial and practical supports to intensive therapeutic interventions — is available and accessible to each family. Clearly this will not be sufficient in every instance but it can be expected to minimise the demands for very extreme action by the State to provide protection and care for children at serious risk.

A VALUES BASE FOR PROTECTING CHILDREN, SUPPORTING FAMILIES

A values base for protecting children and supporting families makes sense in terms of a commitment to children's rights but from other perspectives also — including those of equity and economic efficiency. Fundamentally, though, this approach is underpinned by values that recognise and support children's most basic needs, for example, their need for the identity, experiences and supports that come with family life. For some children this experience can be quite chaotic, even dysfunctional, yet it can also have its strengths and rewards. Any child care system must recognise this and provide a very broad range of supports that allow children to remain within families which, though they may not conform to an ideal, nevertheless offer their children a quality of experience that they are unlikely to obtain in alternative care.

This is not to advocate non-intervention in situations where children may be seriously at risk — on the contrary, early assessment of families that are dangerous and removal of their children is critical — but there is a need for a greater degree of tolerance, allied to substantial supports, of family situations that, while they may not be conventional, do provide a level of warmth and support for their members. In this respect, too, there is a need for a more positive approach to families than is often found. One that never writes off families or their individual members, that is based on legitimate hope, that emphasises what they can rather than cannot do, that will work with them to identify some strength — no matter how hidden — that can be harnessed and nurtured and that is prepared to stick consistently with them as they struggle to provide a better and safer future for their children.

Sadly, this is a scenario that is seen in practice too rarely. There is little evidence of tolerance of diversity, little experience of long-term commitment to families to achieve small, though significant change. There is also ample evidence of a system which is defensive and fearful. This must be addressed if there is to be any prospect of a radical reorientation of the State's services for children.

A MANDATE TO ACHIEVE THE IMPOSSIBLE?

The ten regional health boards have statutory responsibility for services for children and families under the 1991 legislation. They are both direct service providers and commissioners of services from other bodies. Their responsibility for children's services originates in the mandate they were given in the Health Act, 1970, which established the health boards, for personal social services. These included community-based services for the elderly, people with disabilities, and children and families. However, needs grew exponentially throughout the 1980s at a time when resources were experiencing cuts in real terms. As a result, health board interventions with children and families were narrowed considerably and the goals of their intervention became inevitably more limited.

This development, however, also coincided with increasing media interest in child care matters generally and in cases of abuse and neglect in particular. When exposed to the cold light of media scrutiny many health board actions have been shown to be indefensible other than in terms of the failure of successive governments to provide them with a realistic level of resources. It also has to be said that health boards have questions to answer about the way limited resources have been allocated within their programmes and the relative weakness of the children's and families' services in competing for resources with medical services throughout the 1980s. In any event, health boards' actions have frequently been open to public scrutiny and criticism in recent years and it is probably accurate to say that they do not generally enjoy a high level of public confidence. While health boards may feel that much of this criticism is unfair, several have also been the authors of their own negative media treatment through very poor handling of media relations and, in particular, a resistance to public accountability.

Health boards have also been criticised for failures of their child protection responsibilities in a number of high profile reports. For example, the Report of the Kilkenny Incest Inquiry concluded that the central core of the victim's problem:

> was never fully known, investigated, understood or resolved. . . . each aspect of the health services dealt with the individual manifestations of Mary's abuse and her various illnesses entirely separately and without interdisciplinary communication and co-operation. . . . the response of the

community care services . . . seems to have been affected
by weaknesses in management.[6]

The report of the inquiry into the death of Kelly, a fifteen-year-old girl who died shortly after arriving in London from her
home in Co. Mayo, found that the:

> intervention of the Western Health Board with Kelly's family,
> in spite of the best efforts of individual staff, was naïve and
> ineffective when pitted against parents who represented a
> significant danger to at least two of their children.[7]

Similarly, another report identified a series of shortcomings in
the management of a further notorious case of child abuse:

> One of the managerial weaknesses in the case lies in the
> failure to convene . . . a case conference, in order to share
> information, assess risk, make decisions and plan a strategy
> for protection. . . . The children did not receive protection.
> They were trapped in a system that was not responsive to
> their needs until fourteen years later when the full extent of
> the abuse they endured was revealed.[8]

This criticism — and how it was managed — has contributed to
a feeling for health board personnel of being under siege. This,
in turn, has reinforced the development of a culture which is
characterised by defensiveness and fear. Defensiveness, in rejecting criticism, rationalising errors, resisting scrutiny and accountability. Fear, in threatening or intimidating their own personnel into compliance and avoiding risk, or in using their
power against advocates who are seen as threats. In this culture, those who publicly challenge the effectiveness of the system may expect to receive implicit or explicit strictures regarding future utterances.

This is a phenomenon that is abusive and dysfunctional in itself, and it indicates a preoccupation with the story rather than
the reality. It suggests that the actual performance of the system

---

[6] McGuinness, op.cit.

[7] Oireachtas Joint Committee on the Family, *Kelly — a Child is Dead,* 1996.

[8] North Western Health Board, *West of Ireland Farmer Case,* 1998.

is less important than how it is perceived to be. It explains much of the system's response to criticism — usually to attack the critic rather than consider the criticism. Indeed, it is arguable also that its consequence is to lead to the health boards being criticised even more harshly: in other words, it is counterproductive.

Nobody would disagree that the health boards have an unenviable task, especially in relation to children's services. The inadequacy of provision is ultimately a political question yet health boards invariably find themselves defending the indefensible. Instead of attempting to stifle scrutiny and debate the health boards would earn much more public sympathy and understanding if they were to demonstrate that their performance was reasonably effective given available resources, and if they showed humility in acknowledging shortcomings where they clearly exist.

An illustration of how failure to do this can become a serious problem is the recent controversy about the care system and the numbers of very troubled young people who have appeared before the High Court. Sadly, there is now a significant number whose needs cannot be adequately met by the health boards within a timeframe that is relevant for them due to a combination of factors including an inadequacy of planning and resources, but also a failure of vision and commitment. The current situation has been evident and unavoidable for many years because of an unwillingness to hear and act on the analysis and criticism of seasoned observers. Now, arguably already too late, the crisis is beyond denial due to the determination of a High Court judge — but it should never have reached this stage. The majority of health board professionals and management is well disposed to the interests of children and young people but too often their siege mentality has deafened them to the calls of those outside that system. A recognition of the contribution of a wider constituency to the best interests of those for whom they have a statutory responsibility, and an acceptance of the necessity of monitoring and accountability, could only be of benefit to them in their onerous responsibility to society.

It is appropriate to consider whether in fact the health boards now have a task in relation to children which is effectively impossible, given their other responsibilities for the health of the community. In other words, it may be a near impossible mandate and a consequent dysfunctional cultural response that is at the root of many of the inadequacies for which they have been criticised. In this scenario it is difficult to see how the situation can be remedied without radical reform.

Regrettably, it may be that there is a need to review the appropriateness of health boards having the statutory responsibility for children. Regrettably because there are good strategic arguments for the current integration of health and social services. And pragmatically it would be preferable if the actual quality of our service responses for children were the focus for attention rather than the structures necessary to deliver them — this could become a distraction from the urgent need to develop a wider range of more effective service interventions on behalf of children.

It must be acknowledged, however, that the current construct has not been working effectively for a considerable time. A forceful case may be made for major reform, establishing a statutory authority with dedicated responsibility for child and family welfare. However, one has to accept that that is not on the agenda at present. Since it is in the nature of such questions that action is only taken after much argument and discussion — the fact that there is currently no such debate suggests that the current arrangements will persist for some time yet. Any review of the structures for the delivery of statutory services for children is likely to occur in the context of a wider-ranging review of structures for health and social services generally. Nevertheless, it is legitimate to argue, especially at a time of considerable development of our child welfare services generally, for an informed debate on the most appropriate structure to support these services into the future. It is a question that undoubtedly will be addressed, if not for some time to come.

Even assuming the continuation for the foreseeable future of the current structure, one would hope to see a radical reappraisal of the model which has essentially underpinned the health boards' child protection response from their earliest days. This can be characterised by increasing numbers of social workers, perhaps located in a central office within a community care area, trying to respond to an even faster growth in the number of child protection referrals to be investigated. With the full spectrum of necessary therapeutic interventions, support services and functions either not existing or certainly not growing at a commensurate rate, the system as it now exists certainly cannot be claimed to be efficient, effective or coping with current demand levels. There is an undoubted case to be made for substantial increases in resources, but it is equally essential that the way existing resources are deployed be critically appraised.

It might also be suggested that a wider range of resources exist than are generally availed of by health boards. Parents, extended families, communities, voluntary organisations, other state services including schools, all possess resources that, if effectively deployed, have potential to be supportive of children's interests. However, for this to happen there has to be both an appreciation of this potential and already established conducive relationships, which all too often, unfortunately, are absent. In fact the health boards sometimes appear to interpret their statutory responsibility too narrowly. The Child Care Act, 1991, while bestowing the statutory responsibility to take children into care or to apply for a care order on health boards, is quite permissive with regard to other service arrangements:

> A health board may . . . make arrangements with voluntary bodies or other persons for the provision . . . of child care and family support services which the board is empowered to provide under this Act.[9]

Furthermore, the assignment of statutory responsibility should not be perceived as reflective of a superior status, as sometimes seems to be suggested, but simply as an appropriate and necessary mandate for the statutory provider of child welfare services. It does appear unfortunate that this responsibility is all too often interpreted in an exclusive, rather than inclusive, way. As a result, although all of these non-statutory community-based resources are habitually used, it may still be contended

---

[9] Child Care Act, 1991, Part 11, Section 9(1).

that they are availed of neither as frequently nor as effectively as they potentially might.

A further manifestation of this exclusivity has been the retention by health boards of child welfare services that could well be contracted to other organisations, whether voluntary or private. A case in point is the provision of foster care services which until recently has been the almost exclusive preserve of health boards. While the reasons given by health boards for retaining these services for direct delivery themselves are understandable — for example, the preservation of skills and variety of work — they have not necessarily been justified in terms of quality and efficiency. Instead, there have been delays in processing applications from prospective foster carers, and shortcomings in the provision of supports to those approved, due to workload pressures. As a result, potential resources may be lost, thereby placing the system under even greater pressure. It is only very recently that one can find welcome, though few, examples of such work being contracted to voluntary organisations. The implications, however, of anything short of a first class service are major for children and young people, for foster families and for the system as a whole which invariably finds itself providing more intensive — and expensive — responses as a result. Similarly, the health boards have at times been hostile to proposals for new service development, both preventive and therapeutic, even when existing provision was minimal or non-existent and the prospects of them being provided by the statutory body were bleak.

This perhaps raises further issues about the role of health boards as both providers and funders of child welfare services, and the consequent fragmentation and potential conflicts of interest that can then arise. There is a lack of clarity and national policy on the services that might generally be provided by, for example, voluntary organisations and those which should be retained to be delivered directly by health boards. While one would not argue for uniformity, there is clearly a case to be made for some rationalisation. Otherwise we will have a continuation of the current situation where health boards, for example, are both providers and funders of residential care services. This is compounded by the fact that, at present, the newly established Social Services Inspectorate has responsibility only for the inspection of services provided by the health boards. The health boards, in turn, have responsibility for inspecting certain services provided by voluntary organisations in their area. But the division of services between statutory and voluntary providers is frequently quite arbitrary. So as things currently stand, services which may be almost identical in terms of their target groups and objectives may be subjected to separate systems of inspection purely on the basis of their management by statutory or voluntary providers. We really should have a more rational and integrated approach.

This leads inevitably to the need to consider issues of both vision and strategy, but first it may be important to also focus on society's expectations of a child protection system.

THE INEVITABILITY OF RISK

The wellbeing of children has to be both the concern and responsibility of society in general. The status of children's wellbeing and, in particular, the extent to which children are safe, is clearly a dynamic of the functioning of any society. By the same token it has to be accepted that some children in every society are not safe, that abuse and neglect of children may be found in every society. The extent to which it may be found — as, indeed, other threats to children's wellbeing for example, child poverty, infant mortality, civil unrest, etc. — is reflective of the social and economic development of a particular society. It follows, therefore, that a single entity such as a child protection system cannot be reasonably expected to take or be given responsibility for keeping all children safe from harm, even harm inflicted deliberately by a member of their family or immediate community.

Yet this is frequently the erroneous assumption that underpins much of our thinking on child protection. Certainly it is the perspective that consistently emerges in much media comment in the aftermath of a child abuse tragedy. And it is, perhaps, one that has its origins in past excessive claims on the potential contribution to be made by investing in increasing numbers of child care professionals. Much of the development of social services in many countries from the 1960s to the 1980s was predicated on the belief that by appointing more social workers we would somehow reduce the incidence of social problems. Social workers are not so influential! Appointing more is much more likely to result in a heightened awareness of the range and extent of social problems and perhaps, in time, in important lessons for social policy.

There remains, however, an assumption that health board social workers in particular can somehow prevent abuse occurring and, consequently, where it does occur that some health board professional has to be culpable. This is a convenient evasion for the community at large but one which needs rejecting, not least by social workers themselves. It also raises the question of what the objective of the child protection services should be.

If we accept that child abuse exists in every society, it implies that no society has succeeded in eradicating it. Therefore we need to be realistic in terms of our own expectations. Rather than aspiring to the impossible, we would be better served by investing in a comprehensive series of measures that might be expected to reduce the prevalence of child abuse — some examples will be suggested shortly in the context of community-wide actions which could make our society safer for children. These would include steps to be taken to bring matters of concern to the notice of the appropriate authorities. Once these measures are adequate, the objective of the child protection services might then be to ensure that interventions are early, comprehensive and effective.

Clearly there is a great deal more that might be said about the nature of risk and the capacity of the child protection services to respond to, and protect, vulnerable children and young people. Of particular importance is society's acceptance of the reality and inevitability of abuse and neglect, and an acknowledgement that its prevalence is a barometer of how society is functioning. This acceptance will hopefully be accompanied by a determination and commitment both to make children safer and to provide the resources necessary for those charged with the task of protecting children to succeed. By the same token, it is important that child protection personnel should seek ever more effective strategies whilst resisting the burden or privilege of having responsibility for eradicating abuse altogether.

TOWARDS THE FUTURE

Looking to the future, can we be confident that children in Ireland will fare better than in the past?

A starting point might be to suggest that no government enjoying world beating economic success, as Ireland is, can credibly aspire to only second best provision for its children. Put another way, if matching the best provision for children to be found anywhere in the world is not to be the summit of our ambition, which politician will tell us so? That we aspire to second best or less?

It has already been suggested that the establishment of an effective child care system was a significant failure of successive governments over the first 70 years of the existence of this State. Some action has been taken within the past decade to redress this but it has been too little and too lacking in focus and coherence to significantly ameliorate the neglect of the past, nor to respond to the increased needs that have arisen in the interim. Nevertheless, the prospects for a significant reversal of this history are now potentially more positive than ever before. And, if they are complemented by firm political imagination and commitment, there is every reason to believe that the attainment of world-class levels of provision for children are achievable within a timeframe which would still allow us to celebrate the centenary of our State with pride in its support and guarantees for children and young people.

Past experience and prudence suggests that one should be cautious, even cynical, about political commitments to transform State provision for children and young people and their families. If we choose to curb such natural instincts, however, in favour of a positive approach, it may be that we can begin to identify a quite different scenario.

Certainly many of the ingredients for progress are present. For all our past failures it cannot be denied that we possess significant cultural attributes which suggest that if we set our minds to it we can construct a range of supports and services which will bring us a long way towards quality provision for children. The development of a children's rights perspective within the past decade has both put the child centre stage and brought the external international scrutiny of the United Nations Committee on the Rights of the Child into the picture. Significantly, unprecedented economic growth has provided the opportunity to realise what previously might only have been dreamed of in terms of investment in comprehensive and effective policies and provision for children. Yes, the ingredients are indeed there. The remaining questions concern the extent of political commitment and vision to deliver on this potential.

Time alone will tell whether the political commitment has been sufficient and responsible. However, we have come so far that it would be politically unwise for a government to renege on commitments given to date. Not unheard of, but particularly unwise given the constituency involved. It would also be difficult for any successor government to reverse progress that has been widely endorsed and supported. Clearly much would depend on the effectiveness of the child advocacy lobby and, again, the portents are good. Many of the advances of recent years have been due to the development of more mature, effective and increasingly united advocacy for children. The remaining question relates to the breadth and ambition of vision, for this will be as critical in realising the full extent of existing potential as its absence has been in the past.

THE NATIONAL STRATEGY FOR CHILDREN

Clearly, the vehicle which is most likely to deliver on this potential will be the National Strategy for Children[10] to which the Government has pinned its colours and which will be the central plank of its next report to the UN Committee. Its articulation of a vision for children in Ireland is a welcome "first" and the strategy as a whole will, if implemented, represent a significant departure in our policy and provision for children. Even assuming an uncritical acceptance of the Government's commit-

---

[10] Government of Ireland, *Our Children — Their Lives: The National Children's Strategy,* Dublin: The Stationery Office, 2000.

ment, however, its success will require a non-defensive acknowledgement of current shortcomings, sustained investment and coherent action over many years and a level of integration and collaboration between state agencies, in particular, which has never been seen before. Furthermore, it will have to be kept under constant review, and be adapted as required without losing touch with its spirit and essence. A challenging agenda, certainly, but if one wishes to be positive, one that is achievable — assuming the political will.

The Strategy, rightly, addresses Ireland's aspirations for, and commitment to, all children. Within the child care system we may have a particular concern for children who are vulnerable or disadvantaged, but their needs can only be effectively addressed in the context of the State's accommodation of children and childhood generally. In this respect, the experience of being a child or young person in Ireland is seen as being relevant and important in every instance. The State's policies and strategies, whether in the quality of the built environment, the economic supports to families, opportunities to pursue sport and leisure activities safely or the promotion of healthy lifestyles, have a significant impact on the quality of all children's lives.

The UN Convention on the Rights of the Child has children as its focus but it is not in conflict with the rights of parents and families. It is unambiguous on the right of children to a family and its significance to their development. On the other hand, it does recognise that children's rights are not the same as parents' rights and that a small minority of children have to be protected from their families. Fundamentally, it validates childhood, acknowledges and respects the integrity of children as citizens in their own right and recognises the rights of children to be consulted on matters affecting them.

One of the most significant aspects of the National Strategy for Children is that it validates the voice of the child — of all children — and it is therefore difficult to see how this alone would not have the most profound implications for future provision affecting children and young people in Ireland. For children to exercise this right, though — as with other rights — they must be aware of them and they must have the opportunities and support to give voice to them. A series of actions are therefore required to promote awareness of children's rights and to create and promote the conditions which will give them real meaning. It is reassuring that the National Strategy for Children both validates the rights of children and commits future governments to such action.

Although the Strategy can, of its nature, only map out a direction for future governments to take national policy and provision, an optimistic view would suggest that a number of devices — for example, mechanisms to listen to children, the establishment of the office of Ombudsman for Children and Dail na nOg and other national structures to drive its implementation — will have significant long-term influence on developments whilst also having immediate impact. In other words, while the Strategy should make a difference in itself, actions and mechanisms initiated to give it effect will have to continue well into the future. This is, as ever, contingent on commitment, not only on the part of the present government but of its successors over several Dail terms. Failure to demonstrate that continuing determined action should be very harshly judged. Indeed, it is not unreasonable to seek all-party agreement on the agenda for children so that the necessary development of a previously neglected system of provision for children might proceed protected from the buffeting of prevailing political winds.

The Strategy covers the development of government provision for children over the next ten years across the spectrum of relevant concerns for all children. What might we expect to see in place for children in particular need, and particularly for children who are at risk of abuse and neglect?

ELIMINATION OF CHILD POVERTY

Fundamentally, there should be a war on child poverty. Poverty is at the root of many childhood problems. Children have a right to "a standard of living adequate for the child's physical, mental, spiritual, moral and social development".[11] Living in poverty denies them this right, limits fulfilment of their full po-

---

[11] United Nations Convention on the Rights of the Child, Article 27.1.

tential and creates inequality relative to their peers. Poverty also generates family stress, diminishes parenting capacity, leads to family instability and exposes children to a series of major threats to their wellbeing. For the first time in our history we can aspire with realism to the eradication of child poverty — but it will not be achieved overnight, even with the will. The endemic nature of poverty is such that it can only be overcome through consistent concerted action over many years — perhaps a generation — with measures that include the financial, though not exclusively. Poverty is more than the absence of sufficient money, though that may be what hurts most on a day to day basis. It is also about inequality, poverty of opportunity, educational disadvantage and even the poverty of not daring to dream. While short-term action in increasing income will bring significant relief, the eradication of child poverty will demand an acceptance that structures within existing society will have to change. This will have the further implication that the enhancement of opportunities for those who are currently in poverty will mean that those who are currently privileged will have to live with a more even distribution of opportunity. Whether this has been fully realised and, more importantly, whether there will be the political determination to match the rhetoric of eliminating child poverty with effective necessary action, remains to be seen.

MAKING SOCIETY SAFER FOR CHILDREN

Government action that reflects serious and consistent intent to embrace the rights of children as the bedrock of its response to their needs will not only have very substantial significance for the way services develop but, more importantly, for the extent to which children are safe within our society. As has been asserted earlier, we cannot, sadly, eradicate abuse but we can take steps both to reduce its prevalence and to ameliorate its consequences. At a primary level there is a need to raise public awareness about children's rights and also about child abuse and its characteristics. Equipping children from an early age with the knowledge and capacity to protect their integrity is critical. This can be approached in a low-key but effective way, preferably through parents but with the support of teachers, similar to the way potentially difficult issues like the facts of life or adoption can be discussed very effectively with a child in a matter-of-fact way if introduced at an early stage by a confident adult who has the trust of the child.

Secondary prevention can be effected through the provision of a comprehensive range of community-based services which are responsive to local needs. Particularly vulnerable need groups are identifiable and targeted services can be effective in reducing risk and intervening at an early stage in the cycle of abuse. There is scope for substantial improvement in the range and effectiveness of child protection measures, particularly at the tertiary stage. We need to be better at identifying specific instances of abuse or risk; interventions need to be initiated faster and more effectively; the staffing and other resources need to be in place — here we need to be much better at projecting future need and investing in professional training; there is a need for more effective case planning and collaboration between agencies; and there is an urgent need to develop a repertoire of therapeutic interventions for both victims and offenders — and clearly there is a need to differentiate between the various categories within both groups.

Among a number of measures that would contribute to making children in Ireland safer are the introduction of mandatory reporting and the establishment of a sex offenders register. Both have been controversial and have evoked considerable debate amongst professionals but, in this writer's view, there is a very solid case to justify in each case.

Mandatory reporting would require by law certain designated persons to report to the relevant authorities any situation where they knew, or suspected, that a child was at risk. Its introduction would be a clear and unambiguous statement by our society that child abuse is a matter of public importance and that all necessary steps will be taken to ensure that cases of suspected abuse are reported and acted upon. This is a critical element, together with a series of other measures, in strengthening our capacity to intervene effectively in cases of child abuse. Fundamentally, the introduction of mandatory reporting would make a firm statement that the physical, sexual and emotional abuse and neglect of children is not acceptable in Ireland nor, importantly, is the failure to report it. It might be difficult to accept that professionals would have such information and fail to report it. Yet we have seen again and again that this is the case. The Report of the Kilkenny Incest Investigation, when recommending in favour of mandatory reporting, concluded that:

> Experience suggests that some professionals dealing with children may still be prepared to turn a blind eye to the unpleasant reality of child abuse and studies show that professionals and voluntary agencies often refer children on an ad-hoc, discretionary and inconsistent basis.[12]

Mandatory reporting should not be seen as an alternative to investment, for example, in preventive measures such as improved family support services, but as one part of an expanded range of provision which will serve to offer better protection to children. Already the Protection for Persons Reporting Child Abuse Act, 1998 and the publication of the 1999 National Guidelines for the Protection and Welfare of Children,[13] are important contributions in facilitating the introduction of mandatory reporting.

Likewise, the establishment of a register of sex offenders would be an important step in affording greater protection to children and young people and provide an important means for agencies to share information and monitor sex offenders reasonably effectively. At the same time there is a need to have realistic expectations of its likely impact and also to make the case for a number of other complementary measures for it is the combined effect of such strategies that would constitute significant action on the part of the State to protect children. In spite of its undoubted limitations, the establishment of a register of sex offenders would make a small but nevertheless significant contribution to the challenge of making Ireland a safer place for children. In this respect, the Sexual Offenders Act 2001, is broadly

---

[12] ibid.

[13] Department of Health and Children, *Children First: National Guidelines for the Protection and Welfare of Children,* Dublin: The Stationery Office, 1999.

welcome as it will, inter alia, establish such a register. See Chapter 7 in this volume for further discussion.

Given its profile and significance it is perhaps surprising that there have not been more linkages between substance abuse and child welfare.

> It is hard to understand how society could have gone so long without recognising that children in abusive situations often live in families in which alcohol and other drugs are abused. It is embarrassing that fields of study have developed so narrowly that they are not conscious of the life circumstances of all family members. It is inexcusable that bridges between the fields of substance abuse and child welfare have not been established sooner.[14]

Many children are vulnerable due to the impact of alcohol or drug misuse by a family member, particularly a parent. This may be due to the consequence of neglect or inconsistent parenting or it could be due to dangerous behaviour while under the influence. In any event it appears that there is inconsistent and insufficient linkage, by and large, between drug treatment and child welfare services. This has begun to improve, at community level at least, through the investment of increasing resources under the various Local Drugs Task Forces. This is a welcome development but there is both a need and the potential for a substantial increase in complementary actions which recognise the significance of addiction treatment programmes for children's welfare and of the family dimension for more effective treatment initiatives. This will undoubtedly become a very significant development in the integration of disparate initiatives in the future.

Underpinning much of the development of services in the future will be an increased investment in research and evaluation. In reviewing the range of provision for children, the occasional overlaps and many gaps, the lack of effective planning over

---

[14] See, for example, Hampton, Robert L., Senatore, Vincent and Gullota, Thomas P. (eds) (1998) *Substance Abuse, Family Violence, and Child Welfare* (Issues in Children's and Families' Lives, Vol. 10). London, Thousand Oaks, CA and New Delhi: Sage.

many decades becomes evident. Very little data has been collected and even many of the official statistics published over the years lack credibility. Without standardised and comprehensive information there has been no foundation for effective planning — even if there had been the will. However a gathering research momentum, coupled with a belated acknowledgement of the need to substantially improve the quality of our data, has become apparent in recent years. This has been reinforced by the key commitment of the National Children's Strategy to make a better understanding of children's lives, through greater investment in research, one of the three national goals of the Strategy. Clearly to be welcomed, an optimistic view would suggest that this is more likely to solidify, rather than evaporate, with a resultant growth in rigorous professional study as a foundation for effective planning to meet children's needs.

CONCLUSION

It is difficult to avoid the conclusion that we have reached a most critical point in the history of Ireland's provision for, and treatment of, children and young people. Any judgement of performance since independence is likely to return a verdict that verges on the "appalling". No past government emerges with credit. Successive governments have abandoned, neglected and utterly failed children.

Indeed, the record is so poor it is difficult to see how it could be maintained even if, perversely, this was attempted. However, Ireland is now a different country and, while one cannot be blind to continuing aberrations, there is genuine reason to believe that we are on the brink of a new dawn in policy and provision for children and their families.

Firstly, it is important to acknowledge the tentative and faltering improvements of the past decade. Inadequate, certainly, yet inexorably leading to greater awareness of the past, the present and the aspirations we need for the future. From the additional £1 million lottery funding of 1991, to the £35 million of 1993 to the current realisation that immense investment over many years is required, a consistent thread of increasing understanding and realism can be discerned. Much of the credit for this might be attributed to the media for it has frequently been its spotlight that has thrown past inadequacies into sharp relief and demanded political reaction that could no longer hide the reality. The economic growth of recent years has also provided the possibility and the opportunity. Perhaps most of all, it has been the recognition of the rights of children that has had greatest significance.

Ireland probably did not realise the fundamental significance of its ratification of the UN Convention on the Rights of the Child in 1992. Many other countries were ratifying — there remain, today, only two countries which have not, the USA and Somalia — and the fear of not ratifying must have outweighed any concerns that might have surfaced as to its consequences. A combination of effective advocacy and lobbying, adoption of strategies that had proven successful in other jurisdictions and the effective exploitation of the opportunity provided by the scrutiny of Ireland's report on progress by the UN Committee on the Rights of the Child, all had substantial impact. Much more remains to be done, but one of the direct outcomes of the 1998 Geneva hearing was the commitment to develop the National Strategy for Children. This will have long-term impact because for the first time an Irish government is articulating a national vision for children. Hugely significant, it includes a commitment to make the voices of children and young people central to future developments. Once begun, there can be no turning back.

A less optimistic view is that such progress as has been achieved is minimal, perhaps magnified by packaging and public relations but not materially different from what has gone before. We know only too well what that looks like and it must be rejected. The quality of our provision for children is a political issue and must be kept on the political agenda. But it is more than that. It is a moral issue and it goes to the heart of the kind of society we have, or aspire towards. The past is perhaps characterised as the society we told ourselves we had, but hadn't. Now there is an opportunity for us to divine a future and pledge to realise it, knowing it will take time, money and commitment.

Time we have, but children cannot wait. An effective start is already overdue — the Strategy provides the opportunity.

Money we have. To ensure its provision it is necessary to appeal both to the spirit that says that children are equal, all have the right to realise their potential, and to the pragmatism that recognises that investment in developing this potential will always pay dividends and reward society as a whole.

Commitment? That is the test — do we have the political will and commitment? Time of course will tell but we should not be so passive. There is a need to build on the recent past, to compel the political system to recognise the need, the opportunity, the imperative.

To realise this opportunity will require revolution, not evolution. If we allow events to take their course there may well be improvements but there will also be more incoherence, and certainly we will not realise the potential. That has to be made to happen, and it will require concerted, coherent action supported by ambitious investment over many years.

It is not optimism that will make the difference. Rather it is passion, commitment and dedication. Many of the basic requirements are now in place and there has never been a better opportunity in the history of the State. So, one is bound to ask, if not now, when?

Appendix

Counselling Services for Victims of Child Sexual Abuse

The Aislinn Centre (Association for the Healing of Institutional Abuse)

The aim of the centre is to allow survivors a platform to talk of their past experiences, with fellow survivors, in a caring and trusting environment. Services include literacy classes, counselling referral, art therapy, self-development, health services referral and information relating to the Commission to Inquire into Child Abuse.

- Freephone, Republic of Ireland – 1800 25 25 24
- Freephone, UK + Northern Ireland – 0800 039 0301.

Children at Risk in Ireland (CARI)

Provides therapy, counselling, information, research and education services for children, families and groups affected by child sexual abuse. CARI Foundation, 110 Lwr. Drumcondra Road, Dublin 9. Tel.: 01-8308529.

Faoiseamh

Help line established by CORI (Council of Religious in Ireland) in February 1997 to take calls from people who have been abused. Freephone 1800 33 12 34.

Health Boards

The Government has recently developed counselling services for the survivors of institutional abuse in each of the health boards. These can be contacted at:

- Northern Area Health Board (Dublin), Freephone 1800 234 110

- South Western Area Health Board (Dublin) — Freephone 1800 234 112

- East Coast Area Health Board (Dublin) — Freephone 1800 234 111

- Midland Health Board — Freephone 1800 234 113

- Western Health Board — Freephone 1800 234 114

- Mid-Western Health Board — Freephone 1800 234 115

- Southern Health Board — Freephone 1800 234 116

- North Eastern Health Board — Freephone 1800 234 117

- South Eastern Health Board — Freephone 1800 234 118

- North Western Health Board — Freephone 1800 234 119

National Office for Victims of Abuse (NOVA)

Nova was established as part of the overall Government strategy for the support of persons who as children were abused in institutions. It offers the following services to victims of abuse:

- Confidential free-phone line – 1800 25 25 24 from Ireland 0800 039 0301 from UK and Northern Ireland

- Assistance to persons wishing to trace their records

- Referral service to persons wishing to avail of reading and writing services, health services, counselling, education and other appropriate social services.

New Day Counselling Centre

Provides low cost professional counselling and psychotherapy to people living on low incomes in inner city Dublin. New Day Counselling Centre, 11 Meath Street, Dublin 8. Tel.: 01-4547050.

Rape Crisis Centre (Nationwide)

Rape Crisis Line: a 24 hour, nationwide service. Freephone 1800 77 8888.

Right of Place, Cork

This organisation seeks to represent people who have been abused in institutions in the past. It facilitates the tracing of records and preparation for Tribunal Compensation. Freephone – 1800 200 709.